The Rooms of Heaven

The Rooms of Heaven

*A Story of Love, Death, Grief,
and the Afterlife*

MARY ALLEN

Alfred A. Knopf   New York   1999

THIS IS A BORZOI BOOK
PUBLISHED BY ALFRED A. KNOPF, INC.

Copyright © 1999 by Mary Allen

www.randomhouse.com

Some of the names and details in this narrative have been changed.

Library of Congress Cataloging-in-Publication Data
Allen, Mary, [date]
The rooms of heaven : a story of love, death, grief, and the afterlife /
Mary Allen. — 1st American ed.
p.   cm.
ISBN 0-679-45460-8
1. Allen, Mary, [date]   2. Beaman, Jim.   3. Spiritualism.
4. Iowa—Biography.   I. Title
BF1277.A55A3 1999
133.9'092—dc21   98-43129
CIP

Manufactured in the United States of America
First Edition

For all my good friends
and
for my friend and sister,
Christine Allen

Death is nothing at all;
I have only slipped away into the next room.

—H. S. HOLLAND

Part One

I always think of Iowa as a place where strange and magical things happen. Not sleight of hand, card tricks, pull-a-rabbit-out-of-a-hat kind of magic—nothing as literal and obvious as that. What I'm thinking of is vaguer, subtler, harder to pin down and yet more genuine. It's an ambiance, a spirit, an intimation of things unseen, a sense that there could be a little bit of slippage, just the tiniest room for negotiation, in the ordinary order of things.

Most people I know think of Iowa as anything but magical. They think of it—of the whole Midwest—as flat, dull, conventional, a place where mostly boring and mundane things happen. And maybe it is, regarded in a certain way. Maybe life is like a hologram: Hold it up to the light at one angle and it all looks ordinary; tilt it another way and everything shifts, glows, turns strange.

I have a friend who says you always fall in love with the place you fall in love in, and I'm sure she's right, I'm sure that's partly why I think of Iowa this way. And I'm sure it also has to do with who I fell in love with—with Jim Beaman, his particular way of seeing things, his demons and angels. It even, unexpectedly, has to do with what became of him—with death, that mystifying disappearing act which has its own brand of terrible magic, which in the end may be the most magical thing of all.

But even the first time I saw it, entering Iowa from Illinois, I was struck by something unusual in the Iowa countryside. I was driving a small U-Haul truck, moving here from Massachusetts. Earlier I'd passed through a massive thunderstorm. You could actually see it coming—the black clouds towering up ahead in the distance, the rain spattering on the windshield, then turning torrential, thunder rumbling then booming then crrracking, as if the very fabric of the world were splitting, flashes of lightning streaking down again and again in the fields beside the highway. Then suddenly I was beyond it; the sun was back out and the sky was once more an innocent placid blue.

Half an hour into Iowa I noticed a change in the landscape. Whereas Illinois is largely flat, full of marshes and lowlands and small industrial cities, giving it a kind of dull suburban atmosphere, Iowa has a safe, kindly, fresh-scrubbed feeling. The landscape consists of miles and miles of rolling, undulating green, a verdant patchwork of corn and soybeans, the horizon only broken every once in a while by a clump of farm buildings—a large white house, a sagging red barn, a windmill, a silo, a couple of sheds—and sometimes, out in the cornfields, by a pickup truck barreling along a narrow road in the distance, kicking up a cloud of white dust. Often on the horizon the air fades to a pale, hazy, bluish shade of pink, and above it the vault of the mild blue sky curves and rises. The view seems endlessly wide; it makes something expand inside your eyes or your mind.

Gradually, as I was entering Iowa for the first time, I began to notice a large number of monarch butterflies fluttering around in the air. They were everywhere, pottering along at the edge of the road, scissoring across the fields, sailing on updrafts above the highway, blundering into the path of the truck.

1

My neighbor across the street has a dog named Bob.

Bob is a short, old, black dog with an energetic disposition and an alert, foxlike face. His parts are all out of proportion to each other; he looks more like a picture of a dog a kid would draw than a real dog: large oval body, ears like sails on a small bullet head, upside-down V's for legs.

Bob is in love with his mistress, Julie, a pottery teacher and waitress. At least that's what my friend Grant says. Grant's a graduate student at the university. I met him in the physics department, where I used to have a job at a journal. He's the source of most of what I know about Bob and Julie. Grant was Julie's roommate in the last place she lived. I've never met Julie myself, have only observed Bob from a distance of thirty or forty feet.

Once Grant described to me a photograph of Bob and Julie, taken a long time ago, when Bob was just a puppy. It was taken in the morning, soon after they both woke up. Julie's sitting up in bed holding Bob; his face is near her face. Julie's eyes are downcast, she looks sleepy and inward and meditative. "And Bob looks like this," Grant said. He leaped suddenly off the chair in my office, leaned to the side as if straining hard against a leash, bared his teeth in a wide, goofy, manic grin. He practically made his hair stand on end.

I often watch Bob from across the street. The front door of

his house will open and he will emerge, take a brief turn around the lawn, stop a few times to sniff at trees. After he sniffs, he arcs one hindleg up in the air, squirts a little pee onto the tree, looks around fiercely as if challenging an invisible enemy. After he's done this a few times, he returns to the front steps, scratches at the front door, and lets out a sharp little yip. Then he sits down to wait for Julie to let him in. If she doesn't come in a minute or two he yips again and waits more anxiously, head cocked, tail wagging. Where could she be? Sometimes he yips three or four times, each little bark getting louder and sharper. When that happens, I feel like calling Julie on the telephone, shouting into her window from across the street: "Bob is waiting for you!"

I can't stand to watch him wait.

I live in Iowa City, on Washington Street. My house is yellow and has a flat lawn with a sycamore tree, a two-car driveway, a cement front porch with black wrought-iron railings. Bob and Julie's house is large and pinkish tan with a high, peaked, cherry-red roof, a wooden porch, and squiggles of gingerbread trim. It rests on top of a small rise and has a long, green, sloping lawn. I have some history with that house—with this entire neighborhood, in fact.

When I look out my window I see, not just houses and trees and sidewalks and telephone poles—the whole elaborate tapestry of the physical world—but something like a series of overlays: the view as it has appeared to me at different times, colored by different events, over the last twelve years. And when I walk the fifteen-minute walk between my place and downtown, there are various spots along the way that are more than just bits of scenery; they're landmarks in my personal history, signposts that call up certain memories and feelings. One house in particular, a block and a half away from mine—a large, three-story white building with a wide, brick-walled verandah—always makes me do a mental double take. This is where Jim Beaman lived.

The house stands on a good-sized rise above the street; three tiers of cement steps lead from the entrance down to the sidewalk. A two-person swing hangs on chains from the porch ceiling; there used to be a second, matching one of these, but somebody took it down a couple of years ago, or maybe it got stolen. The entrance to the house is a black storm door, and at equal distances from the door are two large windows with foot-wide strips of stained glass at the top. One of these was Beaman's window; his bedroom used to lie beyond the blinds.

There was a time when I could pass this house without even noticing; it meant nothing to me; I hadn't even heard of Jim Beaman. And there was a time—not a very long time, as relationships go—when I was completely wrapped up in the life that went on inside one of its apartments. I'd walk by wondering what Jim was up to, whether he was off at some job or in his bedroom napping or making phone calls or maybe standing at the window, waiting for me to arrive. Most of the time I wouldn't go by; I'd climb the steps to the porch, push open the heavy wooden door that lay inside the storm door, go down the hall and be let in to Beaman's warm, bright apartment.

Then there was a time when the sight of that house was so painful I could hardly stand it. Still, whenever I passed I always looked over—I couldn't help it, as if driven by some kind of reflex—and just before I looked I always felt a tiny spark of hope, as if the laws that govern life and death might have changed from one moment to the next. Then I'd experience a little shock of dismay and disappointment. There was a certain sentence I'd tell myself then, addressing it to Beaman. I'd say it bitterly, sententiously, and in some obscure way it would make me feel better. "Your window is dark," I'd say, "and you, of course, are gone."

I came to Iowa in 1986 to attend the Iowa Writers' Workshop. Two weeks before I left Cambridge, I rented a place over the phone from an Iowa City real estate agent. He told me the apartment was an attic on the third floor of a house. I liked attic apartments; I lived in one in Cambridge, and I thought the place in Iowa City would feel just like home. In my imagination, I pictured a tidy, cozy attic with an old-fashioned quilt on the bed, a white-painted glass-doored cupboard, a pleasant, orderly living room with a green and blue braided rug. As it turned out, the place smelled of bug spray and there were gaps in the bedroom ceiling; the bathroom had no door and the shower was a greasy plastic stall; the windowsills were rotten and filled with piles of dead beetles. I was afraid to sleep in the bedroom because of the likelihood of bats coming through the holes in the ceiling; I sealed that room off; I even put masking tape over the keyhole. Bats can get in through very small places.

My friend Ron followed me from Massachusetts to Iowa City in his car, helped me move into my apartment and stayed for one night, then continued west to California. We arrived at my new home just as the sun was going down. We looked wordlessly around the place, carried my boxes and bed frame up three flights of stairs, and went out to dinner. When we came back it was dark and airless in the apartment. The previous tenant had vacated it the week before and I had neglected to tell the local utilities company to turn the electricity back on. We rested my double mattress on the living-room floor below the window and lay down on it in our clothes— Ron and I are just friends and always have been. The light of a streetlight shone dimly through the window and the air outside was permeated by the sharp, high whine of cicadas; the noise seemed to fill the night with something deranged and ominous.

It was unbearably hot in the room. Ron had given me a fan as a going-away present, and eventually he got out of bed, took the fan out of its box and started waving the box back and forth above the mattress to stir up some air. "I knew this fan would come in handy," he said.

He left the next day for California. After I watched him drive away I went out and bought a newspaper to look for another place. I brought the paper back to the apartment, opened it on the bed, and began to scan the columns of ads for apartments for rent, circling those I could afford. One notice in particular caught my eye; it was for a one-bedroom on Washington Street. I called the number listed in the ad and no one answered; I waited an hour, then called again; no one answered that time either. I kept dialing the same number all day long, and I didn't call any other places. I had an odd little feeling about the apartment on Washington Street, as if I knew it was where I belonged.

Finally at six-thirty a woman answered the phone. She told me how to get to the house—it was ten blocks up from the Civic Center, where the police station is—and I walked there in the pale, luminous evening air. The landlord showed me around the apartment—it was nothing special, just three big rooms on the first floor, with tall windows and no gaps in the ceiling where bats could get in—and I wrote him a check for my first and last months' rent.

Whatever it is that arranges and orders our lives, leads us to crucial meetings, puts us in place for key events, whatever it is—fate, luck, intuition, guardian angels, maybe—must have been operating that day, making me focus on that ad, leading me to this apartment, this street, because none of the things that happened to me would have happened if I hadn't been living on Washington Street.

Washington Street is a wide, straight, tree-lined street that runs through the middle of Iowa City. Its houses are large and old, with handsome front porches and lush green lawns, but there are baby carriages and lawnmowers and battered bicycles on the porches and here and there a pickup truck's parked along the curb among the cars, so you know it's the kind of place where students and married couples and other ordinary people live. My part of the street is flat and open, but a little farther down, after the intersection with Governor Street, the road is split by a series of oblong brick islands covered with close-cropped rugs of grass like the felt-covered bottoms of chess pieces, and the street begins a long, slow, sweeping descent into downtown Iowa City. If you stand at the top of that slope in the evening in a season when the trees are without their leaves, you can see all the way down to the little round stoplight dangling from a wire at the intersection with Gilbert Street, and beyond that and up a rise—Iowa, it turns out, is not flat after all—you can see the glowing yellow marquee of the Englert Theater; you can even see the little black letters spelling out the names of this week's movies. Beyond that and higher still are the regular, square lines of the Jefferson Building, which a long time ago was a hotel but now houses offices for the university.

I had an office in there once. While I was in the Workshop I taught rhetoric, and I was supposed to hold office hours twice a week so my students could drop by and see me. My friend Kathy, who was also in the Workshop and also taught rhetoric, shared the office with me. No students ever came to see us, and we spent the whole time sitting at our desks complaining and laughing. We complained about our students' work and the lack of men in our lives and our various other gripes. I can't remember what we laughed about, maybe the same things.

Once, as we were leaving in the evening—we must have been there to drop off or pick up something, because our office hours were early in the day—we stopped in the stairwell and looked out a window that faced the pedestrian mall behind the building. It was early spring of our last semester teaching and Kathy had been talking about moving away; I kept hoping she'd change her mind and stay. I knew I'd be staying in any case. I didn't want to return to Cambridge or western Massachusetts—I felt as if my business was somehow finished in those places—and I couldn't think of anywhere else to go. But I didn't really want to leave anyway. Iowa felt like home to me; I loved the kind, green, rolling cornfields that surrounded the town, the way everything in Iowa City was safe and clean and affordable. I thought my life would be perfect if only Kathy would stay.

Opposite where she and I were standing, on the other side of the pedestrian mall, was the wide blank face of the Holiday Inn. Most of its windows were dark, but one about halfway up was ablaze with light, and within, like a little play inside a glowing shoe box, a tiny aerobic dance class was going on. Ten or twelve little figures in bright-colored leotards moved to a rapid, silent, pulsing beat, squatting, standing, reaching, kicking, bobbing up and down in syncopated rhythm, like miniature mechanical dolls.

I met Kathy in January of my first year in Iowa City. She was studying poetry in the Workshop. We were both from rural working-class New England—Kathy grew up in small-town western Connecticut and I was from rural western Massachusetts—and we had both worked in publishing, but the main thing we had in common was that we felt different—somehow worse and better at the same time—than many of our fellow Workshop students, who were generally younger than we were and whom we perceived as coming from more normal and more privileged backgrounds than ours. Kathy and I met at a party, and after that we saw each other or talked on the telephone nearly every day. We went to readings and more parties together, sat around Kathy's attic apartment watching TV and eating popcorn, drove to Hy-Vee and Kmart and Target in Kathy's blue VW bug, talked about everything in the world there was to talk about. We didn't have much money and worried hysterically about whatever we spent, but once we bought a box of four pale-green wineglasses and split it—Kathy got two and I got two—and once when they were giving away free goldfish at Drugtown we each acquired one, then went to Kmart and bought goldfish bowls, fish food, and aqua gravel for the bottom of the bowls. Our fish died. Kathy's died quickly; when she got up the next morning it was floating belly-up on the surface of the water in her fishbowl. Mine went more slowly; for a day or two it drifted around looking sluggish and bloated, then floated to the surface as well. We went back to Drugtown and got two more goldfish. This time we were careful to pick ones that looked healthy and frisky; there were thousands crammed into a two-foot aquarium. But the new ones died too. Kathy said she felt like a bad parent.

In the summer she acquired a small used telescope that you could just barely see the rings of Saturn through. One night we set it up in the high school football field and watched a lunar eclipse, taking turns staring through the eyepiece as the moon's light was gradually obliterated by the earth's shadow and the moon looked more and more like a round ball of rock hanging there in space, which is exactly what it is, of course.

The same summer we took up roller-skating by the river. Kathy bought a pair of old used skates at a garage sale and around the same time on a trip I took to Massachusetts my niece gave me a pair that didn't fit her anymore. Kathy's skates were low and black and had metal wheels; mine were tall and white with red rubber wheels. I'd never been on roller skates and Kathy hadn't skated for years, so we started off practicing in a parking lot beside the University Hospital. We went there twice—both times in the evening to avoid the heat—and I had just got so I could inch along for four or five feet when an orderly came out and told us we had to leave; the wheels on Kathy's skates made so much noise they could hear them inside the hospital. After that Kathy bought new black skates with rubber wheels and we moved to another parking lot, next to the recreation center. We went there after supper every night for three weeks and skated around and around till the pinkish twilight faded from the sky and the street lights glimmered faintly in the dusk.

Then we decided to start skating during the daytime in City Park. Nearly every day we'd walk to the student union, skates dangling from their shoelaces strung over our shoulders, change into them at the edge of a parking lot, and hide our shoes in the bushes. We'd skate along a path by the river, stop and wait for traffic whizzing by on Park Road, then skate uncertainly across the street and step up onto the sidewalk. We'd make our way over the bridge and up a rise to the entrance of the park on our right. There we would stop; the path through the park begins with a sharp descent. Kathy would stand at the top of the walk and coast all the way down the hill, flapping her arms like wings, her upper body shifting back and forth. I'd watch to see if she made it, then clump down the hill in the grass with my skates sideways, Kathy waiting for me at the bottom. From there on, the path through the park was more or less clear sailing, though parts were bumpy and narrow and there was only one long stretch—a flat wide curvy section after the path veered away from the river—where you could really pick up speed. In my mind I see Kathy flying along ahead of me there, hair streaming behind her, body swinging from side to side, arms pumping with determination, as small and fierce as an eight-year-old boy.

Finally she decided to leave Iowa City. I felt awful but I tried not to let it show. When a lover abandons you you're expected to cry and yell and beg them not to leave, but when a friend goes there's no precedent, no acceptable way of making a fuss. She visited various friends around the country, got reunited with a college sweetheart, and ended up moving in with him in New York.

That summer—the summer of 1989—I took a part-time editing job at the Office of the State Archaeologist in Iowa City and got into the habit of hanging around on Friday nights with a group of men from work, historians and archaeologists and shovel bums—guys who spend the week digging for artifacts in the field, then come back into town on the weekend. One of them, Ray, had a room in an old four-story boarding house where we'd go sometimes to play cards. Ray had a ferret named Fritz that everyone called the weasel. Once it escaped and was lost for two weeks. Ray put up signs all over town but we were certain he'd never see it again; then someone called saying they'd spotted it two evenings in a row in their garden. Ray went and captured it in the middle of the night. After the weasel came back it was never the same. It was fearful and shy when it used to be bold and confident, and Ray and I made up a little story about how its whole view had been changed by being out in the big weasel world, where it had been chased by barking weasels and almost squished by giant roaring weasels with round rubber feet. Ray said it was only a tube-shaped shadow of its former self.

But mostly I was lonely with Kathy gone—the archaeologists were only good for one night of the week—and it was then that things started happening to me in connection with the house across the street. I was already in the habit of watching the comings and goings there; I'd been doing it ever since I had a one-night stand with a Welsh actor who lived in Iowa City. I met the actor, like Kathy, at a party; his name was Andrew and he was a student in the drama department at the university. He had a beautiful melodious accent and claimed to be totally smitten with me. After the party he wanted to go to my place and it was clear what he was after, and finally I let him talk me into it, though I said that at the most I would only let him spend the night on my couch. As we were approaching my block he got a strange look on his face and asked what my address was; it turned out his old girlfriend lived directly across the street from me. He insisted on going around the block and entering my apartment through the backyard in case she happened to be looking out the window. He left the next morning, promising to call in a few days.

I never heard from him again, but after that I did see his old girlfriend out the window sometimes. In the late afternoon she'd emerge from the house across the street wearing a loose blouse and an India-print skirt, get on an old red bicycle resting against the side of the porch, bump across the lawn, and take off down the street; Andrew had said she was a cocktail waitress. And sometimes earlier in the day she'd come out wearing a white bikini, spread a towel on the sloping grass of the lawn, and lie on her back in the sun. She had pale blond wavy hair and looked a little like a young, unhappy Grace Kelly. Andrew had said he'd broken her heart and I felt a certain camaraderie with her in her loneliness; I got sort of attached to knowing she was across the street. Then one day a green station wagon pulled up and an older woman who must have been her mother helped her carry boxes and lamps down the lawn and load them into the car. They tied a double mattress onto the roof, squeezed a few more items onto the backseat, slammed the tailgate shut with a *thunk*, and drove away. I watched them go, feeling bereft.

A couple moved into her apartment. They had a blue Chevy with a rear bumper sticker that said BIX LIVES. The woman was pregnant; the baby was born in March of 1988. I used to watch the husband walk the baby up and down the sidewalk in the evening. Then, after a year or so, I watched him play with the baby in front of the house. The kid was a cute little thing with wisps of blond hair and the man was muscular and bearded; his wife was tall and slender as a model. I thought they looked like the perfect family. Then the couple broke up; they weren't married after all but had only been living together, someone I knew who knew them told me. Even so, the man would come sometimes on Saturday evenings in the summer and mow the lawn. I was lonely at the time, and I used to sit on my front porch and drink a beer and watch him push the lawnmower around.

Finally I met him in George's Buffet, a bar on Market Street. His name was Steve Howe and he was a carpenter; he took care of the little boy, Walter, five days of the week. We started dating, though not very seriously. On Saturday nights we'd get together in his new apartment on Market Street, sit on the couch and pet the cat and play with Walter, and when Walter went to bed we'd drink beer and listen to music and try, in a forced, cheerful way we somehow never got beyond, to talk. Once I baby-sat for Walter while Steve went out. Walter was almost two then, and he spread a big pile of his books across the floor and went through every one, pointing at the pictures and telling me bits of the stories, like "hick, dick, dock, mouse clock."

Often during the week I'd see Steve park his van across the street, go in the house, and emerge a while later with Walter. Usually I ignored Steve when he was parked across the street— I felt shy at the thought of his ex-girlfriend looking out the window—but one day in May something made me go out-side to say hi. I didn't notice till I got to the other side of the street that he was already talking to someone: a compact, nice-looking man with short brown hair and blue eyes behind wire-rimmed glasses, seated on a little motorcycle.

I said, "Oh, I didn't know anyone else was here."

"I'm lurking behind Steve's van," the guy on the motorcycle said. And that was how I met Jim Beaman.

He got off the bike and Steve introduced us: The two of them were doing a job together, restoring an old house in my neighborhood. I already knew Steve was working there; I could see part of the house out my back window. We stood on the sidewalk making small talk while Walter played on the edge of the lawn. Jim asked Steve about the BIX LIVES bumper sticker on his car, and Steve said he'd gotten it at a music festi-val named in Bix Beiderbecke's honor—Bix was a jazz great who came from Iowa—and Jim said, with his humorous, hum-ble, engaging manner I would come to know so well, "To tell you the truth this is the first time I've ever heard of the guy." I think that might have been the moment I fell in love with him, or it might have been when he said he bought his motorcycle, a Honda 90, because he'd had one like it when he was fifteen that his father made him get rid of. "Can you believe it?" he said, grinning. "I'm forty years old and I'm still doing things because my old man wouldn't let me do them." He said he'd had an accident on the motorcycle by the railroad tracks on South Dubuque Street. "My head dribbled three times just like a basketball," he remarked. "After that I gave up drinking."

At one point in the conversation, Walter ran away along the sidewalk and Steve had to chase after him. I was glad; I wished Walter would keep on running and running, because by that time all I wanted was to be alone with Jim. I wanted to *talk* to him—in my mind I saw the two of us standing there engaged in energetic conversation, talking about intimate things, important things, the things that mattered most to us. What we actually discussed, though, was Volvos: A red Volvo station wagon was parked against the curb in front of Steve's van and Jim said he had a friend who owned one like it that he, Jim, coveted, and he told me a few other details about the friend. Then Steve came back carrying Walter.

It's hard to explain what it's like when you're attracted to someone as suddenly and fiercely as I was to Beaman, what it is about him that makes you fall in love with him. I suppose I could say I was drawn to Jim's quickness—even talking about Volvos he radiated brightness, as if there were an extra-high-wattage lightbulb inside him—to his self-deprecating humor, to the working-class job he did. He was a tuck-pointer: Tuck-pointing, I found out, involves scraping out old mortar from between bricks and replacing it with new mortar. I love smart working-class people, people who defy the stereotypes. They're part of my family heritage: My great-grandfather was a plumber and a philosopher; my grandmother was a nurse, a cook, and a concert pianist; my father made toothbrushes in a factory during the day, read the *Tao Te Ching* and Nietzsche at night, and did organic gardening on the weekends.

Another part of my heritage is making awful, life-ruining mistakes, and I suppose you could say that I had already intuited the mistakes Jim had made and would continue to make—there were hints, after all: the head dribbling three times on the tracks like a basketball—and that rather than discouraging me these added to his attraction in some unconscious way. It's a well-known phenomenon: the urge to repeat the past, find partners that mimic your parents' failures. My parents married unwisely and stayed together; my mother spent time in various mental hospitals; my father tormented her in small, hard-to-recognize, undermining ways. Jim's failures were similar but not the same, variations on the theme of throwing your life away.

But it wasn't as if I assessed his positive and possibly his negative qualities, then made an informed decision. It was more as if, the moment we met, invisible physical forces surrounding our bodies—electromagnetism, energy fields, subatomic particles—began heating up, accelerating, gravitating toward each other. I felt an instant sense of intimacy with him, as if all the rigmarole of courtship—the early phone calls, the terror of rejection, the first awkward touch—had already taken place. As if he and I were already partners, and all that was needed for us to be together—*really* together—was for Steve to go away. Of course, that was not the case.

Jim rode off on his little motorcycle, Steve and Walter drove away in the van, and I crossed the street and went into my house. I ate dinner, thinking about what I'd do when I saw Jim again. I was hoping he'd stop by my office in the next few days. He'd said he might; during our conversation he'd said he was trying to get a contract to restore some brick in the front of the Colonel Davenport house in Davenport, and I'd said what a coincidence; some of the archaeologists where I worked were doing a survey there, looking for historical remains. Jim had said that might be what was holding up his contract—the historical society was waiting for some report—and I said I'd check into it.

He didn't come to my office the next day and he didn't come the day after that. In the evening I looked up his name in the phone book; it wasn't there. I started to get a little worried about whether I was going to see him again, but not too worried; I knew I'd find a way. The next morning I was sitting at home at my desk staring out the window—I only worked in the archaeology office in the afternoons; I tried to write in the mornings—when I saw him ride up to the house he and Steve were working on, get off his motorcycle, and walk across the yard. I noticed he walked very upright, and that although it was a warm day he was wearing a long-sleeved shirt. I thought he looked boyish and cute; I didn't think it was odd that he was wearing long sleeves. The meaning of those sleeves didn't come to me until sometime in the following months, I don't remember exactly when.

Seeing him through the window that morning I briefly considered going out and strolling past the work site, trying to get his attention, but I decided against it; I wasn't absolutely certain he'd remember me. At work in the afternoon I asked the historical archaeologists—Ray and another guy, Marlin—about their survey at the Colonel Davenport house. They said they'd had to put it on hold for a few weeks to do something else. "We've got a neat book about the house, though," Marlin said, pulling a black vinyl three-ring binder off a shelf beside his desk. "Want to look at it?"

"Sure," I said.

I crossed the hall to my office, sat at my desk, opened the book, and skimmed a bit of the text. It described the materials and architecture of the house, the history of how it was built, the details of the colonel's occupation: George Davenport was an important Iowa figure; the city of Davenport was named after him. I turned to another page and came across the following sentence, embedded in a paragraph of biographical information: "The Davenport family included his wife Susan Lewis and sons George and Bailey born by his step-daughter," which I thought meant the colonel had had kids with his step-daughter, though someone told me later this was a misinterpretation. After I read the sentence I sat there and stared at the words on the page. I couldn't believe such a fact would be delivered without further comment or explanation. Marlin said I could borrow the book for a couple of days.

When I got home from work I looked Jim up in the phone book again; he still wasn't listed. During our conversation he'd said we were neighbors and described the house where he lived; it was across the street and about a block and a half from mine. After dinner I worked up my courage, went down the street, and knocked on what I thought was his door, carrying the book about Colonel Davenport. No one answered my knock; later on I found out Jim lived two doors down in another house.

I went back home and considered my next plan. I decided I would have to call Steve and get Jim's phone number. It seemed unethical to ask even a casual boyfriend how to get ahold of another man, but there didn't appear to be any way around it. "I feel like a snake," I said as I dialed Steve's number. He answered and I told him I had a book about the Davenport house I wanted to show Jim, and I told him about the thing between the colonel and his stepdaughter. He laughed and gave me Jim's phone number and that was that.

I was nervous about calling Jim, and an hour later I was still sitting in my living room rehearsing what I'd say to him when there was a knock on my door. It was Jim, saying that he'd stopped by Steve's house and that Steve had told him I had a book to show him.

He sat on my couch and I showed him the book. We talked. He said he'd taken some pictures of the Davenport house a few months ago and offered to go back to his house and get them if I wanted to see them. He left, then returned in ten minutes saying he couldn't find the pictures. We talked some more, this time sitting on my front steps so he could smoke. I said I didn't mind if he smoked in my house—in fact, I bummed one of his cigarettes; I'd quit four years earlier but still lit up occasion- ally—but Jim said he didn't feel comfortable smoking in houses where people didn't usually smoke. We sat outside and talked till it was almost dark; it was late May and there was light in the sky till close to nine. Then I got him to come inside—I was smoking steadily by then—and we sat on my couch and talked until one. Then Jim stood up and said, "Thank you very much for a very nice evening," and left.

The next night he called at seven-thirty and said he'd found his pictures of the Davenport house and if I wasn't doing anything he'd bring them down and show them to me. We looked through them briefly—snapshots of a large brick house, scaffolding in front of some parts, blue winter sky in the background—set them on my coffee table, and talked about other things until twelve-thirty. He came to my house the next night too, and every other night that week. Later on we called this time our couch days.

During that time we talked and talked. We talked about everything and nothing, his childhood and my childhood, people we'd slept with and people we hated, bad writing and practical jokes and construction work, death and college and dreams. One subject led seamlessly to another; at one point, Jim got up to go to the bathroom and stood outside the bathroom door for a good ten minutes because we couldn't stop talking long enough for him to go in there and pee.

He had a cat and had never been married, had lived with several different women over a period of years; he'd been seeing one until fairly recently. He'd grown up in Bettendorf, Iowa, and Des Moines; he'd had a Catholic upbringing, gone to Catholic schools. He talked about good and evil: He believed there was evil in the world, an independent force that could influence people, even those who were essentially good. He'd been a brig guard in the Marines during Vietnam and seen evil there but he didn't go into details; mostly he talked about escorting prisoners, illegally taking their handcuffs off as soon as they got off the base. He said his grandmother was buried in a very old spooky cemetery in Chicago; the place was full of bizarre gravestones, statues of gargoyles and large brooding figures and stone tree stumps wound round with carved thorny vines. He'd been there with his parents when he was twelve and still remembered it: The cemetery felt as if it were full of dark presences; he could feel it even before they drove through the entrance. Listening to him, I could see the cemetery, see him, a sensitive, overimaginative kid, taking it in, and I had a strange, foreboding feeling myself, a mixture of pain and love and some other dark, elusive something. As I look back on it now it seems to me that even then, sitting on the couch next to him, falling more and more in love, taking him in, absorbing every part of him, that even then I knew in some visceral way how our story was going to end.

But it was only a feeling, nothing I could put my finger on, just something I picked up along with other, more concrete, details about him: He loved tennis shoes and had five pairs of them, he had a talent for skipping rocks, he got anxiety attacks when he was sitting in the barber's chair having his hair cut. Language bubbled out of him as if generated by a high-speed computer, if a computer could have a sense of humor. He didn't say "walk," he said "toddle" or "stroll" or "creep" or "waddle"; he referred to certain of his friends as "honyawks," a word I'd heard as a kid but hadn't heard since. He told a story about getting out of the Marines and getting off the plane in the United States wearing his dress white uniform, feeling good about himself, then discovering that something that should have landed in his handkerchief—he had a sinus infection at the time—was resting on his lapel. He could say things like that without being gross or embarrassing; he exuded a clean, open earthiness, there was nothing ashamed or needy or awkward about him. He didn't seem to demand anything the way most men do: sympathy or sex or unqualified approval. He seemed only to want to amuse me.

We talked about sex a lot that week, but only as it had happened between other people—somebody's cheating wife and one of Jim's friends—or between one of us and someone else: how I lost my virginity to a boy with the generic name of John Smith, how he once slept with a former nun. We never talked about it in such a way as to imply it might ever occur between us. At the end of every night, at twelve-thirty or one, even as late as two or two-thirty, Jim would look at his watch, thank me for another nice evening, and leave. He never made any attempt to kiss me, never let on about what he was feeling. I was terrified the whole time that he just wanted to be friends, that he'd gradually withdraw and I'd never hear from him again. Later on he confessed he was afraid of the same things with me. And much later, when his sister came from North Carolina, when Jim was gone and all we could do was talk about him, she said he'd called her during that week—the week of our couch days—and said, "I think I'm in the L-word. I keep walking past her house with some excuse to stop in."

Lately, along with Bob and Julie, a man with a limp lives in the house across the street. He lives in an apartment on the bottom floor; Bob and Julie live above him, I think. Sometimes at twilight I watch him make his way down the porch stairs, a bag of garbage in one hand, the other hand clutching the railing. Then slowly, haltingly, using a cane, he rounds the corner of the house, delivers the garbage to the dumpster out back. Then he retraces his steps and disappears inside again. He's probably in his early forties, but I imagine he lives with his mother in there, that she serves him dinner with the TV on, that they watch the CBS evening news, then a bunch of sitcoms.

Across the street, surrounded by my apartment, by my house in its same old place on Washington Street, I lie on my couch in the evenings and read, stare absently at the wall where it meets the ceiling, at the shadows in the folds of the draperies, at the plant in the middle of my coffee table. I consider the ordinary familiarity of it all, try to reconcile it with the strangeness of the fact that I'm still here but Jim is gone, he no longer lives in this neighborhood or in any other neighborhood in the world.

Despite our fears and hesitations, Jim and I did get together, of course. We made love for the first time under a bush outside the Cantebury Inn during a break in a rainstorm, and after that there were very few nights when we didn't sleep together in my bed. We talked on the phone during the day, grocery-shopped and ate dinner together, walked back and forth between his house and my house. Once, on a clear dark night, walking down to my house from his house to go to bed, Jim looked up at the stars and said, "There's the Little Dipshit" and made me laugh and laugh. And once, after eating dinner at my house, going to his place to watch TV, we were so involved in what we were talking about we passed his house and didn't notice till we got to the corner of Governor Street. We were always talking, always laughing; dozing on his bed after eating, Jim once said he'd had a little romantic dream about us. "What were we doing?" I said.

"We were talking," he said.

In July, a month and a half after we met, he gave me a pink deep-sea coral engagement ring that was a cameo of a little woman; I bought him a stuffed great horned owl from one of his customers. He loved unusual, offbeat things like that. We were going to live in a restored brick building in the country, and Jim would lie in bed at night making plans: We thought we might raise miniature goats, he wanted to build secret passageways in the house our kids would think we didn't know about. We planned to get married in March. But on January 3 at two-fifteen in the afternoon he lay down on his bed, held a shotgun to his mouth, and pulled the trigger. I found out at four-thirty on my way home from work.

That was seven and a half years ago. The aftermath was terrible, but I survived. I have a different job, new friends, I exercise and wash my dishes, I take small pleasure in everyday things. I'm not crazy, not especially gullible. But I don't think about death the way most people do. I believe Jim is still around somehow, somewhere; I feel his presence in many small, ineffable ways. I say this knowing it sounds like wishful thinking, that some people will take it to mean that I haven't accepted reality.

And I say: Maybe.

But maybe death is not the end. Maybe love goes on and on. And maybe life is full of secret passageways and hidden rooms.

2

I'm sitting here trying to picture Jim Beaman, to conjure up his physical presence, tune him into memory like an image on a TV screen. I can almost but not quite see him. What I get is vague, hazy. Some dial needs to be turned to bring the picture into focus and there isn't such a dial, as far as I know. Maybe there's some kind of special meditation, some trick of metaphysics or the imagination, but if there is, I don't have access to it. All I can see are individual features. He had thick, short brown hair parted on the side, and at the back of his head was a tiny dot where there was no hair, and it was as if all his hair issued from that one spot. I don't know why, but that used to really interest me. He had a perfect masculine chin, not too square, not receding but not jutting out, either, and it had a dimple in it. There was another dimple on the side of his face, but that might have been a scar. And he had beautiful lips, just the right size and shape, though I didn't notice them right away—they were just there like everyone else's: a pair of lips. But after I noticed them I continued to notice them, I looked at them all the time. I used to say they were the most beautiful lips in the world.

But it doesn't seem quite accurate to look at him this way, to break him down feature by feature. It's like describing a painting in terms of the brush strokes. It doesn't capture him, it doesn't even capture what he looked like, it doesn't make me see him. I come the closest to seeing him when I picture his eyes. His eyes were large, blue, deep-set; they were clear, bright, translucent, like light on water, water with light in it. It's that light that I can't see anymore when I try to picture him, it's that light that brought the picture into focus.

Another way I can sometimes get him to come in—come in a little, at least—is to picture him in motion: talking, gesturing, grinning, alive and full of animation on the other side of my bed.

I've had the same bed, or at least the same bed frame—a full-size, walnut-stained four-poster—for almost thirty years; I bought it from a used-furniture store in 1971. It's not in perfect shape; it has a few scratches and stains, some small patches of varnish have worn off the knobs on the posts, but I like it. It's one of the few things that have remained constant in my life for many years. It's seen me through bad-job-induced insomnia, the guilty naps of freelancing, the anxious sleep of unemployment; through three (not counting Jim) long-term relationships, two of them more or less harmonious, one an out and out psychological death struggle; through a series of one-night stands; through an affair with a married man; through lengthy stretches of solitude.

Not only has all that taken place in the same bed, but most of it—the part that involved me alone, at least, which is nearly all of it—has taken place on the same side of the bed. For some reason, I always sleep on the right; I never, ever venture over to the left. For twenty years I had a foam mattress and by the time I met Jim the mattress was split-level. The side I always slept on was flat and low, the other side rose away from me at a slight but distinct angle. Every now and then I'd accidentally roll over onto it, notice vaguely that I seemed to be lying on an incline, feel a little bit bad but not too bad about the cause of it—over the years I'd gotten used to being single—then slide back down to the flat familiar part of the mattress and go back to sleep.

One of the first things Jim and I did after getting together was drive to Sears and buy a new mattress and box spring. We brought them back to my house in the back of the truck and carried them awkwardly in their plastic wrappers into the bedroom. Jim had the idea of leaving the old box spring and simply putting the new one and the mattress on top of it, and that's what we did, removing the giant plastic wrappings, angling the new blue box spring and mattress around till we could lay them one by one with a *whump* on top of the old one. We peeled off the paper claim stuck to the mattress, tossed the guarantees aside, made the bed, took the sheets of plastic and the old foam mattress out to the curb to be carted off by the garbage truck Wednesday morning. Then we came back in and admired the bed. The added altitude of two box springs lent it an illusion of grandness that went beyond mere height; it seemed larger than life, almost mythical. When I sat on it next to Jim, our backs resting against the headboard, it seemed not only high but wide and spacious, a magical kingly perch.

It is on my bed that I see Jim the most; it was there, as on an island, that most of our relationship—at least the most important parts of it—seem to have taken place. We did all sorts of things on that bed: We talked, and occasionally we read, leaning up against gray reading pillows, though this never lasted very long because one of us would say something and we'd get involved in conversation. Most of the time we forgot about our books altogether, though Jim brought his faithfully to my house at bedtime just in case. "Every night I take my book for a walk," he said. Once we ate a pizza on the bed; another time, facing each other, sitting cross-legged, we played with a Ouija board on the bed, and twice—over Thanksgiving and Christmas—we rented a color TV and a VCR and watched a bunch of movies lying side by side. Once I hypnotized Jim on my bed, and sometimes I rubbed his back or feet with Icy Hot, a soothing greasy balm for muscle aches; one of his shoulders hurt all the time from tuck-pointing, and his feet, which had unusually high insteps, also bothered him. When he lay on his back his feet assumed a certain position—heels together, toes flopping outward—and I used to say they looked insouciant and rakish, like outlaws and rebels; I used to call them Frank and Jesse, after Frank and Jesse James. We slept in my bed and told each other our dreams in the morning. Jim talked in his sleep as well; once toward the end he said, in the halting, dreamy, childish voice of sleep talkers, "I have a bowl of fish for you."

The other important thing we did on my bed, of course, was make love, have sex, whatever you want to call it; none of the usual ways of putting it ever seem to me very adequate. No one expects you to like the phrase "have sex"; only junior high school students really use it; it's stiff, unemotional, distancing, almost as bad as the clinical, insert-slot-A-into-slot-B-sounding "sexual intercourse." But "make love" is another matter. To admit you don't like that way of referring to sex is to risk being considered uptight, sex-hating, unable to face straight-on without flinching the whole adult, lush, naked business of it. But I am confessing it: I don't like the expression "making love." I'm embarrassed by it; to me it has the ring of sentimentality and something slightly exhibitionist. It reminds me of those lengthy, air-brushed, irrelevant sex scenes early-seventies movies usually included, like the one in *Don't Look Now* between Donald Sutherland and Julie Christie.

Jim called what we did "rolling around," a phrase I liked because it's neutral; it has few or no connotations at all. He had other, more irreverent euphemisms for sex enacted by other people; "strapping it on" was one, "booming" was another. Once in a gas station he told me a guy named Nick Nothnagel who was filling his tank at the next pump over had split up with his wife after he found out she was "laying more pipe than Standard Oil" with other men. "Nick was never the same after-

wards," Jim said, his mood suddenly sober. He regarded infi-
delity as a serious matter; his first girlfriend had cheated on
him and he'd never quite gotten over it; in fact he had a kind of
phobia of being cheated on. I nodded and we exchanged a look
of sympathy for Nick Nothnagel's bad luck; implicit was the
understanding that we—that Jim—would be luckier: He had
me now. We grinned, went back to joking. "She was laying
more pipe than Standard Oil," Jim repeated, and I laughed all
over again.

"She could suck the chrome off a trailer hitch," was another
thing he said along those lines, though not on that occasion.

Of course, we never used such expressions to describe anything we did; they were too ironical, too much a way of commenting wryly on someone else. For us, there was a whole
separate lexicon: in addition to "rolling around," our vocabu-
lary included terms such as hooters, gleep, bullets, and OK
jelly. These stood for artifacts and customs, which together
with the language made up the culture of our own minute
civilization.

For equipment we had two gray reading pillows Jim picked
up at Kmart for reading in bed but with something else in
mind as well. "Bullets" were white contraceptive inserts we
bought but never used, deciding that if I got pregnant we'd
simply get married and be happy about it. The OK jelly, also
known as KY Jelly, was used often and kept in the drawer of the
nightstand by my side of the bed.

There were certain little parenthetical traditions, occurring
before, between, or after sex: the retrieving from the kitchen,
sipping, forgetting, and inevitable spilling of a half-filled glass
of water; the getting out of bed, repeatedly, to pee a little bit—
we called this "peeing six drops," which I, especially, was prone
to. There was the endless talking and equally endless smoking,
by me as well as Jim; I had taken the habit back up with a
vengeance.

And then there was the central motif of sex itself: "rolling around" and its variations, such as a position we called the flying T, which involved both of us lying on our backs, me on top, our bodies forming a kind of X. It was a lazy sort of activity, performed at the end of the night at the edge of sleep, and it really did feel as if we were flying somewhere, gliding through the night above the city on a magic floating carpet of desire, or executing an amazing, dreamy, two-part circus act in the dark dizzying heights of an enormous, ceilingless tent.

But most of what I recall of actual sex with Jim is visceral, atavistic, untranslatable; it presents itself in memory as being in a dark, submerged, nebulous, swirling kind of place, a place where friction gives rise to energy, where needful, mutually attracted elements converge, where, after a spell of frenzied motion, all the little puzzle pieces formerly at odds fall perfectly—*click!*—into place. Only a few concrete details float to the surface: the way Jim's shoulders looked close-up from the vantage point of lying underneath him—curved, brownish tan, scattered over with large, dark, oddly shaped freckles, like maps of little countries; the small but infinitely expressive groan, almost a grunt, which escaped from him at the moment of orgasm, which I would do anything in the world to hear again.

Another set of memories revolve around Jim's truck and work. Pickup trucks are common in Iowa; carpenters and other working men most often have them—loading up the backs with outsize toolboxes, ladders, two-by-fours, wheelbarrows— and Jim was no exception. His truck was a 1977 Chevy Cheyenne with a two-tone paint job: bronze on the bed and fenders, cream-colored on the top and hood. It was a good-sized vehicle, with a fair step up to get inside the cab. The front seat was wide and roomy. Usually a small pile of things rested in the middle between the driver and the passenger side: a newspaper, a cigarette lighter, the black notebook Jim kept track of business notes in, the green bandanna he sometimes tied around his forehead when he was working, to keep the sweat out of his eyes. Tuck-pointing is hard physical labor. It involves rigging up complicated scaffolding, dealing with heat and dust, wielding heavy grinders for hours. But Jim was always cheerful when he had work. What he hated were the off-times: the rainy days; the long, bitterly cold, unemployed winters.

I have a snapshot of him doing a job, tuck-pointing a chimney of a large white house in Iowa City. The picture was taken from the ground by John Gray, his old friend who worked with him during that last summer, the summer he had me and everything was going well and he was so optimistic. His business was taking off and there was lots of money coming in and he had so many jobs lined up he needed to hire John. The picture's a four-by-six-inch color snapshot. In it, Jim is balancing high up on a narrow piece of scaffolding beside the chimney, wielding a mortar board in one hand—the way old-fashioned artists are always pictured holding palettes—a trowel in the other. Next to the house is a huge old oak tree; its leaves, a canopy of green and yellow dots like a pointillist painting, frame the figure of Jim, wearing a white T-shirt and blue jeans. Small within the picture's composition, foreshortened by perspective, he peers down at John through a large, strategic opening in the leaves, sunlight slanting diagonally across his face and chest, the mild blue sky a backdrop to him, the house, the tree. He looks perfectly at home there, relaxed, sure-footed, as confident as an eagle in its aerie.

If business was slow he'd park in the driveway of some old brick house, go up and knock and try to talk whoever came to

the door into having their house tuck-pointed. When I went
with him to Solon Beef Days, a yearly midsummer small-town
Iowa festival—there's a band, and lines in front of tables where
they sell cheap watery beer, and a striped tent you eat barbe-
cued beef and corn on the cob under—he took me down a
street and showed me three large brick buildings he was trying
to talk the city of Solon into hiring him to tuck-point. He had a
made-up word for these marketing activities, as he did for
many things; he loved euphemisms, nicknames, odd quizzical
ways of putting things. The word he used for drumming up
business was "beamonizing." I loved that word. In my mind it
called up images of Beaman going from customer to customer
talking his way into business he didn't quite deserve, like a bee
pollinating flowers or a sly, hucksterish Johnny Appleseed
planting trees. "I've been bee-mo-nized," I used to say.

Once he got a customer on the line it was time to make up a
bid. There were official-looking forms for this, with "Proposal" printed on top in a kind of script. Most of the form was
devoted to space for describing the work that needed doing.
Here Beaman would write, "Tuck-point west side and fill in
hole south side," or "Front porch regrouting. Wash regrouted
surface w/muratic acid ('Sure-Klean 600')." There was space at
the bottom for signatures and the price. I would sometimes
type a bid onto one of these forms for him; he'd sit next to me
at the desk and watch, telling me what to type where, both of
us laughing and joking and smoking. I had a persona that arose
out of these times, and so did he: I was Miss Hellfinger and
he was Omar Pignuts. Jim came up with them—one day, while
I was typing at my desk, he simply started calling me Miss
Hellfinger; Omar Pignuts was born the same way a few minutes later—but we pictured them and filled them out together.
Omar Pignuts was short and shysterish and seedy; he wore a
dark-red suit and smelled like old cigar smoke; Miss Hellfinger

was tall and ropy and old-maidish, with cat's-eye glasses and her hair in a messy French twist. They were, of course, having an affair. For Jim's birthday, I wrote him a short, silly story involving the two of them, sex, working late, and reading pillows. And once Jim sent me a letter in the mail with a small picture of a pig's face and two circles on the envelope instead of a return address; I countered with a skinny finger jutting out of flames beside a pitchfork.

Once I visited him at a job. He was tuck-pointing the side of a private grade school on a leafy street a couple of blocks from downtown, and I stopped by there on my way to work. I came up behind him as he was mixing mortar on the lawn and he turned around and saw me and grinned. I hugged him and patted his back and a puff of dust came out of his shirt.

I have another memory of him at that job, too—where does it come from? Maybe I visited him again on my way home? The first memory—the memory of the puff of dust, of him mixing mortar—is lit by bright, morning sunlight, it has a cheerful workday atmosphere. But this other memory's set in the deep, cool shade of late afternoon; there's a feeling of exhaustion in the air, of the day's early energy and promise having been used up. Again I'm coming up behind him, but this time he's on a ladder against the side of the building; his back is to me, and when I first spot him—in that split second before I recognize him, or maybe as I'm in the process of recognizing him, of registering who and what I'm seeing—I feel a momentary shock: Standing on the spindly ladder, surrounded on all sides by a broad expanse of red brick, he looks small and vulnerable, almost childlike, and there's an aura of unhappiness about him, of boredom and impatience, and there is also something childlike about this. Then the moment was gone. I spoke to him and he turned and saw me; he smiled and came down the ladder and lit a cigarette and we stood in the shade beside the building talking; he was his usual affable, mature, flannel-shirted working self, and I forgot that I had seen a glimpse of that other side of him.

In the evenings when he was done with work we'd sometimes drive to Dane's Dairy for a milkshake, out on Highway 1. Dane's is on the right past a "thickly settled" area; to get there you go by a jumble of restaurants, lumber yards, used-car lots. Then, just before Dane's, the businesses give way to fields and the road splits and opens up, a wide strip of yellow grass separating the two sets of lanes. We'd pull off into Dane's parking lot and circle around to join a line of cars, moving forward inch by inch as each car ahead of us approached in turn the outdoor-service window and the occupants gave their orders, paid and received their change. When we got there a teenage boy would pull across a screen and stick his head out the opening. Jim would get a butterscotch shake; usually I'd ask for chocolate after some quick, last-minute deliberation. The boy would close the screen and disappear and then we'd wait, truck idling, staring through the windshield into the glare of the late-day sun. Finally they'd come and Jim would pay and pull ahead into an empty parking space in the shade; we'd peel the paper off our straws, poke them through the holes in the plastic cup lids, suck up the first swallows of our milkshakes. After a minute Jim would ask me if I wanted to try a taste of his and I would nod, hand him my milkshake, take his. I've never liked butterscotch; I could never bring myself to order it from Dane's, even though I was always surprised to find, trying Jim's, that theirs was white, not yellow, light and frothy, sweet but not too sweet.

Pulling back out of the parking lot, Jim would often turn to me and say with a grin, "Well, should we go for a ride and blow the stink off us?" and we'd turn right and continue heading out past the fields on Highway 1. There were more fields on the other side of them, and if you kept on going you'd eventually get to Kalona, or if you turned off at a certain place you'd end up in Riverside. These are tiny, bright-colored towns with a mild, haunted, time-stopped quality; Riverside's main street has an out-of-business diner, a laundromat with a huge dusty pane-glass window, a grain and feed company, and a Pepsi machine.

We'd ride and ride until it was twilight, then pitch-black night, cool air rushing through the open windows, the truck's headlights throwing their beams onto the straight flat road ahead, the vast dark fields spreading out for miles on either side of us. Occasionally a fork of heat lightning streaked across the sky in the distance illuminating the clouds, the corn, a wooden fence.

Jim made chess sets in his spare time, sculpting them out of clay and then baking them, and one Saturday afternoon in early November we drove to Kalona where he was having one cast in steel and brass. Some of his chess sets were political, the black pieces representing liberals, the white ones conservatives. Each piece was carved and painted to resemble someone famous: George McGovern held his hands up in a "who knows" gesture as a black bishop; Jeane J. Kirkpatrick, the white queen, stared impatiently down at her wristwatch; William F. Buckley grimaced as a white rook; Hunter Thompson, a black knight in a Hawaiian shirt, gave everybody the finger. The pieces were labeled at the bottom—knight, rook, pawn, and so forth—but they were nearly impossible to play with. Jim wanted to make something that was closer to the classical game pieces, a unique but usable set that was also reproducible. He'd been working on one for a while, a set with tall, shapely, intricately carved pieces. The knight was a horse with a mane, square prominent teeth, a long, elegant neck; the bishop had a miter, a beard, and a kindly expression; the pawns looked something like Beaman himself. This was the set that was being cast for reproduction by the place in Kalona.

It was a nice day the day we drove down there, sunny and blue, warm for early November. The casting place belonged to an artist and had a storefront with various pieces on display: a copper sundial, a bronze slice of toast, an iron fish with fingers. The artist showed Jim molds that had been made of his pawn and bishop; they looked good and Jim was pleased. Back in the truck, shifting into reverse, he commented shyly—he hardly ever talked about his sculpting as if it were anything more than a hobby—that he might be finally getting somewhere with it.

But the thing that sticks in my mind about that trip was something else he said. Whizzing along the highway on the way home from Kalona he looked over at me and remarked, "I think I'm getting a cavity." He said it casually, with an air of slight concern, as if he cared what happened to him, as if he planned to have a future.

3

Jim had a roommate, Peggy, and a cat, Kitts. Peggy worked in the neurosurgery department of the hospital and spent a lot of time at Gabe's, a bar on Washington Street with a pool table on the first floor, a dance floor upstairs, and a beer garden out back. Among Jim's things I found a Polaroid of him seated at a picnic table in the beer garden with a few other guys, a pitcher of beer in the middle of the table. One of the men has a round moon face and long hair; another, a black guy, wears thick, square-rimmed glasses. Jim has on a pink baseball cap; his face is out of focus; his eyes look woozy and sad.

Once he said, during the early stage of our romance, when optimism was running high: "My twenties were all right, my thirties were a disaster, and I think my forties are going to be my best decade yet." In his twenties, after Vietnam, he went to college, had two long-term relationships, worked on construction and learned tuck-pointing, played horseshoes at parties, hung out in bars. In his thirties drinking and other problems took over; he had a tempestuous affair with an older woman, moved in with her and then out, ended up living for a while in his truck. Peggy sort of rescued him at that point, took him home and helped him dry out. For a while he slept on her couch, then they moved downstairs to a two-bedroom apartment in the same house. There had never been anything romantic between them but their relationship was as bitter and complex as any bad marriage.

The Rooms of Heaven

Kitts was a large tortoiseshell cat. She wasn't fat but she was long and the bottom of her belly sagged because the vet who spayed her failed to perform the little surgical tuck that would have kept it firm. She was fifteen years old but still in good shape; she had bright eyes, thick glossy fur. Jim was fond of calling her the Miss America of cats. He used to hold her on his lap and sing little songs to her. "She's an old pooh cat, she's a ball of chicken fat," one of them went. Another was a version of "I'm a Little Teapot" that ended, "When you tip her over what do you git? A whole lot of yowling and a litter box full of shit." There was a particular posture she adopted while he petted her: feet planted on his chest, back slightly arched, tail sticking straight up in the air, eyes squeezed shut in kitty bliss. When he scratched a certain spot on her back near the base of her tail she closed her eyes even tighter and stuck out the tip of her tongue, and Jim would say, "No, Kitts, we have no stamps for you to lick today."

"That cat and I have been man and wife for fifteen years," he joked the first time we met.

He was very protective of her. He never fed her anything but dry Science Diet pellets—everything else made her throw up—and he never let her go outside for fear she'd be run over by a car or encounter some other threat. Once, he told me, when a woman he was dating didn't like her and suggested it was time to choose between herself and the cat, he stood up, picked up the woman's purse and held it out to her saying, "Well, here's your pocketbook."

The cat had been with him through all kinds of times. Once, he said, during the months he was living in his truck, he was driving somewhere with the catbox in the back and the little shits went flying out onto the windshield of the car behind him. For years he'd been petting her on the bed in the morning, playing shoestring with a bootlace, singing her the pooh cat/chicken fat song, calling her the Miss America of cats. She was a kind of extension of himself. But it wasn't surprising some woman had wanted him to get rid of her, because she—the cat—was cold and unfriendly, even intimidating, to everyone but Jim; it was as if she'd used up all her love on him and had none left over for anyone else. She ignored Peggy; if a visitor reached down and tried to pet her she opened her mouth wide exposing needlelike teeth and let loose a loud, terrifying hiss. Beaman said even some of his big huge construction worker friends were afraid of her.

I gave her a wide berth at first and she avoided me also, though once at the very beginning when Jim and I were alone in the apartment lying on his bed, she squeezed past the end of the sliding door into the bedroom, padded in, put her head down and delicately sniffed my underpants on the floor. "She likes you," Jim said.

Beaman and I used to say that after we got married we were going to have Christmas cards made up, the kind where you combine a family photo with a preprinted holiday sentiment on a cardboard rectangle, and the photo was going to be a picture of me, Jim, the cat, my engagement ring, and the owl. It pleased us to think of this as our odd little family, depicted for the outside world at Christmas in an offbeat twist on tradition: Jim holding the cat on his lap, me with my hand raised, ring finger thrust forward, the owl with its spooky, arrested strangeness staring down from the wall behind us.

My engagement ring, purchased and given to me on July 27, 1990, is a pink cameo dinner ring. It came from an antique store and was packaged in a small ancient greenish-gray box, the words H. C. WINEKE, OXFORD JCT., IOWA, GIFTS THAT LAST printed in blue on top. The cameo is a little woman carved from an oval of deep-sea coral; you see her head, throat, part of her chest and one small raised shoulder. A simple, togalike garment falls in folds from her shoulder. Her carved hair is swept back in a little bun and the pink of her cheek is slightly darker, like a shadow or a blush. The first time I saw the ring—the moment I lifted the lid off the small grayish-green box and looked at its contents—I was slightly taken aback. It was nothing like what I'd been expecting; it was big, long, and thin; it covered almost the whole space between my first two knuckles. I tried not to let on, of course; I squealed, hugged Jim, did all the usual things you do when you get an engagement ring, but Jim must've sensed my reaction, because he said, "Don't worry, you'll get to like it." And I did. I came to see it the way he did. The ring was a symbol for our relationship, a representation in some way of me: Jim said that I was pink and it was pink and that was one of the reasons he picked it. But it was also an entity in itself; it was not just a stone but a little woman, an imaginary person. At night in bed we dreamed up qualities and a history for her: She'd been a prostitute in New Orleans, a tea-leaf reader in Rome. We kept changing the story.

The owl, my engagement gift to Jim, wasn't just an old stuffed bird, either, this strange, dusty, scary-looking thing, as I sometimes think my friends must see it now. It was life in death, animation captured in stillness, power and spookiness, but power and spookiness harnessed for good. It was another symbol of our relationship. Jim once brought it with him on a dangerous errand, ostensibly to show the people at the house where he went—look, isn't this strange?—but also, as he later told me, to remind himself of us, as an aid to willpower, a kind of talisman against harm.

There was another gift along the lines of the ring and the owl. At Christmastime, Jim gave me a gold pendant watch shaped like a bug. He said he got it for me because it was a June bug and I was born in June and because when I was pestering him about something he would say, "You are a bug," in a way that always reminded me of Richard Nixon saying, "I am not a crook." The watch is an antique; he bought it in the same store where he got my engagement ring. The bug has a head and wings and a pair of antennae sticking up on either side of the head, and when you squeeze the antennae together the wings open, exposing a round watch face. Jim was really pleased with that gift; he kept talking about it before Christmas in this happy way, telling me I'd never in a million years guess what it was, saying it really meant something to him and would mean a lot to me.

When I unwrapped it I felt just like I did the first time I saw my ring—I didn't quite know what to make of it—and he said, "I know it seems kind of weird but you'll see, after a while you'll get to love it, just like you did the ring." What he was saying, I think, was that after a while I'd catch on to the meaning he saw in it. That it would become more than just a plain, regular object in the flat, one-dimensional way of the everyday world; it would take on extra depth, heft, significance, meaning. But he didn't live long enough for that to happen. The watch never came to mean very much to me; I leave it on the bottom of my jewelry box and I hardly ever think about it. I suppose I don't want to think about it because of what took place two weeks after he gave it to me.

But there's a strange thing: The watch I have is not the one he gave me. For a while after he died I wore the watch around my neck all the time on a chain. One day I wore it to the Old Capitol Mall in downtown Iowa City and when I got home the chain was there but the watch was gone. I felt terrible. I went back to the mall to try to find it; I asked at the lost and found but they didn't have it; I walked around the mall sort of half-heartedly looking for it but I knew it was gone, and after a while I gave up and went home. I felt guilty, as if I should have known better than to wear it, but I tried to put it out of my mind. At that point I couldn't take any more losses.

Then one day about a week later, out of curiosity—out of the same grief-related impulse that made me pore over Jim's old photos, wear his clothes, hang on to anything there was left of him to hang on to—I looked inside a little box I'd given him just to see what was in it. There were four cameos, each wrapped carefully in toilet paper; there was a Swiss army knife with a red handle with a cross on it; there were three Belgian relief medals that he'd bought at the Hoover Museum, in round cardboard gilt-edged boxes; there was a set of little Mexican worry men. And there—amazingly—was another gold bug watch, exactly like the one I'd lost.

The first time Jim's cat let me pet her was the day we got the owl. It's a real great horned owl, stuffed in 1963. It has soft little stumps of ears—the horns of its name—brown, silky, variegated feathers, a curved, mahogany nub of a beak. We acquired it from one of Jim's tuck-pointing clients, an artist named Judith Spencer who lived in an old brick schoolhouse in the country. At the time we bought the owl from her she and Jim were negotiating for him to tuck-point a building on her property. The owl was on the wall in her living room; she said she used to have two but her cat tried to eat one and wrecked it. Jim saw the owl and fell in love with it. He offered to do the tuck-pointing job for a reduced price with the owl thrown in; in the end the job was postponed and Judith sold us the owl for $125. I paid for it as Beaman's engagement gift.

He wanted the owl to put on the wall above his desk. The wall was covered with framed pictures and other stuff; he said he liked to look up there in the morning when he was drinking his coffee, petting the cat, thinking about the day ahead. There was a collage of figures, some local, some famous, crowded into a bar, made by a friend of his; Jim was one of the locals, a photo of his face pasted on someone else's body in a tuxedo. There was a ceramic mask of a person of ambiguous sex, a small framed picture of me, a framed copy of a newspaper article that had been written about his chess sets, a piece of window-box art that showed a woman in a slip leaning out the window of a brick tenement house.

We drove out to Judith's and picked up the owl on the first Saturday in August. I carried it home on my lap in the truck. It smelled faintly musty and it was awkward to hold; I was afraid it would break the whole way back. At Jim's, the cat took one look at it and fled to the kitchen. "Don't be spooked, Kitts," Jim called to her, opening a metal toolbox on his desk. He scrounged around and found a hammer and nail, pounded the nail into the wall and hung the owl from it—it's mounted on a branch attached to a disk of varnished wood; the wooden disk goes against the wall—and together we stepped back and inspected it. It stared down at us with eerie, lifelike, raptor intensity, its round black eyes somehow even fiercer because they were made of glass.

Beaman was delighted. He paced a few feet to the right to view it from another angle. "Look!" he said. "The eyes follow you." I walked to a corner of the room; the owl's eyes appeared to rotate slowly in the same direction.

"They do," I said. "It's sort of scary."

Jim walked to the left, turned and retraced his steps. "That's incredible." He laughed and crossed the floor and hugged me and we sat down side by side on the bed, still gazing up at the owl, unable to take our eyes off it. A few minutes later the cat came hesitantly into the room. She leapt up next to us and calmly stepped onto my lap as if it were something she always did. I put my hand on her head and she remained there purring as I petted her. Beaman was delighted with that too. "My family's complete now," he said.

But what I remember most about that day was his appearance the moment he crossed the floor to me, before we sat on the bed. With his boyish stature, close-cropped hair, and wire-rimmed glasses, he always looked younger than forty, but that day it was almost eerie how young he looked, as if he, like the owl, like a cat with nine lives, had been granted another chance.

4

At my house, in my bedroom, is an old metal-banded steamer trunk that used to be Beaman's. I've added a few things, but mostly I leave it full of the stuff he kept in it: mementos, letters, keepsakes, miscellaneous items he saved over the years. I'm amazed at some of the things he saved: an autograph book from the fifth grade; an envelope addressed to a woman he had an affair with, containing a letter from her husband, asking for a divorce; several pairs of discarded wire-rimmed glasses preserved in their cases; a copy of *Time* magazine dated February 27, 1978, with Muhammed Ali on the cover—the article inside is about Ali losing the title to Leon Spinks; an eighth-grade yearbook from Our Lady of Lourdes Junior High School, in Bettendorf, Iowa. The back pages of the yearbook are covered with inscriptions in the large, wavering, self-conscious handwriting of Jim's schoolmates. "To a shy kid with a good sense of humor," one of them says. "If in heaven we don't meet, side by side we'll take the heat," says another. And "To Beans (see you in Hell)," writes a boy who signs his name as "The Blade."

For a long time after Jim died, after anger set in—the terrible foot-stamping rage that went on for months and months like a case of dry heaves; nothing would ever come up, nothing would make it better—I used to lie on my bed and say accusingly to his things or the air around the ceiling, to anything that might contain his spirit: You saved everything except yourself.

The Rooms of Heaven

. . .

There are a lot of photographs in the trunk and the pictures tell a kind of story: Beaman's life from birth to death, or almost; there's a little margin of months on either side where no photos were taken. A Polaroid does exist of Jim after death; the funeral director took it and sent it to his parents in North Carolina to help them accept the fact of his death, but that isn't in the trunk. I don't know what happened to it; I think his parents probably destroyed it.

There's only one picture in the trunk that shows Jim on the other, early end of life. It's a small square black-and-white snapshot of him as a fat, bundled-up baby, his mother holding him up for the camera, his fat little cheek pressed against her cheek. It's winter, there are bare trees and a distant house in the background, Jim's mother wears dark lipstick and a wavy fifties hairstyle. Jim's eyes are closed, his face is set in a mask of baby misery, he looks as if he wants to cry or as if he's dreaming a bad dream.

In the trunk is an album of photographs taken in July 1964, when Jim's family took a trip to the New York World's Fair. In the snapshots they appear to be a normal average family of that era. In one picture Jim's father stands, ruddy-faced and vacation-outfitted, sporting a manly watch and sunglasses, camera slung over his shoulder, against a dramatic natural background: They must've stopped at Niagara Falls on the way to Queens. In another—now, obviously, they're at the World's Fair—his father, mother, and sister stand in front of a futuristic solar-paneled building. His mother and sister clutch matching white pocketbooks by the handle; his father wears black pants and a white short-sleeved shirt, his glasses and haircut reflecting the style of the era. Jim must have been taking the picture. Other photos serve as records of his boyish interests: a Hawaiian hula dancer in bandanna skirt and lei, a new-model T-bird, a statue of an Egyptian pharaoh, and a dirigible sailing high in the blue sky all captured his attention.

Loose in the trunk is what is probably Jim's senior high school graduation picture, enlarged, enclosed in a cream-colored cardboard portfolio. In it he's wearing a dark plaid wool suit and a paisley tie, one shoulder dipping lower than the other; he has glossy brown hair that falls across his forehead, large dreamy eyes, beautiful full lips. He looks like every teenage girl's dreamboat fantasy; I never would have gotten my hands on anyone so cute back then. He was rebellious, hoodlumish, though you'd never know it looking at this picture. Once I told him I hung out with the smart, poetry-writing, Vietnam War–protesting crowd in high school, and he said, "We would not have been friends in high school."

There's a whole album of snapshots taken in Okinawa and Vietnam. As a brig guard, Beaman was based in Okinawa and went back and forth to Vietnam to escort prisoners to Okinawa and the States. The pictures in the photo album show lush blue-green landscapes and unidentified cities, large, open-sided tents and Quonset-hut barracks. Jim wrote comments in blue felt-tip pen on the backs of a few of the photos. One picture, which shows two young men seated on cots beneath an open-air tent surrounded by stacks of cut wood, three large trash cans, various other items, says cheerfully on the back, "Two people trying to get out of work—I was hiding behind the garbage cans."

There are two other pictures of Jim in the Marines that were not pasted into the photo album. In one, a black-and-white snapshot, Jim is posing beside another young Marine in an outdoor setting; both are wearing fatigues—shirts with rolled-up sleeves, pants tucked into combat boots, little caps with bills, everything the same drab color. They're standing in the grass at the edge of a river; the water goes right up to the grass—there's no sandy shore like there would be here. Both guys are holding something small and white in one hand which at first I couldn't identify, then figured out are copies of other snapshots. Jim's buddy is grinning and has a cigarette dangling out of one side of his mouth. He's taller and lankier than Jim, who is short and compact and looks astonishingly young, as he does in all of these pictures of him as a Marine. He's sort of half frowning into the camera, all business. He told me once that the way he got by in the Marines was to melt into the wall, to attract no more attention to himself than necessary.

The other Marine photo that was loose in the trunk is a color Polaroid. The color is dark, maybe because the picture was taken in indoor lighting: Everything, the background, Jim's clothes—he's wearing fatigues again, but in this picture his shirt is untucked—even his brown hair are all tinged with gunmetal bluish green. You can't see much of the background, but I think he's standing inside a barracks in front of a bunk; there's a flat-angled surface behind him, something like a white pillow and a bit of sheet at one end of it. He's smoking a cigarette, held casually in his right hand; he's smiling a neutral little smile into the camera. I pulled this picture out of a group he showed me when we were first involved; I wanted to keep it along with a few others to send to some of my friends, to show them what he looked like. I picked this one because he looks adorable in it, and Jim let me take it, but a month or two later he said, "I hope you don't show that picture to anyone." When I asked him why he said it was taken a few minutes after an occurrence in a Danang PX where some Viet Cong came in and there was shooting, people got killed, though he was safely crouched behind a shelf. He couldn't explain exactly why those circumstances made him want me not to share the picture; he must have thought something showed in his face that he didn't want anyone else to see, but I didn't know what that was, and I didn't ask him.

There's a whole pile of pictures taken during his twenties and thirties. There are pictures of him balancing on scaffolds, staring eye-to-eye at chimneys, peering over the tops of roofs; pictures of various apartments he lived in and girlfriends he lived with and of him looking fatter or thinner, younger or older, wearing different styles of glasses, depending on the time. There are pictures of the cat: lounging and yawning on unmade beds; squatting in a beleaguered crouch in the middle of a patch of grass; staring up at the camera from doorways with round, shiny, indignant eyes.

Jim wrote comments on the backs of some of these old photos, as he did on the ones taken in Okinawa and Vietnam; they say things like "Me and the Lipsious chimney" and "Roy Playing Horse Shoes at Fishers Party." I love these little messages in his familiar, peaked and rounded handwriting. I'm amazed that he would have taken the time to write them, like some old lady with a head full of memories and too much leisure on her hands. I find myself turning over each picture with a sense of expectation; I want to know what he has to say about everything.

A slightly out-of-focus picture of the cat sitting on a chair in the kitchen of some forgotten apartment—there's a pale-yellow brick wall, a wooden Formica-topped table, Jim's steamer trunk with a newspaper lying on top of it—says on the back, "My true love at Lakewood Hills." The cat is curled up, one leg extending beyond the edge of the chair seat. Her half-closed eyes are yellow, her ears stick up like tense little sails.

One picture, taken from the ground, from a distance of thirty or forty feet, shows Jim sliding in a standing position down the peak of a large, ugly, burnt-siena-colored house, one hand grabbing onto a TV antenna. On the back he wrote, "Me falling from the Lipsious chimney." Falling off chimneys was part of his personal mythology, a running joke he had with himself. Printed on his pads of letterhead, at the top of each page beside "From the Desk of Jim Beaman," was a comic black-and-white graphic of a little man in silhouette falling backward away from a triangular roof and a simply drawn chimney, a tiny trowel flying out of his hand. He had a black metal wire sculpture someone commissioned an artist to make for him which also depicted a roof, a chimney—the wire is fashioned into a pattern of rectangles, indicating bricks—and a wire man falling, legs spread, trowel in one hand, brick in the other, off a ladder. And on the wall above his desk he kept a framed pen-and-ink and crayon drawing made by an artist friend depicting a stylized version of him, head larger than body, in white T-shirt and jeans; he's high in the air beside a reddish-brown chimney; a blue crayon sky and the tops of buildings show behind him and once again he's falling, his left leg lifting into the air.

When he was alive I took that stuff about him falling off chimneys—the artwork, the letterhead, the idea of it—for granted. I thought it was a funny little joke, an interesting way of being self-referential. It wasn't until after he died that I saw it was a perfect symbol for his life and his attitude toward it, a kind of joking acknowledgment of his own fallibility, of his lack of caution and his attraction to danger and of the inevitability—his acceptance of the inevitability—that he would screw up and fall.

There are a number of photos taken in the apartment he shared with Peggy. One, taken in July 1988—the date is stamped on the back—shows him sitting at his desk, half turned toward the camera, holding a black metal bust of Chiang Kai-shek. He bought the statue at Jack's, a local department store comparable to Target or Kmart; it was typical of him to happen across an odd thing like that in an unlikely place like that, and it went without saying that he'd buy it. Usually Chiang Kai-shek sat in a small alcove designed to hold a telephone in the living room of his and Peggy's apartment, but for a while he was at my house on top of the bureau in my bedroom, and sometimes when we were in bed Jim would say, "Hoo, hoo, hoo. Nice hooters, too bad I don't have penis," pretending to be the statue. In the picture, Jim is grasping a battery-powered sculpting tool in the hand that isn't holding the bust as if he's pretending to carve it, and the look on his face can only be described as devilish; his eyes have a snapping, wise-guy expression and his lip is lifted in a crooked, about-to-make-a-wisecrack grin. For some reason I find I don't really like this picture. Maybe it's because I recognize in his expression a tinge of bitterness that was there at times in that joking, wisecracking side of him—a rebelliousness he directed at others and at himself, a kind of fuck-you quality. Or maybe it's because in the picture he's sitting at his desk and I don't like to think of him at that desk.

In another picture, also taken in July 1988, he's sitting in a pink chair, a lamp with a white fluted lampshade to the right behind his head, a corner of the couch to his left, the closet door with its mirror and glossy woodwork in the background. All these things are very familiar to me, and seeing them—these details from Jim's apartment, Jim's life—makes my heart catch, gives me a moment of disorientation. It's like walking through a little door into a whole familiar world that's gone, it's been obliterated as if with a single wave of a magician's wand. In the photo Jim's wearing a plaid flannel shirt, turquoise and red on a white background, which I also recognize. Lying over the back of the couch is a newspaper, probably the *Iowa Press Citizen*, judging from the thickness. The picture was snapped from the side. Jim's holding his glasses on his lap in his left hand, he's got a cigarette in his right hand, he's turning to face whoever's taking the picture—in my imagination it's Peggy. Jim doesn't look particularly pleased: His face looks heavy, woozy, weighted down; his forehead is knit and his left eye droops and squints into the camera. There's a world of sadness in that eye and perhaps the shadow of something—someone—else, a darker, uglier, coarser presence that I see sometimes in my dreams, a figure with loose lips and a shambling walk and an aura of potential violence, which is not Jim but which in the dream is somehow connected to him, like a phantom personality superimposed over his.

Jim's sister, looking through a batch of photos with me after his death, said, when we came to this one: "I saw him look like that once. About six years ago when he was visiting North Carolina he brought a case of Budweiser to my house and sat in a chair and methodically drank every single beer, one after another. I tried to get him to stop but it just made him nastier and stubborner."

Here's a photo taken with Peggy on his fortieth birthday; Jim and I wouldn't meet for another nine months. They went out to dinner that night, Peggy told me when we divided up the pictures a month after his death, and in the photograph they're both dressed up: Jim's wearing slacks and a suitcoat, a tie, a white shirt, a vest; Peggy has on a gray suit and a fuchsia silk blouse. They're standing in the doorway between the living room and kitchen of their apartment, and Jim has his arm around Peggy's shoulders. His head is tilted slightly to the side; his hair is neatly brushed; the twin lights of the flashbulb are reflected in his glasses. Peggy's smiling with her lips half puckered as if caught in midsentence; I can just imagine the laugh that's coming out of her, the cheerful goofy annoying thing she's in the middle of saying. She looks happy, chubby, apple-cheeked. Jim's expression is shy and inward-looking; his mouth is open in a small rueful grin.

My favorite picture of Jim is a picture I took. I think I must've been sitting on the bed while he was standing fairly close; he's looking down into the camera with the ceiling behind his head; all you can see is from the midchest up. He's wearing a gray wool vest over a blue and green plaid shirt, a patch of white T-shirt showing in the opening of the collar, and his clothes and the ceiling and the white porcelain light fixture behind him all have a bluish tint as a result of some trick of the lighting or the film or the camera. After he died I had a couple of strange little dreams that had exactly the same bluish tint—not navy blue or baby blue but a subtle greenish, tealish blue. In the dreams the color or the light or both had a kind of fizzy, crackly electric quality, and afterward I used to look at the picture and think about those dreams, imagine that this was a picture of Jim looking down at me from the afterlife. In the photo his lips are pressed together in a little smile and there's a fond, knowing, amused expression in his eyes.

Here's a snapshot of me in the living room of Jim's apartment, bending over the arm of the couch, wearing turquoise cotton pants and a black V-necked shirt. It's summer, the fan is sitting on the radiator and you can see it reflected in the glossy mirror on the closet door. Jim's yellow rocking chair—it had stuffed brocade cushions and worn varnished maple armrests—is in the forefront of the picture. The rocking chair was opposite the TV and there was a little end table between it and the couch. When I was at his place at night and we were watching TV he would sit in the rocking chair, his feet resting on a hassock made of a milk crate and a flattened pillow, and I would sit or lie on the couch. Sometimes, if I was walking past him or happened to be standing while he was sitting in the rocking chair, I would bend over and kiss him three or four times, and when I opened my eyes and looked down at him after every kiss his eyes would still be closed as if he was waiting for another kiss. And I have an odd, persistent little memory—one of those memories that stick in your mind for no particular reason—of him walking toward me through the wide, woodwork doorway of his bedroom and us meeting at the end of the living room and standing there embracing while

I looked over his shoulder into his bedroom at the yellow light the lamp cast on his desk. I remember taking our coats out of the living-room closet at the end of the night and going out into the cold fall air down to my house. The cat would sulk as we were getting ready to leave. She'd glare at us from inside the wooden circle that formed the base of the TV table and occasionally she'd even hiss when Beaman said good-bye to her, as if she'd understood what he said. Once at the last minute he felt too sorry for her to leave her alone for the night. He walked me home and when we got there he felt guilty about leaving me too but he went back up and slept with the cat anyway.

Peggy said when the cops went into his room on January 3 they said, "Oh! He's got a friend," and then the cat came out. I was haunted by that, used to lie in bed at night and picture it: Kitts in there with him, lying on the bed, maybe sitting on his chest, not knowing or maybe she did know what he'd done to himself.

Here's a picture of the corner of Jim's bedroom. It shows two drawers and a corner of his desk; on top of the desk is his black notebook with some change lying on top of it. Next to the desk is a cardboard filing cabinet, regular soggy tan-colored cardboard covered with splashy blue flowers; it's a cheap crummy thing and I'm sure he'd be ashamed to have anyone know he owned it. In front of that, lying on a phone book, is the cat, her ears sticking up and her white whiskers sticking out, her eyes glowing yellow in the light. Next to her on the floor is a little pile of messy stuff, a manila envelope with some pieces of paper sticking out and Jim's blue plastic thing—I guess you could call it a bucket. It's just a rectangular plastic container with a lid with latches and a handle, which he used to call his briefcase. He kept work papers in it, bids and so forth; usually he carried it around with him in the truck. I was with him when he bought it in Target. He was looking for something of a certain size and shape and I happened across this and he was pleased and I was pleased because I'd found it. He said it was just the thing he needed. Also in this messy corner there's something white that looks like a rumpled sheet; I wonder what it's doing there on the floor. I wonder why Jim even took this picture; I suppose because the cat is in it. I looked at this photo a bunch of times before I noticed that way back in the very corner, resting against the wall, partly obscured by the cardboard file cabinet, is the gun Jim shot himself with. It takes my breath away just to see it. Because it's in a corner where no direct light falls on it, it's all one dark color, deep mahogany brown, without any details, almost like a silhouette. You can only see an inch or two of the barrel—the trigger, the trigger guard, and part of the stock—the rest is cut off by the top of the photo. I feel as if I should know something more about that gun—why he had it, where he got it—but I don't. Afterward somebody said his father had given it to him for hunting or as a keepsake or something, but I don't remember Jim ever telling me that. I just remember that it was always there in the corner of the room and that I took it for granted.

Here's a picture of his desk with all the stuff he used to keep on it. There's an ashtray holding a cigarette, and several of his chess pieces in various states of completion. Some are just carved bases with bald, featureless fingers, like penises of clay; they look sort of ghostly, like embryos, unfinished things. There's the phone, black with large white numbers. The original numbers wore off before I knew him and Jim wrote them on. A lot of bad phone calls came in on that phone and there were times when I dreaded hearing it ring. There's the gray metal transistor radio Jim always listened to when he was working and at home when he was sitting at his desk. He always listened to the same oldies station, which sounds like something a middle-aged, middle-class guy who goes to karaoke and wears a toupee would do, but the way Jim listened to it was all Jim. That radio had been up on so many roofs and fallen off so many times it was battered and the antenna was broken off, and Jim didn't really like the songs, he just listened to the music because it was familiar, because that was what he did. He sang funny, made-up lyrics to half the tunes; "Lay lady lay, lay across my big fat head" is the only set I can remember.

Behind the radio are two tin cans full of pencils and pens and paint brushes and sculpting tools, and beside the cans are Scotch tape, a plastic container of glue, a can of Kiwi shoe polish. Jim used to polish his boots in the evening; he'd take them out and sit in the living room cleaning them off with a brush and daubing polish onto the toes and sides with a cloth and then buffing them. They were beautiful brown leather work boots, shaped to the contours of his feet. There's a red address book, a red plastic index card box—he kept notes on all his jobs in it—and a bunch of sculpting tools, red-handled needle-nosed pliers and three or four other tools with scoops and gouges and points on the ends, on the far right side of the desk. By the phone there are three miniature bricks, and standing next to the plastic index card box is a little model of a man in a gray business suit. It all seems so cheerful and interesting and wholesome, just all Jim things, which I loved, but that desk has other associations for me that are not wholesome. Something else took place at that desk that there are no photos of, something he did in secret for hours at night on certain occasions in spite of himself. It was something he wanted to stop doing but couldn't seem to, and it involved a whole different set of implements: a half-filled glass of water and a little copper measuring cup, some filters ripped off cigarettes, a bunch of syringes lined up along the desk, a plastic baggie containing white powder. The needles were for shooting up; the powder was cocaine.

5

Jim acquired the intravenous habit during the Vietnam War, when he injected heroin and smoked dope with his Marine buddies in Okinawa. I doubt if he was ever truly addicted to heroin because he only used it occasionally and he stopped altogether without much problem. He had a lot more trouble giving up alcohol. That he had to quit in his late thirties. After years of heavy drinking he was having seizures, and—as it says in the AA *Big Book*—his life had become totally unmanageable: He was alienating business clients, falling off roofs, getting into potentially fatal accidents on his little motorcycle. Somewhere along the line between the heroin and the booze, he started shooting up cocaine.

Besides the intravenous habit, Jim might have picked up the taste for taking foolish risks in Vietnam, an addiction to the thrill of living on the edge, close to death, the way a lot of Vietnam veterans did. Or maybe his propensity to throw himself full force into whatever trouble presented itself was due to something innately self-destructive in him, encouraged by the nihilism of the sixties. Or maybe it was a way of rebelling against his critical, controlling father. Or maybe it was some combination of stubbornness and romanticism, traditional ideas of what a man should be and low self-esteem.

He loved hard-boiled mystery stories, and I think there was a picture in his head of a person he wanted to be who was something like a character out of a novel by Elmore Leonard or John D. MacDonald, a guy who was smart and sensitive but strong, who never allowed himself to be pushed around, who wasn't afraid to take risks. And behind that was another picture of himself that he didn't want to see, didn't want to be, a kid who was small and weak and fearful, who was a victim of his father and other adults. In that scenario, the drugs, the alcohol were a mistake; he used them to make himself feel better, stronger, tougher, to keep himself from seeing the second picture, the one of the small, powerless kid.

I remember two stories Jim told me about his childhood. One involved his Grandma Beaman and a berry tree. Jim loved fruit; as an adult he would go to the refrigerator almost every night at nine or ten, take out three or four pieces—apples, grapes, oranges, kiwis, anything but peaches, which he said were too fuzzy—wash them at the sink, and eat them. He said he loved fruit even as a kid, and once he climbed a berry tree in his grandparents' backyard and picked and ate a bunch of berries and got into trouble for it with his old man. He didn't tell me what the trouble consisted of but he implied that it was painful and humiliating, and the grandmother, who had witnessed the trouble, said to him when they were alone together afterward, "Jimmer, where's that berry tree?" And she went outside with him and he showed her the tree and she helped him pick some more berries.

The other story also involved his father. When Beaman was six, his father took him fishing in a rowboat on a stream. Jim sat up front and his father sat in the stern and rowed and at one point, where some trees grew near the brook, the boat appeared to stall. Jim's father rowed and sweated and rowed some more but the boat wouldn't go anywhere. He was mystified, impatient, irritated. Finally he looked up and saw what the problem was: Jim was grinning an impish little grin, holding on to a fat branch that hung down beside the water.

I loved that story and so did Jim. His father didn't get mad

when he saw him holding on to the branch and that made it a
happy memory, but I think the real reason it was such a good
story for Beaman—he always talked about it with a cheerful
grin—was that it captured something essential about him and
the part he often played in things. I used to think about that
after he died, that in a way it seemed as if his cosmic role in this
life was to hold on to a tree branch while somebody else was
rowing in earnest, to throw a little wrench into the works.
There's a figure like that in Native American Indian mythology and whenever I read about him I think of Beaman; he's
called the Trickster. The Trickster is kind of a fuckup, he's a
liar and a thief, but he has an important job in the world: It's to
keep people from taking themselves too seriously, from getting
stuck in rigid ideas of right and wrong; he stirs up trouble,
brings in fresh air, new perspectives, makes people question
their judgments. And that's what I think of when I think of that
moment in Jim's childhood, his old man rowing and rowing,
Jim holding on to the tree. His father was disciplined, hardworking, middle-class, a careful citizen who worried about the
neighbors, who wanted to impose order on the world around
him, to impose order on Jim. And Jim was a mutineer, an
insubordinate, a force for chaos.

One of Beaman's trademarks as an adult was that he always
put the toilet seat down after using the toilet. I only knew him
not to do it once, during his last week. It should have given me
a clue as to the dire shape he was in because he never failed to
do it otherwise, no matter what. He said his father had drilled
the habit into him. Other rules his father tried to implant
didn't take as well. As a teenager he smoked cigarettes and hid
them in his room; he fought and hung around with ruffians; he
drank; he skipped school. The more his father tried to control
him the more he rebelled. "I don't know what I'd do if I had a
kid like me," he said to me once.

Pasted into one of the old photo albums in Beaman's trunk

is a group of family pictures taken during the Christmas Jim was fourteen. You see his mother standing in front of the tree; his father seated in a leather armchair, holding the dog, Bonnie; Jim clowning with friends, grinning next to his sister. Only one snapshot provides a hint of anything less than perfect: It's a picture of Jim in a plaid shirt with the sleeves rolled up, sitting on a folding chair at an angle to the camera; his sister, wearing a nightgown and bathrobe, is sunk in an armchair to the left and behind him. Beneath raised eyebrows Jim's eyes are dull and wounded, around his mouth is a wary angry sullenness, a clenching of the jaw in shame and frustration. There's a look of challenge to him, a sense of battle with the picture taker. You get the feeling that the picture taker's winning—so far.

When he was eighteen, they had it out for real; there was a fistfight, Jim's father got the worst of it, his mother broke it up with a poker. Jim left home. Shortly afterward he was drafted and ended up in the Marines. I know he and his father made up after that, because in Jim's trunk I found a letter to Jim from his father, sent to him in Vietnam in 1969. The tone of it is chatty and friendly; it contains news of the weather, of Jim's mother's health, of a new used car, and it makes reference to Jim's finances and his plans to attend the University of Iowa when he returns to the States. But somewhere along the line, long after he got home and went to college but at least a year before we met, they had another falling out, and this time they did not make up. The fight had to do with a letter Jim wrote to his niece, who was going through a phase of getting into trouble, sneaking out with boys, hanging around with a wild crowd. The letter was long and full of advice; he tried to put things in his niece's terms while at the same time discouraging her from making the same mistakes he'd made. His father intercepted the letter, he and Jim argued over the phone, his father refused to give the letter to the niece. Jim's mother sided with his father. Jim was hurt and insulted, his sense of privacy was violated, old feelings were stirred up. After that, he stayed in touch with his sister but he and his parents didn't speak. I don't think they ever spoke again.

When Jim died his family got one half of his ashes and I got the other. His sister told me his parents had a military funeral, including a twenty-one-gun salute. She said it was horrible, every single gunshot a reenactment of his death. She said it was really sad, too, seeing that little tiny box get lowered into a grave. We had an informal memorial service in Iowa City also, in the basement of the Unitarian church. Jim's sister came from Raleigh, North Carolina, stayed over that night, and flew home the next day. I never did anything with my half of the ashes; I never tried to scatter them; I left them in their original container, a tan cardboard box sealed with brown masking tape. I think of leaving them in that box as a joke between me and Jim. I used to keep them on top of his trunk; now they rest on the corner of my worktable. I like to see them sitting over there, a kind of reminder that death is part of life, the way people are always saying it is.

I'm sure the drug culture of the sixties and seventies also heavily influenced Beaman, but nobody I talked to seemed to know exactly how. One of his first girlfriends said that even in high school he was a legend as a crazy man who would say anything, drink or smoke or swallow anything, take any risk. She said he had an incredible amount of energy and all of it was turned in on himself. Jim's friend John Gray said he thought Beaman was more into drinking than drugs in the seventies but he would do drugs if they were around. Jim's friend Karl Rhomberg said he had the impression Jim took some drugs in high school, then started using more seriously in Vietnam. But back then, as he said, everybody was doing it: If you can remember the sixties and seventies you didn't have any fun.

I was influenced by the drug culture, too, but with a different outcome than in Beaman's case. I didn't do a lot of drugs as a teenager but I had an emotional alliance with drug takers, with drug taking in general; I understood the appeal, the romance of self-destruction, I internalized the values of the counterculture.

I came to my identification with the drug culture via a Doors album, which I inherited from my paternal grandfather's second wife, Hildegarde, when she died in her early sixties. Hildegarde was youthful, open-minded, liberal, intellectual. My father was all those things, too, but he was haunted by personal demons—character defects, as they say now in twelve-step programs—that overshadowed his other neutral, admirable traits and ended up transporting him out of the broad-ranging, intellectual upper middle class my grandfather and Hildegarde belonged to into a class that more resembled that of the working poor. He had problems with passivity and depression; he didn't believe he could get what he wanted so he worked in a factory instead of pursuing his dream, which was to be a farmer. He made an awful marriage, as they used to say, then stayed in it for the wrong reasons. He and my mother created together, out of their combined mental and spiritual illnesses, the kind of life usually associated with poverty: Their house was small, cramped, dirty, an aura of hopelessness hung around it like a smell.

I did not live there with them. I had an older sister and a younger brother who did, but I lived down the road as a kind of unofficial foster child with a family named the Paysons. I first went to live there in 1954, when I was eighteen months old. My sister went, too; my brother hadn't been born yet. My sister and I went because my mother had been admitted to a mental hospital and my father couldn't take care of us during the day while he worked. He found the Paysons by putting up a notice on the bulletin board in the Westhampton Congregational church. The Paysons' oldest daughter, Mary, was about to go to nursing school and it was her idea to take us; she thought the experience would help her prepare for her career. She never did become a nurse; she got married instead, and I ended up living with her parents for a lot longer than she was around to help. When my mother returned from the hospital after six months, my sister and I went back to my parents' house to live. My sister readjusted, continued living with my parents. But I could not adjust and after a month I went back to live with the Paysons, where I stayed, with the exception of some overnight visits at my parents' house, until I was eighteen. When I was ten the state found out about me and I became an officially registered foster child. After that a social worker came to the Paysons' house once a year and looked at my bedroom and inquired about my living conditions. I was always afraid they would find something wrong and make me leave.

I was a kind of self-selected foster child. I desperately, vehemently, did not want to live with my parents. I had wild sobbing hyperventilating anxiety attacks if I even thought I might have to live there. Most kids want to live at home and it's considered by the courts and the social service agencies and the population in general to be a tragedy if they have to be separated from their mother. But I wanted to be separated from my mother. I was terrified of my mother, the way you'd be terrified of a murderer or a tornado ripping through the trailer court or a cobra that can strike you dead at any moment if you get too close to it. I wish it weren't true but it is, and since it is, I wish I could explain it, say exactly what it was about my mother that made me so afraid of her, but I can't. Not in any simple way that I can state without hedging and claim to be the truth. I don't remember a lot of what happened when I was very young so I have to rely on other people's accounts, my father's mainly, and over the years I've come to realize my father wasn't a very reliable narrator. But here's what he said: Right after I was born, or maybe it was before, my mother had what used to be called a "nervous breakdown." My father had to take care of me all by himself: feed me, burp me, change my diapers. Perhaps because she never took care of me, my mother failed to bond with me. And, as my father said, she went completely off her rocker: She screamed in the night, she psychobabbled, she asked my father whether I was a bartered baby: My father's name was Bart, and "bartered" must've been a merging of two ideas, I was sold, traded, given away; I was his, not her, baby. She made my father put me out on the cold sunporch in the winter in a cardboard box so my crying wouldn't wake my sister; my father sneaked out and rescued me after my mother went to sleep. She tried to make me drink pHisoHex—an awful, bitter soap that came in a green plastic bottle—to cure a cold; my father wrestled the bottle away from her during a violent argument. I remember the way my father would tell those stories: the pHisoHex, the bartered baby, my mother's rejection of me. He would do it with a certain tone of voice, as if it gave him a kind of secret satisfaction to report my mother's bad behavior, as if the whole point of those stories was to let me know how much nicer he was than she was, how cruel my mother was to me. And I believed it. And it's not exactly that I don't believe it anymore, that I think it was all a lie, a frame-up, that my mother wasn't really crazy, she was actually nice to me. I'm saying I don't know what to think.

My grandfather and Hildegarde lived in Rockport, Massachusetts, during the last few years of their lives. Before that they lived in Bermuda, where my grandfather had a job in the Navy. After they moved to Rockport, they invited my sister and me to spend a week with them during the summer for two years in a row. The third year, before we could go, my grandfather passed away suddenly; Hildegarde died a couple of months later. She left a will detailing who got what of her and my grandfather's things, but my father and uncles said they didn't have time to mess with all that; they just asked everyone what they wanted and gave all the unclaimed stuff to Hildegarde's daughter by another marriage. I said I wanted that record by the Doors, which Hildegarde had showed me during a previous visit. It was 1968 and I was fourteen.

Hildegarde had bought the Doors album because she was curious about the new phenomenon of rock and roll and also because she'd read somewhere that the Doors made a metaphysical connection between sex and death; she was really interested in death, especially life after death. My grandfather used to make fun of her; he was a crotchety old Yankee type, and whenever Hildegarde talked about life after death—not like it was spooky, silly, the way people usually talk about ghosts, but in a serious, inquiring, intellectual way—my grandfather would say, fondly, "Oh, Hildegarde, shut up." But sometimes I think, Well, I bet he's convinced now. I had a dream about the two of them the night before Beaman died; they didn't do anything in the dream, they were just there, hovering over me.

My father was sympathetic to the drug culture in the sixties, or at least to the hippie ideology it was couched in. He had back-to-nature leanings and was a rebel at heart; he had no stake at all in upholding the status quo. I don't know whether my mother was sympathetic to it or not—I know very little about my mother, actually, her personality quirks, her likes and dislikes—but I suspect she wasn't sympathetic to it. She wasn't sympathetic to much of anything, as far as I can remember. The Paysons were opposed to the drug culture in every fiber of their being. They were good people, but they came from the Puritan tradition of old-fashioned rural New England. Doing much of anything for the sake of pleasure, for pure recreation, was not a concept they really understood, let alone doing anything as profoundly shocking to them as taking drugs. Taking drugs wasn't even something they could have imagined real people doing. Only evil, frightening, cardboard stereotypes—drug attics, as Dad Payson called them—took drugs.

I'm picturing myself upstairs in the Paysons' house listening to that record by the Doors. It was their first album, the one with "Light My Fire" on it, and I listened to it over and over. The Paysons would have been downstairs in the living room watching the evening news with Walter Cronkite or the *Lawrence Welk Show* or the *Beverly Hillbillies* on TV. I would have been sitting on the bed, the record player on a table beside it. I don't remember anymore where I got that record player, one of those little ones that came in a kind of suitcase, with three speeds, a fat removable spindle for 45s, an arm with a primitive needle. The bed was a double bed, with a dark curved walnut headboard, and in the memory the room is shadowy, poorly lit; the only light issues from a black metal gooseneck lamp that sits on a bedside table opposite the side where the record player is. I associate that lamp with Charlotte, the Paysons' grown-up daughter, who used to study under its light. At one time I shared the room with her, but she has since married and moved away and so have her two older sisters and older brother. I think of the lamp as her lamp, and I think of the bed as her bed and the room as her room and I think of the whole house and everything in it as the Paysons', certainly not as mine. I don't belong in that house and I don't belong in the tiny innocent Congregationalist town of Westhampton, Massachusetts. Neither do my parents, but I don't belong in their house, either, and I sort of know all that but I don't know what to do about it, where to go instead or how to get there, as I sit there on the bed, listening to the Doors.

I can only imagine now what the Paysons would have thought—Mom and Dad, as I called them—hearing the strains of that music drifting down the stairs. Maybe I kept the volume down too low for them to hear it, maybe they were too old or deaf or had the TV on too loud to hear it, but I doubt it. I'm pretty sure they did hear it, that they were shocked, disapproving in their straightlaced, innocent, Congregationalist way, and I'm sure I knew it too and it made me nervous, guilty, scared that they would kick me out, send me back to my parents' house, which was the one thing I was most afraid of. But I kept playing that record anyway. I played it over and over, because it spoke to me of something that I wanted or needed, something that I already felt without quite knowing it.

Recently I've been listening to the Doors again, trying to figure out what their music said to me back then, what it still says to me, to tell you the truth. A lot of it is silly, sophomoric, I know, the product of a morbid, overheated imagination—sons murdering fathers and doing the unmentionable with their mothers, snakes being ridden to lakes and all that. It's perfectly designed to appeal to an adolescent sensibility and I'm sure that's partly why it appealed to mine, although even back then I was a little bit embarrassed by liking it. But I did like it. And I still do. There's something about that music that stays fresh, timeless for me; I can go for years without listening to it, then pick it up and put it on the CD player and there it is: I still like it, and I'm still a little bit embarrassed by liking it.

I like the bluesiness of it, and the frenzied, take-it-right-to-the-limit quality, which must appeal to some urge or desire like that in me. But a lot of other rock-and-roll bands play music with those attributes. I read in Jim Morrison's biography—probably the same biography Oliver Stone read before he made the movie—that when Morrison was a kid driving through the Southwest with his parents they came across a car accident in which some Indians had been killed—he saw the wreckage through the window—and the adult Jim Morrison used to say that one of those dead Indians got into his body, and when he was out there onstage, dancing madly around in his drunken rage, it was that Indian in him, doing a shaman's dance. Sometime after his death the piano player in the band said that if Morrison was like a shaman—and it was true, he *was* a kind of shaman—then the band was like the musicians in the tribe who played the drums, made the music that whipped the shaman higher and higher into his ecstatic states. And maybe there is something to that; maybe that is part of what I heard, what I still hear when I listen to that music.

But there's more to it even than that. It's that sex and death thing Hildegarde read about in some magazine, which made her buy the album in the first place. She never told me what she thought of the record, but I doubt if it was what she had in mind when she bought it: all those veiled references to the sexiness of death, all that bad poetry with sex as a metaphor for death, death as a metaphor for sex, drugs and alcohol as vehicles, as metaphors for both. It was those morbid, adolescent, death/sex lyrics that made the Doors' music so bad, but at the same time, maybe, they were also the very thing that made it so good, what ultimately accounts for the appeal of it. Freud said there's a death instinct as well a life instinct, a force that drives us toward destruction along with a force that drives us toward survival and procreation, and I have a suspicion that it was that urge Jim Morrison tapped into, that at the bottom of what I feel when I listen to the Doors and similar music, and like it in spite of myself, is some basic, primal, almost sexual desire that is all wrapped up with death.

The last time I had a go-round with the Doors was not too long after Jim Beaman's suicide. I can't remember how I came to it, but at some point a month or so after he died I went out and bought a compilation CD by the Doors—Hildegarde's old record had gotten lost many years earlier—and I started playing the new CD over and over. Then I narrowed it down to one song that I played over and over, "Riders on the Storm," and every time I listened to it, for the duration of the song only, the feeling ended when the song did, I felt a little bit better. I used to imagine the ghost of Beaman standing there beside me, hearing it too—back then I was always imagining the ghost of Beaman hanging around. The living Beaman thought the Doors were hokey, phony, and I couldn't imagine the dead Beaman liking their music either; I could practically hear the comments he would have made about some of the lyrics. But although the music wouldn't have spoken to Beaman about himself, it somehow, in some way I couldn't put my finger on, spoke to *me* about him.

Even though Jim Beaman couldn't relate to Jim Morrison, there were certain parallels between their lives. Both of them had strict, military, sometimes absentee fathers: Morrison's father was a Navy admiral who was often gone; Beaman's father was a traveling salesman and a retired Navy man. Both Jims compulsively rebelled against authority, possibly because of their fathers; both of them took drugs as part of their rebellion; both of them were alcoholics, and it was probably alcohol more than drugs that got them both in the end. And it occurs to me that in a way what I loved about Jim Beaman, what grabbed my imagination about him—part of it, anyway—was the same thing that grabbed my imagination about Jim Morrison. It was drugs and sex and death, the sad, awful romance of self-destruction. It was that rebellion against authority, that wildness, that willingness to do anything. I was too much of a good girl to act out like that, but I wanted to, I had the urge to, so I was attracted to boys who would do it for me.

These days when I listen to the Doors what I hear in their music is Jim Morrison telling us, over and over, that he's going to die. He's going to die and it's alcohol, it's drugs, that are killing him. And I think Jim Beaman said the same thing to me, over and over, in so many ways, but I didn't really listen, didn't process it until it was too late. I heard it in the same way I heard it when Jim Morrison was saying it: I heard the idea of it, the romance, the tragedy, the fantasy, which is not the same as the real thing at all.

This time around when I listen to "Riders on the Storm," I notice something I never used to notice. "Riders on the Storm" was on the Doors' last album. By the time it came out I'd put the Doors behind me; the balance between embarrassment and liking had tipped in the embarrassment direction, and I felt ashamed of ever having liked them; all I heard in that song were the adolescent lyrics, the hokey thunder and rain at the beginning and the end of the song. It was 1971 and I was about to go to college; I had left the Paysons and was living on my own. Jim Beaman was finished with Vietnam and had enrolled at the University of Iowa. Jim Morrison would be dead at twenty-seven before the year was over. By the end of Morrison's life his own myth had gotten to be too much for him: He wanted to stop being the Lizard King and start being a normal person; he grew a beard, got kind of fat, just wanted to live in Paris like everyone else and write poetry. But he couldn't be a normal person, because by that time he was too far gone into alcoholism.

The new thing that I hear in "Riders on the Storm" comes in one little word, one little syllable that falls twice toward the middle of the song. The word, the syllable, is "Yeah," and it sounds like his mouth is away from the mike; there's a lilting, downward quality to it, a kind of dreamy dismay, like the sound of someone falling, someone who knows he's falling but can't stop himself, can't even quite bring himself to care, like a man drifting down from a very high place, like a man plunging backward off a chimney.

6

I can't remember exactly when I first realized Jim had a drug problem. To figure it out I have to go back to our couch days, that week we spent on my couch talking, getting acquainted.

I see us there, me sitting on the end of the couch I always sit on, him on the end he always sits on. It's our third evening and already we've established a routine, a habit for these nightly talks. Behind us is my huge living-room window, the window I look through at the house across the street, but it's night now and the curtains are drawn. The drapery cord dangles down and there's a thingamabob, a little fluted plastic skirt, that I fiddle with, running it up and down the cord as we talk. He's got short hair, good posture, large pale-blue eyes behind wire-rimmed glasses, a dimple in his chin. He's wearing jeans, tennis shoes, a bright-blue short-sleeved shirt with big splashy flowers. I sit there talking, listening, absorbing impressions, taking everything about him in.

I tell him all of my stories and he tells me all of his. We talk about our childhoods, about notable experiences growing up. I tell stories about living in Cambridge before moving to Iowa—how lonely I was, how I took modern dance classes year after year with the same group of four women; other students came and went, but the five of us kept signing up and we never got any better; we lummoxed across the floor, landed every time with a thud. Jim talks about hitchhiking to Florida with a girlfriend, about working construction. The construction stories have a roguish, slapstick charm; they involve tricks the underdog workers played on mean, unreasonable foremen, bar fights in which chairs and windows got broken, tables got tossed through the air, and bunches of people were knocked out cold; afterward money had to be paid to the owner of the bar for damages.

He talks about his friends: Cynthia Sales, a tall, fat, loud-laughing black woman who cornered him once in a bar and gave him a good-natured kiss. Sharon Meagher, a reporter for a local newspaper, who has one of a series of weird clocks he made a long time ago and gave away. Mary Beck, who makes beautiful, artsy quilts and who once told him something she'd never told anyone else: She was still a virgin at the age of thirty-six. Ace, his mechanic, who owns a hot-air balloon and once assaulted a cop for frightening his eight-year-old daughter. Hank Klosterman, the master bricklayer who taught Jim how to tuck-point. Bobby Osborn, a black guy who's doing time for drug dealing. Bobby keeps getting caught; Jim thinks maybe he feels more comfortable in jail than on the outside. Once Jim and Bobby went on public-access TV and Bobby played the part of a convicted drug dealer, which he was, and Jim pretended to be his lawyer. Everybody believed them till he, Jim, gave it away. "I've always been a big blabbermouth," he said.

He has a way of making everybody and everything interesting, exciting, larger than life. And I'm a willing participant in this transformation; falling in love is like reading a novel, it's an act of imagination, a suspension of disbelief. His life rolls out before me like a magic carpet, his friends are characters in a story. The men he knows are tough, protective of the people they love, full of dry humor and funny expressions: How much did they stab you in the ass for that? It beats a poke in the eye with a sharp stick. Either that or they're like Bobby Osborn: outlaws, scoundrels, tricksters who are not quite who they seem to be. The women he knows are shy, cheerful, but mostly asexual—or else they're beautiful but brainless. I'm none of these things, he lets me know, I'm in a whole new category: I'm smart, I have class but I'm down-to-earth, and—this part he tells me later, after we've slept together—I'm beautiful. I don't believe it; I keep waiting for him to look at me and see something different.

Maybe this is partly why I never look at him and see something different: an addict, an alcoholic, someone whose life is completely out of control; I'm so preoccupied with my own inadequacies it doesn't occur to me to take stock of his. But it's more complicated than that, of course. Infinitely more complicated.

Once I asked him, "What went through your mind the first time you saw me? Was it love at first sight?"

It was during a certain type of conversation we used to have endlessly on summer nights in bed. In my mind's eye I see us leaning up against the headboard smoking, him wearing jockey shorts and one of those soft, ribbed, tank top–style undershirts—I used to call them Stanley Kowalski undershirts—myself in a pair of short-sleeved cotton turquoise pajamas. Those pajamas had a little hole in the crotch but I wore them anyway because Jim thought they were charming.

In those conversations we'd go over and over how we met, talk about how lucky we were we'd found each other, how we'd never expected to fall madly in love with someone who was also in love with us. It was usually Jim who initiated talk like this. Once he said, for instance, "I wonder what would have happened if one of us had been married when we met." And then he said, "Well, I guess we would have just gotten a divorce." I've never met a man so willing to love so openly, who didn't hold at least a little something back. The idea that we were soul mates, that we were somehow meant to be together like some kind of star-crossed couple, was at the heart of our common myth.

In my version of our story, it was love at first sight for both of us. But when I asked him, picturing the two of us standing on the sidewalk beside Steve's van, he said that actually, the first thing he thought when he saw me was that I was cute—"cute" was a word he used to describe women he was attracted to—but that I probably wasn't the type to be interested in someone who was involved in what he was involved in. That I would be shocked and repulsed if I knew the truth about him. That therefore he didn't even consider me as a possible sexual partner.

And I remember the satisfaction I felt, like the pleasure of giving someone a gift, when I denied feeling anything like that about him, ever.

But how did I find out about the drugs in the first place? They came floating in like scraps of driftwood, bits of seaweed, along with all the rest. A story here, a detail there. Alcoholism, drugs, hard times.

Him spending Christmases alone with the cat. Living in the truck and the little cat shits flying out of the litter box in the back. Losing jobs, falling off roofs because of drinking. Going to the play *Jesus Christ Superstar* high on heroin a long time ago with his first girlfriend; two nuns sat behind them. Staggering down the middle of a street in Mexico, fucked up on mescaline, feeling alien and desperate. What he says when I ask about his ring.

He wears it on the ring finger of his right hand. It's shaped like a class ring but without the insignia; later when I get a better look at it I'll see it's got a raised X with a tiny diamond in the center. I'm not used to seeing rings on men unless they're wedding rings, and I think it's sexy. It's a contradiction—a ring like that on a working man.

He's full of contradictions. A priest once pointed this out to him in the most succinct way possible, when he was in the eighth grade. The priest was Father McConville, history teacher and football coach during the late fifties and early sixties at Our Lady of Lourdes Junior High School. Unlike the other priests at the school, Father McConville was young and smart and vigorous; he made history interesting, he could throw a football half the length of the football field. He summed Jim up to himself one day in after-school detention, the two of them seated in an empty classroom, the priest leaning forward over the top of the teacher's desk, delivering his statement with an air of puzzlement and affection and an edge of exasperation: "There's nothing I could say about you that wouldn't be true."

How did he know, I wonder. What could Jim have done all the way back then that would have been so contradictory? I can only imagine. Probably he was a good boy and a bad boy. Shy and outgoing, rebellious and obedient, foolhardy and fearful, lazy and hardworking. And on and on.

Sitting on my couch at night with his combed hair and clean jeans and blue Hawaiian shirt, he looks incredibly boyish; he's full of fantasies, uncontrollable enthusiasm. During the workday he looks older, competent, manly, serious; he's got lines on his forehead, mortar dust on his hair and glasses. There's a straightness to him that cancels out the badness, a badness that cancels out the straightness. He's a trickster and a thief, a wiseguy with a scatological sense of humor. Yet he's polite, shy, a little old-fashioned; every night he stands at my door before leaving and says, "Thank you very much for another nice evening."

And the drugs, the alcoholism are another contradiction.

On the fourth night I point to his finger and say, "I like your ring." He takes it off and hands it to me. I hold it up and turn it around, look at the little diamond in the center. "It's nice," I say. "Where did you get it?"

He takes the ring back and puts it on, grins his lopsided, disarming grin. "I made a trade for it in a drug deal."

And I'm not shocked, I don't take a step back, I don't think about what drug dealing means in practical terms about who he is, how the propensity for that sort of thing might affect me in any relationship we might have. I don't have any practical, everyday, down-to-earth thoughts at all. I'm charmed, excited, attracted. And somehow—most important—I don't think that he is still dealing drugs. That he might have a drug problem; that alcohol too will sneak back into the picture like a dark horse coming up from behind. Somehow I have the idea that all that—drugs, drinking—took place a long time ago, in some other, closed-off part of his life. I don't understand what a person who knows anything at all about addiction would understand—that unless he's in some kind of recovery program, even if he isn't doing those things now, chances are he'll be doing them again. And when he does, it won't be romantic at all.

Then there's Sheila Branch. Jim tells me about her during our couch days too. Sheila Branch isn't a friend of his, she's an adversary, an influence, a former lover.

Recently I was sitting in a friend's dining room, full of light and glossy hardwood, drinking coffee and eating bagels on a Sunday morning. We were talking about my friend's house and her neighborhood and she said, wrinkling her nose, "The people next door are alcoholics. And the woman's sister is a drug dealer." I had a sinking feeling, asked a few questions to confirm my suspicions: I knew who she was talking about. But I didn't have the nerve to tell her that that woman, that drug dealer, was Jim's old girlfriend, Sheila Branch. That Jim, whom my friend knows only as my dead fiancé, had been intimately involved with that drug dealer, lived with her, taken up some of her habits. I was too ashamed to say that.

But when Jim talked about Sheila Branch during our couch days, I was only worried about whether I was threatened by her in any way, wondering how I would stack up against her in competition for Jim's affections. I would win, of course, hands down—I knew it even then—and that gave me pleasure. I didn't mind hearing about the strange, nefarious stuff she was into— she was out of town; Jim said she was in L.A. meeting with some Mexican drug traffickers—about how turbulent her and Jim's relationship had been. I just felt good and virtuous by contrast.

I remember Jim saying, sitting on my front steps during our very second conversation, before I'd even lured him into my house and onto the couch, before I took up smoking again: "A few years ago I was dating this woman." I was still trying to figure out whether he was single and heterosexual and I interpreted his statement as a positive indication on both counts, and I remember also thinking "dating" was a quaint, anomalous way of describing a romantic involvement, like a leftover expression from his high school days. Later on, when I knew more about Sheila and about their relationship, it seemed an even more unsuitable, a spectacularly inappropriate, way of describing it.

Sheila was four years older than he. She had two sons and a daughter; the youngest was in his early teens when she and Jim met. At that time she was also still married, to an investment banker who worked in New York. Jim told me that when the husband came home to visit, Jim would go by their house—the rest of the time he lived there—and Sheila would bring him out a cup of coffee, which Jim would drink standing on the sidewalk. Sheila and her husband got divorced a year later, whether because of Beaman I have no idea. The affair between

Sheila and Jim went on for six years. They fought and drank and made up and fought again, they struggled for power, Jim moved out and back in several times. I don't know exactly when the whole thing ended; I don't think there was ever so much a clean break as a slow ugly deterioration.

I met Sheila not long after Jim and I got together. She had thick, shoulder-length dark hair, a puffy face with large, attractive features, an expensive, slightly shopworn elegance. She was the opposite of those women who are all soft edges and nurturing; you sensed an element in her of something dangerous, as if she could do you a lot of harm if she wanted to. But at the same time something hurt flickered in her eyes.

I remember Jim telling me, during our couch days, that once during the winter he had a series of horrible dreams. He didn't say which winter and I imagined it happening back in the distant hazy fairy tale past, the way you sometimes do when someone tells you stories about their life, especially if they're stories you have a stake in taking place a long time ago in a hazy past. The dreams were so bad he would shout and fall out of bed and wake up in a sweat. And the dreams were about Sheila Branch: She and some other vague, shadowy figures were talking; they knew something he didn't know, and—this was the main thing—they were evil. Evil in a way that was truly, utterly real and absolutely terrifying, more real and terrifying than anything he'd ever encountered in waking life. After that, he said, he started thinking of Sheila Branch in a way that was colored by those dreams, he felt a little afraid of her in some vague metaphysical way. She'd given him a red scarf for Christmas and he felt spooked by that scarf, he didn't even want to touch it. He also said that at the time he was giving up heroin.

That was the sort of world Jim lived in, a world in which there were demons and angels, real ones. And I believed it, I still believe it: They were real. I sensed them around him, like a disturbance in the air, like a sound just beyond the register of human hearing, while we were sitting on my couch.

He talked about growing up Catholic, going to Catholic schools. He was full of funny, irreverent stories: he and his friends throwing spitballs at the cross—you got extra points if you hit Jesus in the crotch; breaking into the sacristy and eating the holy wafers, which turned out to be already blessed. But I pictured—heard, imagined—murmuring voices, young boys standing in the dim air behind the altar surrounded by images of peril and suffering, the slaughtering of Jesus, damned souls writhing in hell.

Beyond his end of the couch on the floor the whole week was my neighbor's white vacuum cleaner; I'd borrowed it and hadn't given it back yet. The couch was low and every now and then when Jim shifted in his seat I saw the curve of the white ridged vacuum cleaner hose peeping over the top of his head. But I didn't register it as such. I was distracted, absorbing impressions more than factual information, it was as if I was engaged on some plane of reality that wasn't quite literal. And every time I saw that little white crescent peeping over the top of his head, instead of identifying it as the hose of my neighbor's vacuum cleaner, I thought vaguely of tonsures, yarmulkes, halos, religious garb of some sort. And along with that vision I had a strange, strong, almost sexual feeling, an impression, something I picked up and absorbed the way you absorb but could never describe a piece of music, the way the music makes you feel: It was a fascinating, complicated, multilayered impression, both very light and very dark, numinous, otherworldly. It wasn't anything about Jim so much as something I seemed to feel around him. The closest I can come to describing it is to say it was demons and angels.

I don't know what the angels were or where they came from. Maybe he absorbed them as a kid in Catholic school along with the atmosphere, the preoccupation with heaven and hell, good and evil; maybe they were connected to the holy wafers he ate that turned out to be already blessed. Or maybe they were all bound up with the demons, maybe you can't have one without the other.

I have a better idea what the demons were. They were drugs: a whole host of gargoyles, fiends, furies that came crowding in the door along with cocaine, alcohol, heroin, Valium.

The myth Jim and I made up together about ourselves was more than just a story of destiny and true love. It was a story about the battle between good and evil, the struggle as to which was going to get Jim's soul in the end: life and love, or drugs and death. In that battle I was the force for good. "Now that I have you I have something to live for," he used to say.

It never once occurred to me that I wouldn't be able to save him, that our story wasn't going to have a happy ending.

The first inkling I had of his actual drug use—the first time I got a taste of the real thing and the ways it would affect me, how it would frustrate me and make me feel scared and power-less and how I would ignore it, pretend it hadn't happened—also came during our couch days, on about the fourth day of that week. I was walking down Washington Street in the late morning, approaching the stop sign at Governor Street, and Jim drove up in his truck and stopped. He rolled down his win-dow and I went over to talk to him. He said, "I was up all night partying, I didn't sleep at all and now I've got to go work on the Haverhill's chimney with John Gray." I wondered, what do you mean, you've been up all night partying, but I didn't ask him. Instead I said, "Aren't you tired?" and he said, "No, I feel fine." He looked past me instead of at me and his eyes at that moment were a beautiful pale translucent blue like lake water, and I saw something in them I'd never seen before, something vacant and maybe not entirely friendly. Then he said, "I'll drop by tonight when I'm done with the job," I stepped back away from the truck and he drove off.

7

The year I met Jim I was coleader of a Girl Scout troop, which was how he and I came to have sex for the first time under a bush outside the Cantebury Inn in Coralville.

I got involved with the Girl Scouts through Maxine New-man, a woman I'd known in the Workshop. She'd come to Iowa from Arizona, gone through the program at the same time I did, and like me had decided to stay in Iowa City. I didn't know Maxine very well, but in August after Kathy left I called her thinking we might become friends. She said she was lonely too and was looking for things to do, especially ways to get more involved with the community; one thing she was consid-ering was becoming the leader of a Girl Scout troop. She liked children and missed their company—she'd taught grammar school before coming to Iowa—and she'd been in the Girl Scouts as a kid and had good memories of it. She'd already been in touch with a woman in the local organization; the woman said they had several spots opening up.

I'd never been in the Girl Scouts. The town where I grew up didn't have Girl Scouts when I was a kid, but it did have 4-H. Every year for four years I took 4-H sewing with the same group of nine girls; every fall each of us picked out a pat-tern and bought material, then spent the entire school year cutting, pinning, ironing, stitching, and hemming a single gar-ment. It took that long because Dot Miller, our leader, who was nobody's mother but enjoyed spending time with kids, had only one sewing machine; we spent most of our time at meetings hanging around waiting to use it or ripping out mistakes. One year I made a sleeveless, turquoise, V-necked shift out of coarse, burlappy material; the stitch-on pockets frayed almost immediately, messy little fringes of thread sticking out along the edges. Another year I sewed a terrible dress with an off-white light cotton short-sleeved top attached at the hips to a heavy navy-blue skirt. I never wore either garment, and the sight of them hanging in the closet filled me with boredom and dread. To me, 4-H meant endless, overheated afternoons in Dot Miller's small living room wrestling with unwieldy patterns and dull scissors, the tedium of hemming and stitching and basting. When we recited the solemn 4-H pledge at the beginning of each meeting ("I pledge my head to clearer thinking, my heart to greater loyalty, my hands to larger service, and my health to better living"), I felt vaguely hypocritical, and when I clutched a flickering white candle at the yearly districtwide gathering in the Westhampton town hall and sang the slow sad closing song, "Lights Out, 4-H," along with all the other local 4-H members, their faces around me glowing with reverence and apparently heartfelt sincerity, I felt like an outsider and an impostor.

I didn't remember any of that, though, when Maxine said she was going to be the leader of a Girl Scout troop. I said it sounded like a nice idea, and that maybe I would be her coleader.

Maxine called the Girl Scouts and signed us up to lead a troop of nine- and ten-year-olds at the beginning of the school year. But first we had to attend a meeting at which we were instructed about the aims and philosophy of the Girl Scouts and given a packet of handouts about the cookie drive and badges. Maxine and I sat at the end of the table, anomalous among the middle-aged mothers who were the other new leaders. Maxine in particular looked out of place; she was twenty-five, chubby, and had on bright-red lipstick, long dangly earrings, black tights, and a leopard-skin tunic with a deep V neckline, which was the same outfit she'd worn that day to work. Nevertheless, the women seemed to welcome her as a former Girl Scout. They were slightly less friendly to me, maybe because they were already acquainted with Maxine as their initial contact, or maybe because the reservations I was having were showing on my face.

Our troop met in the music room of the Southeast Elementary School. Fifteen straight, neatly spaced rows of small wooden chairs faced a large desk at the front of the room. There was an upright piano to the right of the desk. A boxy tape recorder, a guitar in a case, and stacks of dusty sheet music were piled on a long table beneath a bank of windows.

To our first meeting Maxine wore black vinyl high-heeled boots, a tiny black leather skirt, a sleeveless pink V-necked blouse, feather-and-bead earrings, and her usual bright-red lipstick. There were ten girls in the troop, eight in fourth grade and two in fifth. "I like your lipstick," one of the fifth-graders said. She was a tall chunky girl with little moons of chipped red nail polish on the ends of some of her fingernails.

"Thank you," Maxine said. She spoke to one girl after another, asking carefully worded questions in a teacherly way. The big girls answered eagerly; the younger ones hung back shyly, their voices nearly inaudible. I tried to involve myself in the talk, but the girls' attention remained riveted on Maxine. A sturdy little kid wearing sandals and a purple halter and shorts moved closer to her and stood waiting for a chance to speak. "What are we going to do with our cookie money this year?" she said when there was a break in the conversation. "Last year we went to Wacky Waters."

We herded the girls to a circle of chairs Maxine and I had arranged earlier and I took attendance. There were Claires and Jennifers and Beckys; the girl in the purple halter and shorts was named Tiffany, the two older girls were Amy and Heather. Maxine discussed certain items of business—where to get uniforms and badge books if you wanted them, who still needed to pay the registration fee—and her plans for the troop that year; she said *her* plans, not ours. Afterward she brought out a paper bag of refreshments we'd bought before the meeting at a grocery store across the street, and each girl had three ginger snaps and a little plastic cup of cream soda.

A few parents arrived to pick up their kids and they observed from the sidelines as we joined hands, arms crossed in front of our midriffs, and silently passed a squeeze from hand to hand. Across the circle from me, Maxine smiled knowingly from girl to girl as if sharing a happy, private secret. My own smile felt forced and stiff, and somewhere in the back of my mind a memory stirred of lit white candles in the Westhampton town hall, of me pretending to feel regretful during "Lights Out, 4-H" when really I couldn't wait for the moment when the candles were blown out and we could all go home.

Our next few meetings didn't go very well. Maxine and I weren't well prepared and the girls weren't interested in any of our ideas for them. They said the water badge sounded boring; they didn't want to go for a walk and collect fall leaves; they liked the idea of rehearsing and putting on a little play but couldn't decide which one. "All we ever do is talk about what we're going to do," Tiffany complained shrilly. By the end of the third meeting even the quieter girls were running around the room giggling hysterically, knocking over chairs, pounding on the piano and playing "Duck, Duck, Goose" while Maxine and I screamed at them to stop.

Maxine called me before the next meeting and said she'd decided to stick to activities related to clothes and jewelry. "Fine," I said. We bought white T-shirts and stencils and fabric paint, beads and glue and earring posts, and after that the girls spent all their meetings sitting on the floor painting T-shirts and concocting jewelry over spread-out newspapers, arguing about who got the red paint next and where the tube of glue was. Maxine and I sat on the floor beside them and made everything they made; I ended up with several new pairs of earrings and a stretched-out T-shirt covered with thickly painted purple and red flowers. The big girls breathed through their mouths and talked distractedly about their boyfriends ("You know John? Well, he said if I break up with Danny he wants to go out with me . . ."), piling up separate mounds of blue and black beads. The younger girls frowned in silent concentration, searching among the square plastic containers for the perfect size and color bead, showing their finished products to Maxine and me; even the littlest ones produced long glamorous-looking earrings, which they claimed their mothers would allow them to wear.

Although the girls were happier stenciling T-shirts and making jewelry than they'd been during earlier meetings, their behavior was still less than ideal. They complained about everything we did and everything we bought for them, disregarded our requests to glue only on top of a newspaper, did as little as possible to help clean up at the end of meetings. I nagged and Maxine was short with them, snapping out orders, her face set in an angry frown. They ignored us both equally. Maxine said she felt like a teenage babysitter.

The cookie drive came at the end of the term. Maxine and I had little to do with it; one of the girls' mothers came to each of our last six meetings and handed out order forms and cookies and collected money as it came in. The girls were better behaved with her around, as if they considered her a genuine adult worthy of respect and authority.

Of the money earned by cookie sales, the Girl Scout organization got half and the troop got half, some of which was traditionally used to take the troop on one big final outing. Maxine insisted recklessly when we were alone that she was going to blow the whole outing thing off; by that time she was even more disillusioned with the Girl Scouts than I was. "Let their parents take them to Wacky Waters," she said, her eyes shining with a stubborn look that was now familiar, "because I'm not going to."

I didn't want to do it either, but I knew we would, for the same reason we had stuck it out the whole school year even though we hated it—because it would be too embarrassing to stop, because then we'd have to explain to the parents that we couldn't stand their kids. So in the end we merely tried to get the girls to choose an outing that wouldn't be too painful. Wacky Waters inevitably came up, but only a few girls were enthusiastic—they'd gone there last year. Maxine and I were relieved. A camping trip, the Palisades Park, a museum in Chicago were all considered and vetoed for one reason or another. Finally Maxine took matters into her own hands and decided we would spend one night in the Cantebury Inn in Coralville. For once the girls were unanimous.

"Goodie!" Tiffany said. "We can swim in the pool." She rotated her arms as if practicing the butterfly stroke.

"We can stay up all night and have pillow fights," one of the older girls said. "It'll be like a pajama party."

The other girls giggled and elbowed each other.

Enter Beaman. We meet, I lure him to my house, we sit on my couch and talk every night for a week. Sexual tension builds. Every night he stands up and says, "Thank you very much for another nice evening" and leaves. The outing at the Cantebury Inn approaches.

I haven't told him about my involvement with the Girl Scouts. I'm afraid it will color the way he looks at me, give me a misleading tinge of goody-goodiness when in fact my sympathies lie on the other, bad-boy end of the social spectrum. I feel more at home down there with the rebels and the nonconformists. Meeting Jim, spending evenings with him, is like returning home after a trip into alien territory.

"There's something I have to do on Saturday night," I say on Thursday as he gets up to leave, "but I'm embarrassed to tell you what." We stand at the door looking out through the screen. It's raining. It's been raining and raining for days and days, the streets are covered with giant puddles, the rivers are poised at the tops of their banks. This is not the summer of the big flood. It's a trial run; this year it will stop raining after a month.

Jim seems a little relieved when I tell him about the overnight at the Cantebury Inn; later on he confessed he thought I was going to come out with something about some other man. He's charmed and amused by the whole Girl Scout thing. The next evening he presents me with a little gift he happened to find that day in a junkshop—a round, iron Girl Scout pin—and he tells me how he told his friend John Gray about my involvement but first he only gave him a couple of hints and let him guess what it was. "Oh no!" John said. "Is she married?"

"Nope," said Jim. "Guess again."

When I say I'm not looking forward to Saturday night, he says he's supposed to watch a boxing match on TV with John but afterward he'll meet me in the bar at the Cantebury Inn to cheer me up for a little while, if I can get away.

This is Friday, the night before the outing. We sit on my couch and talk, go for a ride and get some ice cream, come back to my house and talk some more. It gets later and later: one o'clock, one-thirty, quarter of two. I'm sitting sideways facing him with my knees drawn up, playing absently with the plastic skirt-shaped doodad at the end of the drapery cord, listening, talking. Finally, casually, in a perfectly neutral tone of voice, he asks, "So, can I stay overnight?"

This is what I've been waiting for but suddenly I feel scared. I can't look at him, all I can do is stare at the plastic skirt-shaped thing, slide it up and down the cord. "I'm not ready," I say, and he doesn't miss a beat, he goes right back to talking about the book he's reading. Twenty minutes later he thanks me and walks home in the rain.

The next day is the day of the Cantebury Inn and it's raining again. Maxine and I arrive late; the girls and their parents are waiting for us in the lobby, the girls carrying little suitcases. Tiffany has a pillow under her arm as well. The parents say good-bye and we check in. We've reserved two rooms, one with a pair of double beds for the Girl Scouts, the other an adjoining room with two single beds where Maxine and I will sleep.

We change into our bathing suits and go for a swim, then go back to the rooms and order two large pizzas and turn the TV to the movie channel. *The Princess Bride* is on, and the girls settle down on the beds in their damp swimming suits, eating pizza off paper plates and sipping cans of soda. At nine-thirty two mothers show up for a visit, and at ten the telephone rings: Jim's down in the bar.

I tell Maxine, slide open the glass doors, and step out into the courtyard. I feel sprung, free, I'm skipping class on the last day of school, jumping out of a burning airplane, floating down through the sweet blue air to a world that's soft and lush and full of Jim: Jim as he appears in my imagination, witty and perfect, his flaws only making him more perfect. I glide past the pool breathing in the smell of chlorine, descend a set of stairs and enter a bar named the House of Cards. The room is smoky, there's a TV and a long pale wooden bar, a clutter of high boxy tables and chairs. Beaman's seated beside a post drinking coffee from a white mug. I order a glass of chablis, then drink two more in rapid succession.

When it's time to go, I walk him outside to the parking lot.

It has ceased raining but the warm air is heavy with moisture, the sky dark and starless. We stand by the truck and suddenly I'm kissing him and I can't stop; the accumulated outpouring of all that frustrated desire bursts through our defenses like a million tons of water forcing their way through a dam, cows, trees, houses swept along in their path. It's necessary to go further then, it can't be put off. I gesture toward the front seat of the truck. "Too bright," Jim says, looking around. He leads me across the pavement to a large bush beyond the darkest edge of the parking lot.

Underneath the bush, I undo the button on my slacks, he unbuckles his belt. We roll around on the grass; drops of water from the bush shower onto our shoulders and heads.

"Can you believe we did that?" I say when it's over and we're struggling back into our pants.

Jim laughs. "Yup," he says. "Let's get out of here. It's wet." He takes my hand and helps me out from under the bush's low-hanging branches. I stand up and look down at my pants. They're light-pink cotton, the fabric stamped with pictures of little golfers in various poses, teeing off, putting, driving miniature golf carts. My pink cotton knees are black with mud.

"I can't go back in there like this! What will they think? And my keys are in my purse, so I can't go to my house to change."

"My clothes will probably fit you," Jim says. "I'll take you to my house and you can get suited up in some of them."

We park on the street in front of his house, a block and a half from mine. "Oh," I say. "Somehow I had the idea you lived in a different house."

I follow him up a bank of steps to the front entrance, turn left, and go down a hallway to a door at the end. He unlocks the door and swings it open and I see a living room with a high ceiling, dark glossy woodwork, three windows facing west, a large tortoiseshell cat standing in the middle of the floor. "Hello, Kitts," Jim says to the cat.

The cat and I follow him through a wide oak-framed doorway on the right into his bedroom. In the doorway is a heavy sliding wooden door that makes a loud *whoosh* whenever you open or close it; I have a door just like it in my house between the living room and the bedroom. Jim slides it closed behind us and we forget what time it is until three in the morning, when I suddenly remember Maxine and the Girl Scouts. I've put them out of my mind so thoroughly returning to the thought is like waking up from a dream, making a transition from one world to another. I can't believe I've stayed so long at Jim's.

He rummages in his closet and pulls out a pair of jeans and a thick cotton, long-sleeved jersey and hands them to me to put on. As he predicted, they fit me perfectly, the jeans snug and comfortable, the shirt heavy and warm. After we're dressed he feels around in the pocket of his pants and says, "Damn. I lost my jackknife. It must've fallen out under the bush."

There's another surprise when we look out the window. It's pouring and it looks like it's been pouring for several hours: Large puddles cover the sidewalk and street, a steady jet of water gushes from the gutter spout, swift streams rush along the troughs inside the curbs. A deep, distant clap of thunder rumbles as we're getting into the truck, and once again I have the guilty feeling of returning to the world from some other place: Is it possible a thunder shower has been going on without my noticing? At Dubuque Street Jim has to turn around and go back: the river's overflowing, the street by the park is a lake of water. He tells me it's okay, he knows another way to get to the Cantebury Inn.

As we creep along through the torrential rain I'm suddenly a mass of worries. I'm worried about what Maxine and the girls will say, afraid of being a bad example, frightened that Jim will hurt me now that we've had sex. "So, do your relationships last a long time?" I ask belatedly.

"The important ones do," he says.

I'm scared to inquire whether ours is going to be important, so I fret about the Girl Scouts instead. "What'll I say when I get back to the hotel? Where'll I tell them I've been?"

"Tell them you got caught in the rain," Jim suggests helpfully, "then went home and changed."

The girls are still up inside the hotel. They greet me at the door of their room, their faces flushed with excitement and their hair disheveled. "Where were you?" they exclaim in unison.

"I had to go out for a while to meet a friend," I offer weakly. It's a lame excuse but it seems to satisfy them; they're not much interested in me anyway. They race back into the room and jump on the bed to continue playing. They appear to be in the middle of some practice that involves the occult. "Hold your hand out and imagine with all your heart that the pillow is rising off the bed," I overhear from Heather as I leave the room. "If I can do it you can too."

I experience a sudden rush of affection for them. "Good night," I call.

"Good night," they answer cheerfully.

Maxine's awake but she's not speaking to me. She sighs loudly, frowns, turns her back when I ask if she minds if I switch on the light. I don't blame her. I deserve whatever punishment I get, but for once in my life I don't care what I get or whether I deserve it, despite my worries earlier. Right now, everything feels right. I'm happy, and I know my happiness is big enough and sure enough to cancel anything negative Maxine or anyone else has to dish out.

I brush my teeth and get undressed, leaving on Jim's shirt, taking off the jeans. I slide them over my hips reluctantly, thinking that they fit me better than my own clothes, are sturdier and more comfortable. I would like to keep them and wear them forever. I don't know it then, but some day in the not too distant future I'll get my wish.

I get into bed and lie there listening to the Girl Scouts in the next room. They talk and laugh, squeal and shriek, thump pillows, bounce on the bed. They don't sleep a wink, and I hardly sleep at all myself.

In the morning while we're waiting in the lobby for the parents to pick up their kids I go outside and look for Jim's jackknife. The bush is easy to find; it's right beyond the far end of the parking lot, just as I remembered, and underneath it the tall, reedlike grass is flattened in a large circle. Resting partly hidden in the grass is Jim's red-handled jackknife.

When I get home there's a message on my machine from him that says, "Call me back and let me know whether the Girl Scouts burned you at the stake."

8

In the middle of June I took a Greyhound to Chicago to spend a weekend with my sister, who had flown there from Massachusetts to attend a library supplies conference. The visit had been planned for months and happened to fall two weeks after the night Jim and I got together outside the Cantebury Inn.

During one of the days my sister and I spent together, we went to the Lincoln Park Zoo. The zoo had a gorilla cage like an enormous indoor terrarium: Encased within a huge thick cylinder of glass was a small hill planted like a natural habitat. Four or five gorillas dotted the hillside—huge lumps of reddish-brown fur partly concealed behind boulders and trees. Outside the cage's perimeter was a six-foot-wide strip of corridor where spectators circled in dim, purplish light, peering through the glass. Christine and I stood there in a sea of noisy children, staring into the enclosure at the gorillas. They seemed shy, furtive, harmless, abashed by their surroundings and by all the attention. Then, just as we were about go to a different part of the display, an enormous, full-grown male slowly lumbered down the hill toward us. It came to a stop on the other side of the barrier opposite my sister and me, crouched, thrust its huge head forward, and trained a rakish, penetrating gaze directly—or so it seemed—at me, raised its giant fist, and began to pound on the glass. The noise was deafening; children and adults screamed and jumped back. The glass of the cage bowed outward with each blow but didn't break. My sister and I scurried away. Behind us the pounding continued: *boom! boom! boom!* It thundered and echoed throughout the vast, high-ceilinged room.

Beaman chuckled when I told him about it that night on the phone. My sister and I were lying on the double bed in her room watching television when he called. Christine picked up and she and Jim had a friendly little conversation before she handed him over; when I looked at her the next time she was asleep. Jim was more interested in my reaction to the gorilla than he was in the actual event itself. "You're a weird little woman," he used to say whenever he was amused by something I said or did, and I used to say, "I am not little," though I doubt we'd worked out that routine by then. Talking to him on the bed beside my sleeping sister, I felt happy, lucky, safe, in love, gratified to be the object of such warmth and attention.

Later on in the conversation I asked him whether "it" had come in—by that I meant and he understood I meant a bunch of cocaine a guy he always called the Boxer was expecting. He and the Boxer were in business together, or had been—now that he was turning over a new leaf, Jim said, he was pulling out. The business was: The Boxer imported cocaine in large quantities, and Jim took care of the petty transactions—fielding phone calls from local people who wanted to buy small quantities, exchanging money for drugs.

The Boxer's real name was Chuck Patterson. He was a short stocky guy with a scarred face and huge meaty fists; hence, Jim's nickname for him. It seems likely that the Boxer had a nickname for Beaman also, but if he did I don't know what it was. I do know that when he called Jim from a phone booth at the corner of the park down the street to communicate information about a deal or make arrangements to meet, they used code names for each other: The Boxer called Jim Tonto, and Jim called the Boxer the Lone Ranger. All this was the Boxer's idea, Jim told me with a small ironic grin; the Boxer was paranoid and had ideas derived from the movies. He wore mirror sunglasses and rode an immense BMW into town once or twice a week; the rest of the time he lived an isolated life in the country; he watched a lot of TV, even daytime TV; he did not take drugs himself. Jim told me that when he first volunteered to be the Boxer's runner, the Boxer said he was surprised a guy as smart as he was would want to get involved in a thing like that.

The shipment that was due had been in the offing for a while, and when Jim told me about it sometime during the previous weeks he said he felt an obligation to the Boxer to help get rid of it. After that, he said, and I believed, he was through with cocaine. I wasn't worried about the cocaine coming. I was curious, waiting to find out what would happen, strangely disconnected from the reality of the situation. Somehow I managed to avoid not so much seeing it for what it was, but rather, seeing it at all, at least on some important level.

Jim said that it hadn't come in but that it might arrive next week; then we went on to talk about something else.

I brought two pictures of him with me that weekend to show my sister, a photo of him wearing brown plastic–framed glasses in a yellow-lit kitchen, which I liked because of the humor in his eyes, and the snapshot taken so many years earlier while he was in the Marines, the picture he told me later not to show anyone. My sister agreed that he was cute. She was happy and excited for me; over the pictures we stared at each other with pleasure and surprise, as if the last thing either of us ever expected was for one of us to achieve romantic love. Looking at my sister, I remember, I felt a slight sense of superiority, not in terms of myself—my being—but in terms of my life and my luck. I felt like a small plane that had finally taken off from the runway and was rising into a permanently happier stratosphere, while my sister remained on the ground.

At some point during the weekend I mentioned to her that Jim had had some involvement with drugs, then quickly assured her that it was mostly in the past, that he was giving it up, that there was no real problem. What kind of drugs, she wanted to know. Cocaine, I said, and she, my marketing-manager sister, my sister who has a dull, steady, younger boyfriend and a closetful of rayon dresses, silk blouses, fake-linen suits, said, "Oh! That drug is really, really hard to give up—it's practically impossible. You'd better be careful."

She had an air of authority, as if she knew exactly what she was talking about. I don't know how she knew. Maybe she'd had some experience with a user herself.

I remember that we were resting against pillows watching TV on the double bed when she said it, and I felt a tiny chill around my heart, a certain sour, cold, nasty sensation in the area of my head and shoulders. But the moment passed and my sister's words receded. I put them out of my mind, and my sister, too, seemed to forget what I and she had said. We talked about Jim a lot during the rest of the weekend but the subject of drugs didn't come up again.

The first time I saw Jim under the influence of cocaine he was standing on his lawn with Sheila Branch. He'd called me at work forty-five minutes earlier, whispering into the phone that something bad was happening at his house, and would I mind stopping by on my way home. Earlier that day the Boxer had handed over a quarter of a kilo of cocaine to him to distribute—the shipment they were expecting had finally arrived, two weeks after it was supposed to come—but I didn't know that, and if I had I doubt that I would have connected it to what was happening then.

"What's the matter?" I asked, alarmed.

"You'll see," said Jim. "I can't say over the phone. I'm glad you're coming." He hesitated, then added, "I love you." It was the first time he told me that.

"I love you too," I said.

I left work early and walked to his house as fast as I could. I felt worried and anxious, but I also felt a little excited because something out of the ordinary was happening and because Jim had called me and asked me to come; I felt strong and competent, confident I'd be able to rescue him from whatever he needed rescuing from.

Then I saw Jim and Sheila on the lawn. My eyes went to her first, then to him. I didn't recognize Sheila—I'd never seen her before—and for a minute I didn't register Beaman either. When I did it came as a small shock. He looked incredibly disheveled, jumbled somehow—mentally, as well as physically—as if he'd been taken apart and reassembled with all the pieces slightly out of place. One side of his shirt was untucked, he had on a pink baseball cap, and on his face was an expression of intense, childlike shame.

That look of shame, I found out in the months to come, was one of the indicators that he was high on cocaine. There were other signs also: The hair at the front of his head stood up because he'd been running his hand through it; his voice had a taut, strained, raspy quality, as if someone had turned a key and tightened everything in him, tightened his vocal cords, especially; there was something fuzzy about him, something blurry around the edges. And he looked intensely, painfully, ashamed. It wasn't that he was ashamed of being high or anything else that was rational; it was a more basic, elemental shame than that, an old shame left over from childhood that somehow got dragged up out of the waters of unconsciousness, like a fish caught on a hook, by cocaine. At first I didn't identify it as such, didn't know what I was seeing in him.

I only knew I always felt an enormous pity for him when he was high on cocaine. Pity, and exasperation because he was doing it again, and as the months wore on I felt other emotions: rage and abandonment and frustration. But it was never a clean feeling; I never had the urge to judge him or blame him; whatever I felt was always mixed with sadness because of that shame.

When he saw me his eyes momentarily brightened and he walked across the grass to meet me, touched my shoulder, and introduced me to Sheila. Sheila shook my hand and smiled a small, brittle, frightened smile. I felt threatened by her too. She headed down the sloping lawn to the street, got into her car, and drove away.

"Let's go to my house," I said when she was gone. I wanted to rescue him, make whatever was wrong with him better, spirit him away to some safe place. Jim nodded willingly, but after we'd walked a hundred feet along the sidewalk I stopped. My landlord and his wife were on my porch repairing something. I couldn't imagine the two of us sauntering past them, stopping for a while to make the inevitable conversation, going inside and sitting around where they could look at us through the windows, so we turned around and retraced our steps back to Jim's. We went inside and sat on the couch in his living room. I remember it was very bright in there; shafts of yellow sunlight teeming with dust motes came through the windows and spread across the floor and the arm of the couch.

Jim told me that earlier a car with two men sitting in it had been parked out front and at one point he'd seen one of the men walk across the yard and go around the corner of the house to the back door. He was pretty certain they were DEA men.

"Oh, I doubt it," I said. "They were probably just selling something or visiting somebody else in the house."

"Then why would they sit in the car for so long?"

"I don't know. What do you think they were doing?"

"Surveillance," he said. "Don't you see? It's a drug bust."

It occurred to me for the first time that Jim's involvement with drugs was not only tragic and inconvenient but also illegal, and that not only he but I—as an accessory, as a person in the wrong place at the wrong time—might be arrested and prosecuted. Panic rose in me and I stood up; I wanted to get out of there immediately. But the only place I could think of to go was to my house, and since the presence of my landlord and his wife on my porch made that seem impossible, all I could think of to do was wait for them to leave and hope they'd go soon. It never occurred to me to go off to my house or somewhere else alone, to leave Jim behind to whatever was in store for him, to be arrested or not. Somehow, I felt inextricably bound to him and his fate, like a person on a runaway horse. It was going to be a rough ride—I was starting to see just how rough it would be—but for some reason—maybe the horse was going too fast, maybe I was stuck to it through some mysterious, partly sick, partly heavenly alchemy—I could not get off. I had to stay on until it threw me.

It also didn't occur to me that Jim might be hallucinating those DEA men. It was he who suggested this possibility. He said Sheila had said that when you reach a certain point with cocaine you can start to hallucinate and that was probably what he was doing. Sheila was an expert on all matters relating to drugs, though she, like the Boxer, didn't do them herself. Jim thought it was possible he was hallucinating, but he wasn't sure. He said he knew people went nuts sometimes if they did too much cocaine and that this might have been the case because he felt very strange, but on the other hand he was certain he'd seen a black car parked at the curb with two men in it. "I don't know," he said. "I've had some funny feelings on cocaine before but I never saw anything that wasn't there."

I went out twice during the late afternoon and scouted around to see if my landlord and his wife were gone, but they weren't, and as the afternoon wore on I stopped worrying about being busted by the DEA. It wasn't so much that I believed Jim had hallucinated them as that I just let the whole thought of their existence recede into some dim out-of-the-way corner of my mind. I still felt uneasy, but since nothing happened, the expectation that something would happen gradually faded away. And as it turned out nothing did—the door never crashed open, no DEA men showed up with guns drawn and warrants for our arrest.

Jim and I never discussed those DEA men after that day; they just faded away, the way so many things involving his drug problem did. It seems likely to me now that they were part of a temporary "cocaine psychosis," a fairly common phenomenon in people who habitually take large doses of cocaine, I've read since Jim's death. The day after the incident of the DEA men, he thought a group of ex-cons from Muscatine were in town ripping people off and that he was on their list. He and I stayed up half the night at my house looking out the window, his truck parked across the street. At one point he thought he saw someone lurking around his truck and went out with a flashlight and a penknife to investigate. Both of us were scared to death; I was just as surprised as he was when he came back inside saying there was nothing out there but shadows. Maybe I was even more surprised, since he probably knew on some level that it was just a fantasy or a hallucination, whereas I had no idea what to think. By one-thirty in the morning we'd smoked all of his cigarettes and he called a friend who worked in a bar and asked him to bring a pack over on his way home. "Phil? This is Bea-monovitch," he said when his friend answered. We kept waiting and waiting for Phil to show up but he never did, and by the end of the night Jim was searching for long butts in the trashcan.

The Rooms of Heaven

．　．　．

The next day we were supposed to go to a party, one of those huge yearly get-togethers in someone's backyard out in the country. Nearly everyone Jim knew would be there and I had been both looking forward to it and dreading it. I spent most of the day sleeping, catching up from the night before. It was hot and Jim kept coming to my house, sitting on the side of the bed and telling me little things that were happening downtown or at his house. He was euphoric, probably at least partly as a result of cocaine, though I would never have thought of that as the reason then. In the midafternoon he took off his shoes and pants and crawled into bed with me.

I remember standing in the bathroom getting ready for the party after he went home. I put on a pair of white cotton pants and a long gauzy plum-colored shirt my sister had given me for my birthday—the shirt was semi-see-through; you had to wear a camisole underneath it. I brushed my hair and applied some makeup and stared at myself in the mirror, my face close to the glass. I suppose I'm pretty enough, certainly I'm not ugly, but back then I was always worrying about my appearance, thinking people were judging me in terms of how attractive I was. I was preoccupied by the impression I was going to make on Jim's friends, fearful about whether they'd think I was good-looking enough. It's true, though I'm ashamed to admit it: Those were the sorts of thoughts that were going through my head, not concern about the night before, not uneasiness about the DEA men Jim might or might not have seen, not anxiety about him distributing a quarter of a kilo of cocaine for the Boxer. I'm sure I felt all those things and more, but I had squashed them down into some compartment of my mind below the realm of conscious thinking, where they resided in the dark, nightmarish and distorted, like trapped, neglected animals. Deep inside my body I could feel the walls shuddering with their pounding.

When I got to his house Jim's friend Cynthia was there. Cynthia was involved with a guy named Wayne who was another friend of Jim's. I hadn't met her before and I felt shy around her; I knew that she had kissed Jim in a bar once and I think I may have been a little intimidated by that kiss. She and I ended up sitting in Jim's bedroom talking, her at the desk, me on the bed, while Jim did something in the kitchen. Cynthia was telling me about her problems with Wayne and I was listening and nodding sympathetically, and Jim came in the room and said to her, about me: "You see why I love her so much."

The whole time we were talking she was carefully spooning something out of a plastic bag inside a paper bag into smaller plastic bags and weighing them on a metal desktop scale and closing them up with twisties, and every now and then Jim would come in and take over for her. At one point he went out on his little Honda 90 to pick up a pizza, and when he came back he put the pizza down on the table and hugged me and I remember how incredibly happy he seemed.

9

We didn't go to the party; we just never got around to it. I don't think Cynthia went, either. During the afternoon she kept talking about what time she was going and who would be there and whether she should get a ride with us or someone else, but by evening she said she thought she'd probably just forget it and go home.

Later on—several hours after Cynthia has left—Jim and I are sitting in his bedroom, me on the bed, him at the desk; there's bright light issuing from a lamp behind him but the corners of the room are dark, shadowy, and we're talking—sharing intimate details, childhood memories, our deepest, most personal thoughts. This is the night he tells me about the Vietcong coming into the PX and shooting people, the night he tells me not to show that picture of him, the one I've already showed my sister, to anyone. He rummages around in the trunk that holds his mementos, pulling out this and that, holding up each item for me to see. He takes out an ancient, leather-bound missal he had in third grade, a thick wooden plaque, the words SHITBIRDS OF THE YEAR, 1969, burned into the varnish, J. BEAMAN among the names. This is something he acquired in the Marines. Then he finds an odd-looking white-painted metal candleholder with leaves and branches and a single cup for a candle. "I forgot about this," he says with an expression of surprise and pleasure. "Isn't it strange? Someone gave it to me." He watches as I hold it up and examine it, and I know it has some meaning for him beyond the simple facts of it, that it sparks something in his imagination or triggers some association, and though I don't know what, it becomes for me as well something more than what it is, it takes on a gloss, a veneer, a hint of something pleasing and mysterious, the way certain toys or places could when I was a kid.

I remember that moment well. I see myself sitting on the bed in that room with its high ceiling and shadowy corners. I see Jim sitting across from me in his curve-backed, leather-seated chair in front of the large, dark-stained wooden desk, the bright light from the lamp behind his head. I remember feeling full of a deep, lush, painful, complicated love that had in it an element of fear and an element of pity and an element of something else: the demons and angels around him, the white powder I was suppressing knowledge of behind him on the desk.

Then Jim said something that broke the spell completely. It was, "Time for a drug break." He stood up and went into the bathroom. He was gone for a long time and when he came back things were completely different, because it was while he was in the bathroom that I understood exactly what a drug break meant—Jim leaning over the sink searching for a vein, sticking a needle in his arm, the blood, the body being invaded—and I could not, absolutely could not, stand it. The insanity of it, the violence and the creepiness, the essential disregard for self-preservation sent me back to some scene in my childhood—my parents fighting in the bathroom, my mother wielding a bottle of pHisoHex, which she wants to make me drink—and I started crying loudly, hysterically. I lay on the bed and sobbed while Jim sat beside me. I was truly upset, but there was also a touch of something manipulative in that crying, as I remember it, an attempt to get across a message—you see what this does to me?—that would make him stop. It did not make him stop.

The Rooms of Heaven

He sat there, arms at his sides, eyes fixed on the wall opposite, a stubborn, defensive look on his face. Raising my head off the pillow to glance at him, I felt mildly shocked. It was the first time his response had been anything less than totally sympathetic when I was upset, and I felt the cold finger of fear touch my heart. He doesn't love me, I thought, and a little wave of pain and shame radiated out from the thought. I stopped crying and sat up.

Later that same night, sitting on my porch with him in the dark, I say, "A person who freaks out at the thought of needles can't exactly be with someone who shoots up." But I have no intention of breaking up with him; I just want to hear him reassert what he has already told me on other, more optimistic occasions: that he is going to, definitely, stop. It doesn't occur to me that even if he says he will he won't be able to stop, that this will not be his fault or my fault or a question of what either of us wants but an integral part of a condition, a disease he has, a kind of mental and physical illness, which neither of us knows anything about and which he will never admit to having, never even admit it is a disease, making it fatal.

Jim says, "Well, of course if it's a choice between you and cocaine I'll choose you." There's a pause, then he says, "I need to be alone for a minute. I'm going to go for a little walk." I sit there in the dark on the porch for a while and wait for him to come back and then it comes to me that he's not coming back, he's at his house with a needle in his arm, and I rush up there. There's a towel slung over his window so you can't see in and I go in the front door and down the hall and let myself into his apartment with my key and there he is at his desk with a needle getting ready to stick it in his arm, and somehow I get the feeling that this is not just any dose, this is an overdose. I let loose a loud, terrified wail, take a syringe off the desk and say I'm going to jab it into my arm if he doesn't stop. He says, "Don't do that," and his face looks sort of irritable; he puts the needle down and says, "I probably wasn't going to do it anyway."

A while later I sit beside his desk and watch him wrap a rubber tube around his arm below the bicep and pull it tight, stick a fresh, newly filled syringe into a scarred vein—it takes him a couple of tries to get it in—and slowly depress the plunger. I've come a long way in a couple of hours; I can see him do this now and hardly even flinch. The only thing I can't do is disengage, and awhile later when he says he wants to walk to Sheila Branch's house because she has some tar heroin and he wants to buy some and smoke it so he can sleep, I try my hardest to talk him out of it. I try to get him to go to my house and go to bed instead. I whine, bribe, threaten, try to trade on how much I think he loves me, but none of it works, so I walk with him to Sheila Branch's.

Sheila answers the door wearing emerald-green silk pajamas. It's four o'clock in the morning but she doesn't seem to mind being dropped in on so late. She sits in a chair on one side of the room; Jim and I perch side by side on a couch opposite. The room has a high ceiling, track lighting, shadowy white walls, sparse modern furnishings. A square glass coffee table rests in the middle of the expanse of hardwood floor between Sheila and us. She tucks her legs under her, takes a cigarette out of a brown vinyl case, and lights it with a lighter. She and Jim discuss money and quantities, what she wants for one hit of tar, how much tar she's got and how much she hopes to make with it. They argue a little. Her manner toward him is tough, familiar, imperious. He acts restless and defiant; he smokes, picks at the sofa, glances around the room. I don't know what to think or say or do. I feel like an actor who has blundered into the wrong movie, a third-grader who finds herself on the mean, scary teenagers' side of the playground. My mouth is small and tense, my expression frozen and fearful. Jim gets what he wants and we walk back to his house in the dawn.

At home, he takes the left-over pizza out of the refrigerator and brings it into the bedroom and we sit on the bed with the open box between us. I remember watching him eat a piece of cold pizza with a strange, ugly, childish look on his face, and I remember that a little later he said, full of self-hatred and bitter regret, as we were sitting there among the rumpled covers smoking, tapping our ashes into a dirty glass ashtray resting on the sheet, "It's Sunday morning and my wife and I are going to go to church."

We lay down in his narrow single bed—him on his back, me wedged in beside the wall—and pulled the covers over us. I dozed, woke, dozed, got up and went to the bathroom. When I came back he was sitting at the desk messing with a syringe. I said, "I'm going home. I can't take any more of this."

Jim said something paranoid like, "Yeah, sure, you don't care about me anyway."

When I got home I called his friend John Gray. "He's up there killing himself," I said. "Can you talk to him?"

John said, very firmly, "There's nothing I can do." Then he said, "For years I had hope he'd grow up and stop this shit but I don't have hope anymore." I felt shocked, scared that John had no hope that Jim would change, that he saw him in such a negative way. But I didn't lose hope that Jim would change, my hope didn't even waver. I just hung up the phone and sat there in my pink rocking chair and stared out the window, feeling terrible and somehow ashamed, trying not to think about what John had said.

That was the only time I ever tried to enlist anyone else's help with Jim's drug and alcohol problems, partly because I agreed with John—I still do—there wasn't anything he could do. No firetrucks and policemen, no family members, no concerned, well-intentioned onlookers can do anything to fix someone's addiction. Addiction is the tar baby, another person might step up to it and take a swing but they'll just get stuck too. But I didn't exactly know that then, and there were plenty of other reasons as well why I didn't enlist someone else's help. I didn't want to tell anyone what Jim was doing because I was afraid of what they would think. On some level I guess I felt like Jim was being a bad boy and I felt like a bad girl too; I felt like what he did reflected on me, as if it wasn't just him doing it, it was me doing it too. And I had no sense that whoever I asked would actually do something *helpful*; I thought they would just say, "Oh, bad, bad"; try to make me break up with Jim or put him away in some jail or hospital, none of which I thought would be helpful or desirable. And I kept thinking the whole problem was just going to go away, that every binge was the last, that it was just a matter of Jim wanting to stop, and since he obviously wanted to stop, he would stop, he had stopped already, except for the times when he wasn't stopping, when he was sitting up there at his desk like he was now, killing himself.

After a while I started worrying about what he might do to himself. I kept picturing him falling asleep with a cigarette between his fingers, dropping it on the floor or into a shoe or something and the house starting on fire, and so I walked up to his house and nosed around outside his window. I didn't smell smoke and there was nothing else I could do so I went back home.

Then there's a stretch of days when I don't remember what happened, except for one little memory of lying on my bed late at night, struggling in some half-asleep, half-awake state to get up. At one point I succeeded in sitting up, but I think it was just some phantom dream version of me, like the astral body they talk about in spiritualist literature. I had the sensation that there was a body lying on the bed, and a body sitting up. I was worried, hysterically worried—Jim was still bingeing after days and days—and even though I was absolutely powerless, I couldn't give up the feeling that there must be something I could do, should do to stop the disaster.

When memory reconnects I see him standing at the kitchen stove in his apartment, boiling water. I'm behind and to the side of him, standing next to the small drop-leaf table that sits in the middle of the room, and Peggy, his roommate, is somewhere in the picture, too, though I can't quite locate her; she's simply there, a third presence in the memory. Maybe she's nearby in her room off the kitchen, or maybe she is standing in the doorway, drawn out of her room by my arrival on the scene. I don't know what she thinks of all this: Jim at the stove boiling water, the whole furious, runaway drug binge. She seems to be taking it calmly, even casually, as if nothing out of the ordinary is going on. But maybe I'm remembering wrong.

The water on the stove, I somehow know, is for shooting up heroin. Some old filmclip or other scrap of folklore is surfacing in my mind with images of junkies, cracked sinks, and spoonfuls of water being boiled over candles, of poverty and debasement, and a dingy, black-and-white hysteria seems to descend over the room. Jim isn't acting like himself; there's a cynical, antagonistic edge to him, a kind of grim determination to self-destruct.

"This isn't the real you," I say weakly, attempting to conjure up another, saner version of him, to call him back from the edge.

"Oh, yes it is," he says in his cynical voice.

He says he wants to break up. He's going away somewhere, either to North Carolina where his sister lives or someplace else, someplace really bad. He won't tell me where. I write my work phone number on a scrap of paper that's sitting around the living room—a Pizza Hut form asking customers to rate the local franchise: It has questions like "How was the service during your most recent visit?" and little boxes you check for "excellent," "good," "fair." I write that number down picturing him calling me some better, sober day in the future when he's passing through town, us getting together, him perhaps deciding to stay. I'm not sure if I'm remembering the number correctly, so underneath I write the name of the office where I work so if he has to he can look it up in the phone book.

A month or two later, when the binge is well behind us and we're acting like normal people again, more or less normal at least, he will say it made him feel really good when I wrote that number down and gave it to him, though I never would have guessed it at the time—all he did was look at it and put it down on the table.

I was devastated that we were breaking up, that he was going away. I remember sitting on the couch feeling hurt and cold and sad and abandoned, though I pretended—to myself as well as to Jim—that I didn't feel that way. I wish I could say I felt or acted differently—that I was more rational, less pathetic, that I was the one who initiated the breakup out of self-respect, self-protectiveness—but I can't. I just sat there on the couch trying to make myself numb, accept this huge awful loss, like a snake trying to digest an elephant it just swallowed.

I had no idea where that bad place he might be going to was. I had a vague sense of it as someplace distant and sinister and hazy in the imagination, Vietnam or El Salvador or Bogota, Colombia, somewhere like that. What I think now is that he was talking about death, suicide, that that was the place he might go which was really bad. Really bad because he'd grown up Catholic and on some level he believed that it was really bad to commit suicide, but he saw it as a place you could go to get away. And when he said, months later, it made him feel good when I wrote my number down on that piece of paper, maybe he was saying that it made him reconsider.

The Rooms of Heaven

I went home, and later on in the day he called me and said he was going to be staying at some friends' house, a couple he knew who lived in a trailer park; they were coming to pick him up and could he drop some of his stuff off at my house. I said fine and he said he'd bring it down in about an hour and then I waited and waited. Finally he showed up with some things, odd things from his past, a pennant that had "'68" on it, which must've had to do with high school football, and some other strange objects from his trunk—that white candleholder with the leaves on it was one of them. He brought them into the house and gave them to me and then he left. Later on he said, "If I ever start giving my things away or taking them back you'll know I'm thinking about suicide." But I didn't pay attention when he said that; it was just one of those things I ignored because I didn't want to take it seriously.

The next day he called and said he'd changed his mind, he'd been thinking about it and he wanted us to stay together, he wanted to give up all that bad stuff he'd been doing and go on, have a real life. Then he told me both his hands were swollen and there was a big red mark, an N on its way to becoming an M, slowly spreading along the top of his right hand. We agreed it was probably blood poisoning.

His truck is in the shop so I borrow my upstairs neighbor's car and drive him to the hospital and we go inside, into the emergency ward. It's about ten P.M. when we get there. Jim has an intake interview, we wait, a tall willowy black nurse calls him in. I look around for a magazine, pick up a copy of *People* off the table, take a seat among a bank of navy-blue waiting-room chairs, and settle down to read. Forty-five minutes later the willowy nurse comes out and says, "Where'd your friend go?"

"What?" I say.

"Your friend, he disappeared," the nurse says. "I thought maybe he was out here with you."

"No, I haven't seen him."

The nurse shrugs and starts walking away. "What's he on?" she says over her shoulder. "That guy's totally wired." She grins and shakes her head.

"I'll try to find him," I say. I get up, go out the sliding double doors, walk a little way out into the dark empty parking lot, and look around. Then I go back inside, walk down a long hallway, stand and stare at an exit door. I can't imagine where he could have gone. I keep picturing him escaping on a motorcycle that has somehow materialized in the middle of the hospital emergency room, him roaring down the hallway like something out of a Charles Bronson movie, stopping in the waiting area to gather me up, the two of us roaring out the front door and off into the night. Except he didn't stop to gather me up. He's gone. Disappeared. At that moment, standing in the long empty hospital hallway, I know it's hopeless. He really is crazy. It really isn't going to work out between us. I start giving up, finally, on the relationship.

I return to the waiting area. I see the tall willowy nurse and I ask her hopelessly, "Any news about Jim Beaman?"

"Oh," she says, smiling, "he turned up. He's down in X ray. An orderly brought him down there without telling us."

10

Denial is an astonishing thing. Over and over I'm struck by Jim's and my ability to ignore the true, hopeless side of the situation, to delude ourselves into believing that what was going on wasn't going on. It's as if we were operating in two separate, simultaneous realities. One was what was really happening—the mood swings, the binges and the slips, the out-of-control addictive behavior, mine as well as Jim's: He was addicted to drugs, I was addicted to him. The other was what we thought was happening: We were in love, we were happy, we were going to be married; we had a few problems but we were solving them, they were practically solved already. And because we thought the latter was happening, in a way it was. In a way, both of those realities were true. Both of them exist, like two different movies running at the same time on the same screen, in my memory. Sometimes one shows, sometimes the other. The happy movie appears more often—I watch it more often—but the other, darker film always bleeds through into the light.

The four days Jim spent in the hospital are the happiest part of the happy movie. The hospital was a protected environment—we were safe from drugs there—and Jim wasn't that sick after the first day. He needed an IV and the doctors wanted to run some tests and keep an eye on him, but the red mark on his hand was receding and there didn't seem to be anything all that serious wrong with him. I had an almost holiday sense of relief that the binge was over and he was acting like himself again, down-to-earth and sensible and remorseful.

He said he thought at bottom the binge had been about testing our relationship, that he'd said to himself, I might as well do the worst and get it over with, lose her if I'm going to. The explanation appealed to me: It implied the binge was a one-time choice contingent on circumstances instead of something he had no control over, something he might repeat; and it implied his basic motivation had more to do with fear of losing me and thus love of me than with anything to do with cocaine. But I doubt there was much truth in it; it seems clear now that he'd simply reached a point where his cocaine use was out of control, especially when there were large quantities around within easy access. But neither of us could have faced believing—*really* believing—that, though I'm sure we both knew it on some other level.

I visited him in the hospital every day after work and the nurses let me hang around for hours; Beaman said they let me stay so he wouldn't be such a pain in the ass. He had the room to himself; on the morning of the first day an old man with yellow skin and sunken eyes was in the other bed behind the half-pulled curtain, but he was gone in the evening and no one took his place. Jim and I watched TV, lying together on his narrow bed, and went on little jaunts around the hospital, down to the smoking room at the end of the hallway or to the cafeteria on the first floor, via the elevator, dragging the unwieldy IV stand everywhere; Jim kept calling it Skippy. We observed and discussed and joked about everything: a large dim room off the first floor hallway billed as the meditation room, which had three benches facing two large TVs with pictures of blue skies, puffy clouds, and fields full of flowers permanently projected onto their screens; the white-smocked orderlies eating packaged sandwiches in the florescent-bright cafeteria; the plastic grids on the elevator ceilings, which looked like little ice cube trays. Jim kept calling the smoking room the Joseph P. Mengele memorial smoking area. It was a small, deliberately dingy room with orange plastic chairs lining the walls, rusty floor-stand ashtrays placed among the rows of chairs, and an old scratched console TV in the corner. Sometimes we'd run into an acquaintance of Beaman's, a lawyer recovering from minor heart surgery, puffing on a cigarette there. Rather than discouraging us from smoking as it seemed intended to, the ambiance of the room made us cheerful and defiant. The three of us—me, Jim, the lawyer—sat around the perimeter chatting and joking, blowing smoke into the middle of the room.

On the third day, when I showed up at noon, Beaman said he'd discovered a new place to smoke. It was outside, to the left of a patio where patients ate lunch, a long paved open passageway, breezy and secluded and shady, between a waist-high cement wall and the side of the building. We pulled two chairs over and sat with our feet on the wall, sharing a cheap tin outdoor ashtray. By that time Jim's IV had been removed and he was wearing jeans and a T-shirt. The swelling in his hands was almost completely gone but the doctors wanted to keep him for another day. We talked and joked and laughed. But then, subtly, imperceptibly, Jim's mood shifted. He grew silent, restless, his face took on a distracted, irritable look. He said he thought he'd lost a bunch of money he needed to give the Boxer; he wasn't particularly looking forward to going home and dealing with that or the rest of the mess he'd made, but at the same time he was anxious to get on with it. I said nothing. I was living from moment to moment only. I didn't let myself think about what would happen next.

On the door of his hospital room was a sign that said, in big red alarming letters, DANGER! CONTAMINATION RISK. Every time I looked at it I was filled with a terrible heartsick dread. I knew it was a warning to hospital staff to beware of Jim's bodily fluids because as an intravenous drug user he was at high risk for AIDS. He said he never shared needles with anybody but he thought it made sense to have an AIDS test anyway. When the results came a week after he got out of the hospital he called me at work to tell me the test was negative. He said that when the doctor told him he was so relieved he said, "Do you have a candle? I want to light one." I asked him why he was worried since he never shared needles and he said, "Well, there might have been a few times in an emergency." Three years later I had an AIDS test and it was also negative.

The last day he was in the hospital was the Fourth of July. In the evening we went for a walk and ended up on a bridge overlooking City Park—the same park where Kathy and I used to skate. From there we watched the fireworks across the river: big white chrysanthemums of light bursting against the velvety sky, feathery red and blue star shells, rockets exploding in flashes of sound and light. It was hot and humid and the air was thick and heavy. Something in the night felt poised, held back, on the verge of letting go; as we walked along the path toward the hospital thunder growled. It started pouring as we crossed the courtyard to the side entrance of the hospital. Stroke after stroke of lightning lit the sky and thunder clashed and boomed; thick sheets of rain sluiced across the windows of Jim's hospital room. There was no question of my going out in that, and we sat there, him on the side of his bed, me on a plastic hospital chair, and waited for the storm to die down.

On the way home I stopped by his house to search for the three thousand dollars he owed the Boxer but had somehow misplaced. The lost money was weighing on him; while we were saying good-bye he asked me to go to his house to see if I could find it. Peggy wasn't home and I let myself into their apartment with my key. Jim's room was a mess; there were dirty ashtrays, papers, the scale and other drug paraphernalia on the desk and clothes flung all over the bed. In getting ready to go to the hospital he had taken half the shirts and pants out of the closet, debating whether to wear them; he said the doctors and nurses would treat him better if he was nicely dressed. The little gray cloth bag he'd described was right in the middle of the floor beside the bed. I unzipped it and found a fat stack of money encircled with a rubber band. I zipped up the bag and put the money in my purse. When I got home I called Jim and told him I'd found it.

I don't know what I was expecting to take place when he got out of the hospital, but it certainly wasn't that he would go right back out and do it again. For one thing, he assured me that he wasn't going to do it again: He didn't want to, couldn't afford to, knew that if he did he would eventually lose me, wasn't all that stupid, given the trouble it had just gotten him into. And I believed him because I wanted to believe him, and also because it simply didn't make sense for him to keep on doing cocaine. I hadn't caught on that what was happening didn't have anything to do with making sense.

So when he disappeared the first day out of the hospital and was gone all day, I had no idea where he was; I was frantic with worry, convinced he'd been in a car wreck or had met some other awful fate. I kept calling his phone number, leaving messages on the answering machine. Finally he called from home at eight o'clock and said he was sorry; he'd been out driving around with some friend all day, bingeing on drugs again. Later on he said that was one of the hardest things he ever had to do in his life, to call me and tell me what he'd been doing and say he was sorry.

After that he stopped dealing for the Boxer and made a serious effort to give up cocaine. He tried to do it on his own—didn't enter a treatment program, didn't attend twelve-step meetings—so his efforts were probably doomed and maybe he knew on some level they were doomed, maybe there was some part of him that was still holding out. But all the other parts of him tried. He remained drug-free for weeks at a time, and his slips lasted only a night. At first, during the sober periods, we were recklessly optimistic; we got engaged, made our plans, stayed up late talking about how happy, how lucky we were, weaving the spell of our myth in which everything was going to be all right, more than all right—addictions vanquished, sanity restored, happiness at last prevailing.

11

I have a thin file of notes Jim and I exchanged during that time. I typed most of mine; I don't even handwrite a Post-it note if I can help it. Jim wrote his on "From the Desk of Jim Beaman" letterhead, that notepaper printed with a little man falling backward off a chimney.

Also in my file are a few pieces of correspondence Beaman wrote to two of his friends: Jeffrey Palmer, a former roommate of his who now lives in Des Moines—they shared an Iowa City apartment on Fairchild Street, which Beaman always called Stepchild Street; and Jim Robb, or Robo, another old Iowa City friend of Jim's. Robo had moved to San Diego ten years ago. I met Jeffrey at the memorial service, got to know Robo over the phone long-distance during the week after Jim's death. I can't remember how Robo and I got connected; I only remember sitting in my living room talking on the phone to him about addiction and shame, him speaking from his experience as a recovering alcoholic. He said, "When you're drinking and feeling bad about it, it doesn't take much to hit a raw nerve."

Both he and Jeffrey sent me photocopies of correspondence Beaman wrote them during the summer and fall he and I were together. Those letters meant a lot to me, especially in the first months after the death. I read and reread them, scrutinized them, pored over them as if contemplating an enigma: the spirit of Jim, which I was always looking for back then. And it was there, a little, in the handwriting—the little peaks on the *m*'s and *n*'s, the looping *d*'s and *l*'s—in the syntax and the humor, even in the spelling errors, though not enough to be satisfying, just enough to make me want more.

The letters document Jim's and my state of mind during the summer and fall of 1990. They provide a record of our denial, a picture of reality as we wanted it to be.

In the middle of July, about two weeks after he got home from the hospital, Jim wrote both Jeffrey and Robo to tell them he'd fallen in love.

"I've met a woman that I think I'm madly in love with," he tells Robo on July 22, 1990. "She feels the same about me which makes the situation better than ever." To both friends he brags that I'm a "published writer." He also notes proudly to Robo, "She's clean of drugs and a slight drinker." Of himself he comments, "Still not drinking—drug every now and then but that's on the shelf due to my sweet Mary."

"Best friends are under blood obligation to inform dramatic romance shifts to one another," he concludes his note to Jeffrey. "My obligation is fulfilled."

I had already informed Kathy. She and I still talked often on the phone, and I'd been giving her practically minute-by-minute updates on my relationship with Beaman—told her when we met, when I lured him to my house with the book about Colonel Davenport, when we had sex under the bush. I didn't tell her much, however, about Beaman's problem with drugs and alcohol. I did mention something about it to her during our couch days—said he had a history of being a wild man and an addict but that was all behind him. Kathy thought it was sort of sexy too. The next time I told her about it was when he was in the hospital with blood poisoning. I said, "Something really terrible is going on and I don't want to tell you, I don't even want to think about it myself," and then I did tell her. I don't remember saying that; Kathy told me recently when I asked her.

The Rooms of Heaven

I wrote Kathy a letter on July 20, 1990, as well. It starts off, "I'm writing this in the shade of a garage door on Sunday while Jim strips forms off a concrete sidewalk. I'm supposed to help set string lines (whatever that means) pretty soon. I feel sort of like I'm at the beach except instead of water there's a huge cornfield over to the right." The letter goes on to describe the weather, the surburban neighborhood, little things that happened at my job, my writing—I was working on a novel then, which I abandoned in the fall—my and Jim's plans for the winter; he was hoping to go to Mexico and I was considering going to a writing colony. I don't remember any of those things when I look back on that time. Kathy said, when I asked her to send me the letter, that it seemed unbelievably cruel to remind me of my happiness when Jim was alive. But what it reminds me of more painfully is how little I was living in reality back then.

One day in August of that year I found in my mailbox an envelope addressed to "Mrs. Beaman"; inside was the first of the notes I got from Jim. Written on a piece of his stationery was the following: "My Dearest Mary, I had a very interesting dream about you. I was yodeling in your canyon. Playing patty cake with your hooters. . . . Then we had sex."

I responded along the same lines: "Dear Jim, Last night I had a dream about you. I was an index in a Sears catalogue and you were a bookmark between my pages. You were moving around and then . . . ! all of a sudden we were at my office." (The Sears catalogue reference relates to a comment Jim made about an odd dream I had about simultaneously being and editing a piece of paper bearing a list of names. When I told him about it the next morning he said, "You have such strange dreams! It's like you dreamed you were the dictionary or a page in the Sears catalogue.") "At that point we had sex," my note goes on. "The reading pillow played a major part. Don't ask me what it was doing in my office."

At the bottom of the letter I added a P.S. with an entirely different tone, an apologetic one, though the apology wasn't mine to give: "I'm sorry we had such a bad ending to the night last night, especially since we didn't talk about it. We'll have a better night tonight."

Jim put a note in my mailbox the same day, offering his own apology and an explanation: "I'm just scared. Everything I've ever wanted I've found in you. . . . It's all happening so fast. Just hang with me till I get my sea legs."

Try as I might I can't recall what the "bad ending to the night" consisted of. I only remember finding the envelope with the note in my mailbox, tearing it open, and reading the contents, relief flowing through me like warm bathwater. We must've had some little fight, occasioned by some bad mood of Jim's. I responded by fearing rejection, thinking he'd changed his mind about the relationship and was going to start acting cold and withholding, and that would mean he didn't love me. What I see now that I didn't see then, what Jim didn't see either, or at least didn't admit, is that those bad moods probably had at least as much to do with cocaine, not to mention alcohol, as they did with me. Maybe Jim was scared, not quite trusting *us*, floundering in search of his relationship sea legs, but in the end none of those feelings really mattered. Because whatever he—we—felt or did was never just about him and me, it was always about him, me, and a third party, a huge secret significant other like a black hole between us, sucking in all the attention, pulling all the strings: the third other, of course, was addiction.

They say in twelve-step programs that alcoholism is "cunning, baffling, and powerful." I'm not exactly sure what Bill W.

meant when he wrote that phrase back in 1940, but I think I have an idea. There's something slippery about alcoholism, about addiction in general; it lies and hides, seduces you with pleasure, sneaks up on you from behind. "First you take a drink, then the drink takes a drink, then the drink takes you," F. Scott Fitzgerald wrote. Some invisible transformation goes on, a sleight of hand too quick for the eye or the mind, and in the end it's you that changes.

These days almost everyone, including the American Medical Association, knows that alcoholism is a disease, but somehow it's still hard for most people to believe—really believe—it. An illness is a condition, not a series of moral decisions. Diseases aren't choices; we don't regard them as blameworthy the way we regard the actions people choose to do. But alcoholism involves actions, and many of them are blameworthy, self-destructive at the very least. I've heard alcoholism compared to diabetes, with booze being to the drinker what sugar is to the diabetic. But alcoholism is different from diabetes: The alcoholic is like a diabetic who can't or won't stop eating sugar; he'll do almost anything to keep eating it. And the alcohol—the sugar—doesn't just make the patient sick, it makes him, it can make him, obnoxious, destructive, crazy, scary. Moral deterioration is a medically recognized symptom of advanced-stage alcoholism. Alcoholism is implicated in 60 percent of all child abuse, 80 percent of all domestic violence, 30 percent of all suicides. But still, it's a disease. I believe it, as much as I believe schizophrenia, Alzheimer's, and any other conditions that affect the way you act and think are diseases. Alcohol affects your brain chemistry; it inhibits the receptors, slows down the brain cells' firing, messes with the chemical messengers.

Cocaine is probably even worse. It causes your neurons to release a flood of dopamine, a neurotransmitter that makes you feel good—much more dopamine than they normally would.

That's why the drug makes you confident and euphoric. But it's a short-lived feeling: After the high there's a horrible crash; you feel just as bad during the crash as you felt good before. The crash occurs because you've created a temporary dopamine shortage, which is why you crave more cocaine, why you keep on doing it and doing it in binges. At the same time, over time, some researchers think, something starts changing in the basic chemistry of your brain: to accommodate the extra dopamine you grow extra little dendrites with extra dopamine receptors. To keep the receptors happy you need more dopamine and hence more cocaine, but eventually, no matter how much cocaine you do, instead of more dopamine, there's less available; you've used most of your supply up. Since dopamine is necessary for a normal mood and mental state, this is a major problem. Symptoms of heavy cocaine use or withdrawal include anxiety, confusion, irritability, agitation, lying, paranoia, and suicidal depression. Monkeys will choose cocaine over food or sex; they'll press a lever as many as twelve thousand times for a single dose of it.

Codependency, or whatever you want to call it—the tendency to be attracted to alcoholics, addicts, people with lots of problems, to get involved and stay involved, no matter how bad it gets—is an embarrassing affliction. It has no glamour, no dignity whatsoever. Its causes, its symptoms and manifestations are rooted in the sort of hurt, weak, childish impulses nobody wants to admit: fear of abandonment and authority, the desire to pacify and to please, low self-esteem. At its heart is the struggle to control the uncontrollable, to ensure love and security, to make the unsafe safe; it's the powerless striving for power in devious, circuitous ways.

The uncontrollable thing the codependent tries to control, of course, is someone else's drug taking or drinking.

The Rooms of Heaven

I remember every one of Jim's slips.

One night we were in his living room. It was eleven-thirty, time to go to my house and go to bed, and he said, "I need five minutes alone and then I'll be right down." "I need five minutes alone" was our code for saying I have to go the bathroom—seriously go to the bathroom, as Jim used to say—and I want to do it without you around making me self-conscious.

I said, "Okay," and went to my house and waited for Jim to come. I kept thinking he was going to arrive at any minute but he never did. When I called his house I got the answering machine. Finally he showed up at two in the morning; he'd been out in a car with some friend getting high. And it happened on his birthday, August 28. I was at my house waiting with his presents wrapped and his birthday dinner made. That time he arrived four hours late. And there were other occasions, other slips as well.

I got caught in the trap every time. Every time I somehow "forgot" what had happened the last time and I'd start fresh, go back to zero with the slate wiped clean. At first I didn't even suspect what he was doing when he didn't show up; then later on, as the months went by, I'd know but I still wouldn't quite believe it—I'd say, well, he wouldn't do *that* to me, would he? And then I'd think something else must've happened to him and I'd panic. Once when he didn't come home all night I was convinced he'd been in a car accident. I remember staring out my window at the empty, four-o'clock-in-the-morning sidewalk shiny with damp and the streetlights sending out their feverish yellow glow into the night, the windows in the house across the street dark and blank, thinking I wouldn't be able to stand it if he was dead because then I couldn't talk to him anymore.

At the same time I felt incredibly resentful, just absolutely furious. But my anxiety about being abandoned was even stronger, so I pushed my resentment aside—let alone any rational thinking about the situation. And when he came back he always looked so miserable and ashamed—as if he felt like a failure—and I would forgive him, or maybe forgive isn't exactly the word I'm looking for—the word is more like excuse, or pretend, as in pretend it hadn't happened.

What I remember most is all the waiting. I was always waiting by the phone for him to call, waiting for him to come to my house, waiting for him to get back to normal and be himself, waiting for him to stop taking drugs altogether. It never truly occurred to me that he wouldn't stop, that there wouldn't be relief at the end of the waiting, that I was waiting for nothing. I was like one of those monkeys that pushes a bar twelve thousand times for a single dose of cocaine, that keeps pushing and pushing, hoping, hoping, never giving up hope that the good feeling will come back.

I guess in that sense I was addicted to Jim, to the relationship, to the relief and happiness I felt in those times when things were going well—to the unconscious feeling that he, it, love were going to heal some wounded part of me, if the relationship and what was standing in its way would only heal itself.

And what about Peggy? Where did she fit in? I can only conclude that she was just another monkey pressing on a bar, the same one I was pressing on, the one that had "love" and "approval" and "Jim" inscribed on it. I wasn't there all those years she and Jim lived peaceably together, but somehow I know what it was like for them, for her. All those Friday, Saturday nights. Jim at his desk or in the rocking chair in the living room, high, bleary eyed, incommunicative but there. Peggy bopping cheerfully in and out, going back and forth to Gabe's. They spent holidays, Sunday afternoons, his fortieth birthday together. There are photos in the trunk of Peggy smiling and holding up a homemade pie with a crisscross crust for the camera, Peggy watching TV in front of the fan wearing shorts and a sleeveless blouse. There's that snapshot of the two of them, Peggy in a nice blouse and gray suit, Jim in a suitcoat, tie and vest, standing in the doorway of the kitchen on his fortieth birthday.

Before I came along, they had a version of home, a kind of small, illusory, dysfunctional family, and if it wasn't a real family, a real relationship, if they didn't share a bed, that was okay. Peggy just let it slide, filled in what was missing in her imagination. I don't know about Jim, what he was up to in all this. Probably their living arrangement filled some need of his as well, but whatever it was it wasn't the same need it filled for Peggy. That I know for sure.

Then I enter the picture. Suddenly everything's different. Jim's in love, he spends Friday nights, Saturday nights, holidays, birthdays at my house, he's happy, he's trying to give up drugs. Peggy freaks out—not too badly, she doesn't go absolutely nuts—but she cries, she says a few catty things to Jim about me, she makes some scenes. Who can blame her?

Sometimes at night when Jim and I were at their place watching TV she'd come home and storm around the kitchen, banging cabinet doors shut, rattling the dishes in the dish drainer, then come into the living room and make a scene. She'd yell at Jim for not cleaning the apartment often enough, for not doing the dishes, for various other misdemeanors; she'd say that she was just his slave and nothing else. Then she'd reach a kind of crisis and start to cry inconsolably and shout, "You don't care about me!"

Jim did not do well with those scenes. He dreaded and resented them; he talked about them a lot when he and I were alone as if they really bugged him; once he got up and went in his room and took a Valium at the sound of her fumbling at the door with her key. Usually we tried to be gone before she came home but it wasn't always possible to get the timing right and sometimes we'd be sitting there in the living room when she came in. She wasn't always in a bad mood; sometimes she'd plop down on the couch, light a cigarette and sit there making friendly small talk, laughing her goofy, cheerful laugh. Or sometimes she'd start off friendly and I'd think she was in a good mood, but then it would become apparent that she was in the other kind of mood. Jim would try to reason with her or joke her out of it—"Where's the telephone? I want to call Rome and tell them to make you a saint"—but fairly quickly he'd move from strained equanimity to rage himself. He had a fierce, hair-trigger temper of his own, as many alcoholics do. Usually he'd stand up, get his jacket from the closet and we would simply go, but once he started to shout at her, then stopped, and when he turned to face me I could see it cost him an effort to rein himself back in.

If by fall Jim's and my optimism was waning, you'd never know it from our letters.

On September 14, after I was rejected for a job I thought I'd get with no problem—I didn't even get an interview—Jim sent me a funny little note signed by Omar Pignuts offering me "lifetime employment" in the position of Miss Hellfinger. "Your job related experience fits our requirements to a flying T," the note assured me, and "your office equipment such as the mention of a non-slip grip reading pillow tipped the scales in your favor."

"I humbly accept your offer," I wrote him back. "I will be on the spot with my pillow and other special equipment when you give me the OK (jelly)."

In October Jim bought a used electric typewriter at a thrift store down the street. The store owner promised to repair a couple of sluggish keys before Jim picked it up at the shop, and on October 28 Jim wrote me, "Would you check on my typewriter?"

"Thank God it's a new day," the same note says. "I have a secret and I won't tell you." The "secret" was probably my Christmas present, a beautiful rose silk coat Jim bought me weeks in advance and kept in a giftwrapped box under his bed. He was terrible at keeping secrets and told me about the coat soon after promising not to tell me about it. Only the giftwrapping prevented him from opening the box and showing it to me.

I have no idea what "Thank God it's a new day" refers to. Probably some argument or depression, some bad mood or unpleasant incident that took place the previous day. There was always something we were recovering from; life with alcoholism, drugs, addiction is a series of wrong turns, new starts.

On October 30, Jim wrote Robo that he was trying to get the hang of his new typewriter. "It's a Panasonic with word storage and the whole nine yards. . . . So for the next few days it will be typing lessons for the big Beams. . . . Practice, practice, PRACTICE IS THE KEY.

"Business is going great," Jim continues, adding that he has bought a new dump truck. "As with every vehicle I've ever owned the body is rather humble. . . . But the tires are all new and the exhaust is new and the engine runs great. I have all these grand plans to paint the damn thing this winter but we will see."

Jim's new dump truck never made it farther than a few miles down the road to a new parking place in the yard of one of his construction buddies. I helped him drive it there, following in the Chevy pickup, the rusty old dump truck lumbering along belching exhaust, Jim looking small behind the wheel. After that one trip it refused to start, and the friend in whose yard it was parked diagnosed its condition as fatal, requiring too many repairs to be worth fixing.

The typewriter met a similar fate. Like a photograph, the letter to Robo captures a single moment; it was a moment when all was well, when optimism was high, when the relationship between Beaman and the typewriter was at its pinnacle. The letter was written in the morning. By evening it was clear the typewriter hadn't been fixed as the store owner promised; the keys that stuck when Jim bought it still stuck and the shift key had stopped working as well. Jim was frustrated and irritable.

In the pile of photos I found in his trunk, there are two pictures of me I'm almost sure were taken that day. I'm lying on Jim's bed in both of them. In one I have the comforter pulled up around my chest, my bare shoulders and the tops of my bare breasts are showing, my hair is squashed and flattened on the pillow, and I'm laughing. In the other I'm dressed and lying under Jim's plaid blanket; I'm wearing lipstick and staring at a brochure with a studious, pinch-mouthed look. Although it escaped me the first time I examined the photo, I'm pretty sure now that brochure was the typewriter's operating instructions, and the look on my face wasn't just self-consciousness because I was having my picture taken, it was a look of anxiety, of unhappy, determined concentration. I was trying to block out Jim's bad mood—his mounting annoyance over the typewriter, as tangible and threatening to me as an approaching storm system—and at the same time avert it, searching among the operating instructions for some hint or clue as to how to solve the problem with the shift key.

Other things went wrong that evening too. Jim had asked a client, a woman with a lot of property around town with whom he was on good terms, to write him a recommendation, which he needed to be eligible for the job of restoring the brick on some valuable old buildings for the state historical society. The woman said she'd be glad to recommend him but then kept putting him off, and I think it embarrassed him to keep having to call her about it. Earlier on the day of the broken shift key she'd told him to drop by her house after dinner to pick up the letter, but when he called her at nine o'clock to see if it was ready she snapped at him dismissively. I don't remember exactly what she said but it was something along the lines of, "Don't bother me, I'm busy." When Jim came back into the room his eyes were large and shiny with rage and something else that I think was shame. He stomped around the kitchen calling the woman a bitch and worse, and then he went in the bedroom, picked up the typewriter, and slammed it down on the desk. When it hit the desk the bell that rings when you reach the end of a line made a little dinging sound as if in protest; the platen came off and some other parts got broken too. Afterward he threw the whole machine away in the trash.

Looking back on that incident now, I think that Jim's reaction was probably related not only to shame but to alcohol. He'd drunk five or six beers in a restaurant the night before and afterward he wanted to go out and drink again. When I met him he wasn't drinking at all, he'd given alcohol up because he'd had to give it up. But gradually, bit by bit, when we went out to dinner and at certain other times, usually when there was something going on with cocaine—a problem coming down off it or when he was craving it—he started drinking again. At first it was only once a month, then every two or three weeks, then once or twice a week. And at first it was only one beer, then it became two or three, then five or six or a bottle of wine. It worried me but not very much; I was too dumb or deluded to see how dangerous it was. I didn't know there couldn't have been a worse poison for him, not even cocaine. Alcohol seemed more "normal" to me than drugs, especially drugs injected with needles, and I hadn't had much experience with alcoholism; I had no idea how awful it can get.

But I noticed that sometimes when he drank or the day after he drank he'd be in a very good mood, then, all of a sudden, as if something flicked a switch in his brain, he'd get in a very, very bad mood.

12

Jim and I are sitting at my kitchen table late at night. It's mid-September, he's fucked up again on cocaine, and we've been through the whole routine: him trying to hide it and me knowing anyway and him denying it, then admitting it, and me getting mad in a frustrated, powerless way, then forgiving him because he feels so bad about it himself and because there's nothing else to do—nothing else I'm willing to do—but forgive him. But it's a grudging, conditional kind of forgiveness, pregnant with requirements and anxieties for the future.

I'm toasting an English muffin. The toaster pops up and I grab the hot muffin and set it quickly on the plate, pick up the knife, and start buttering. I look up and see that Jim is watching. I ask him if he wants half the English muffin and he shakes his head. He's never hungry when he's been doing cocaine, and this always makes me sort of mad. I feel rejected, the way a mother feels rejected after she's cooked a big dinner and everyone's having too much fun to come to the table. I guess I think Jim is having fun. I think giving up cocaine is a matter of will, something he's doing because he wants to, and when he fails, I think it's because he doesn't want to give it up enough. That's what he thinks too.

I place the knife on the edge of the plate, pick up the English muffin, take a bite. "That looks really good," he says, and when I glance over at him I'm startled by the intensity in his eyes, as if that English muffin represents a whole wholesome life he's barred from. Still, I don't want to acknowledge that this probably isn't going to be the last time we find ourselves in these circumstances, and when he says, a few minutes later, "I've decided I'm not going to marry you if I can't give this up," I don't take it all that seriously, I don't consider what he might do instead. I say, "Don't worry, you'll be able to give it up."

It's a weekday at the end of October and we're sitting in Jim's living room. Two empty beer cans rest on the table between the rocking chair and couch, the kitchen sink and counter are littered with empties, and Jim is holding a can from which he sips. He's not drunk, though in the last hour his speech has started slowing down and his lines are growing softer, blurrier, like an outward manifestation of his interior landscape. He drinks slowly, steadily, mechanically, consuming one beer after another in a businesslike way. He would like to stop but he can't. He's drinking for maintenance, for self-medication.

It's the day after one of his all-night cocaine binges. Usually he takes Valium, but his supply has run out and he can't get any more right now—the woman he buys it from, a housewife with a permanent prescription, isn't answering her phone—and—this probably has more to do with cocaine than Valium—he's depressed. Badly depressed. He's crashing, or maybe he's past crashing and into withdrawal. Depression and anxiety are symptoms of both. His brain has a shortage of dopamine, his neurotransmitters are flapping in the wind. Dysphoria: the opposite of euphoria, a state of anxiety, dissatisfaction, restlessness. Anhedonia: a chemically induced inability to experience pleasurable sensations. These are awful words. Even now they send a chill through me.

But at the time—back then—I have no idea. I know he has a problem but I don't know what it is, I don't understand the connections between the mind and body, I don't know his mood is being jerked around like the endman in a game of crack the whip: by cocaine, alcohol, even Valium. Still, when I spoke to him earlier on the phone I could tell something was really wrong, and I've taken the afternoon off work to spend the rest of the day with him.

He sits in his rocking chair and sips beer, pets the cat, smokes. I sit on the couch, drink water, tap my cigarette ashes into the same ashtray he uses. We talk, the cigarette butts mount up. Sometime during the long afternoon he says something that will haunt me later, after the suicide.

It relates to his friend Tom Hunnicutt. Tom is a tree surgeon and a recovering alcoholic. Tom, he says, has fallen off the wagon; he's been drinking for days holed up alone and Jim is afraid he's going to shoot himself. In fact, he's virtually certain of it. He's so certain he thinks he should go over there and try to talk him out of it, and then he feels guilty for putting off going over there. "I'm not looking forward to dealing with Tom drunk waving a gun around," he says. He tells me about another time Tom was drinking and talking about suicide and he, Jim, persuaded him not to: "Think of all the people who love you who it would really hurt," he said to him, then named Tom's wife and some of his kids. And it worked—Tom didn't kill himself.

What I hear in this is not a veiled warning, a projection of his own thoughts and fears and desires onto another person. Instead, I hear a reassurance. I hear Jim counseling Tom against committing suicide. I hear the part about suicide hurting people, I hear him saying he would never hurt me that way.

Nevertheless, something prompts me to say, "It's a real tragedy to kill yourself over booze or drugs, never kill yourself over booze and drugs, because there's always a second chance," and Jim says, "Yes, but sometimes when you're sitting there with the needle in your arm or the bottle in your hand you think you're never going to be able to stop." And even then I don't make the connection, I don't feel scared this means he might actually kill himself, I still think I have the power to keep him from doing that. But I do get a strange, almost physical sensation, a sudden expanding and contracting in the stomach region, a sort of phantom ache in my arms and legs.

Many months later, after Jim's death, I asked Tom Hunnicutt whether he was drinking and contemplating suicide the previous fall, or maybe I just told him what Jim said, and he looked shocked and said, "I never even thought about that." Though someone else who knows Tom told me afterward she doubted he was being totally honest.

In the early evening I cook a pot of spaghetti sauce, the kind Jim likes, with sausage and red peppers, but in the end he can only sit at the kitchen table and watch me eat, sipping beer and talking. Then the phone rings and it's his friend coming through with the Valium at last and Jim and I go out and sit on the porch to wait for her. After twenty minutes she drives up in her little yellow car, money and a bottle of pills change hands, Jim and I go into the house and he shakes out three small blue Valiums and swallows them. I start picking up beer cans and putting them in the sink.

Thanksgiving arrives. Things have been going well and we're optimistic. I've been squeezing aloe vera gel from my plant onto the crooks of his arms every night for a week: He wants to join a health club but he's embarrassed to take his shirt off and have people—healthy people—see his tracks; he says aloe vera will heal them quickly. I take this as a good sign, a definitive indication that once and for all he's made up his mind to give up drugs.

We prepare the Thanksgiving turkey and put it in the oven, stick a movie in the VCR, lie down on the bed. Jim falls asleep the minute the credits start rolling and I sit there propped against the headboard smoking cigarettes, watching the movie, smelling the turkey cook. The movie is *A Dry White Season*: A black gardener's child takes part in a protest in South Africa; the child is arrested and killed; the gardener investigates and gets arrested by the secret service, tortured, and killed; the gardener's white employer brings the case before the state but in the end there is no justice. I stare at the screen completely absorbed in the story, in the movie's atmosphere of tension and dread, but every so often I stop watching it and look at Jim, and at one point about three quarters of the way through I take off his glasses. They're new glasses; he picked them up at the optometrist's office only a few days earlier; he bought me a pair of contact lenses at the same time. The glasses have wire-thin dark-red and brown tortoiseshell rims. It suddenly occurs to me they might get bent by the way he's sleeping—on his back with his head turned on the pillow, one side of the glasses mashed against the bridge of his nose—and I think it is also at this point that I give up on the hope that he is going to wake up and watch the rest of the movie with me. I reach out and carefully, delicately remove the glasses. He doesn't even stir, and I sit there looking down at his sleeping face, trying to memorize its details, as if I know someday I'll need them—the two fine lines between the eyebrows, the deep-set eyes, the slope and curve of his nose, the shapeliness of his lips.

Later on, after we've eaten, gone for a walk, watched a second movie, he sits on the edge of my bed and I squeeze the clear greenish gel from an aloe vera leaf onto the purple scars in the crooks of his arms. Usually when I do this he's witty and buoyant, almost manically optimistic in the way that only he can be, when things are going well, but tonight we're both subdued.

"Thanksgiving's over," he remarks sadly as I bend over him in the lamplight, ministering to his arms.

The phone hasn't rung all night, and this thought wakes me out of an uneasy sleep in which I'm dreaming about setting off a bomb and running down the road, away from my parents' house. The digital alarm says 5:17 and I lie there wondering whether I should try to go back to sleep until I think of something I feel guilty about from yesterday—how I cut him off on the phone—and then my anger turns to worry and I get out of bed and pull on yesterday's clothes, a pair of blue jeans and a turquoise sweatshirt. I walk the half block up the street to his house. It's December 13. Ice crunches under my feet, my breath issues visibly from my mouth, and I think that I have done this now in all kinds of weather: the thick humid sultriness of summer, the cool bright starriness of fall, now this bare, frigid bleakness.

I walk around back to see whether the truck is there. It isn't, but a blanket has been slung over the curtain rod of his window and there's light around the edges, so I know he's probably inside. I open the front door to his building thinking irrationally, or maybe not, that it is me he wants to keep from seeing through the venetian blinds. I smell cigarette smoke in the hallway and it gets stronger as I get closer to his door. I knock quietly. In a minute he opens the door, and I see immediately that what I was afraid of—what I knew but didn't quite believe, what I'm always somehow surprised by, no matter how many times it occurs—is in fact the case. He looks anxious, gray-faced, fuzzy around the edges. I'm shaken and saddened and angry, but along with that is a tinge of relief: He's there, he's alive.

Through the double doors of his room I see his desk littered with syringes, the orange plastic caps of syringes, a spoon, several plastic baggies, a small copper measuring cup.

"I'm sorry I didn't call you," he says, and I can see he means it.

"Don't you think I have any fucking feelings at all?" I scream.

"Shhh, Mary," he says, "you'll wake the neighbors."

13

Early on we talked a lot about Christmas.

I've never been a big fan of the holidays. I don't look forward to them; when I think of them I don't imagine a close-knit family sitting around a cheerful firelit living room, I don't hold out hope that they'll be better—happier, sweeter, cozier—than other days of the year. But Jim still did, potentially, at least. He'd spent a few Christmases alone when he was drinking, just him and the cat. He'd buy a present for her—usually a can of tunafish—and a present for himself from her, wrap them both and open them both, feed the cat her tunafish, and that would be it. But when I came along he was all excited about the Christmas we were going to have together. He started talking about it right away, even as early as our couch days, before either of us had even let on that we were interested in the other. But he would give me little hints that he *was* interested in me; he'd say, "Someday I'd like to take you to such and such a place and show it to you," and so forth. And he created a little fantasy about Christmas. I'd told him all my stories about Christmas at my parents' house—I used to stay overnight there on Christmas Eve. One year we had a chimney fire. I was sleeping in a single bed with my sister and all night long we could smell this terrible smell, the smell of the ceiling smoldering around the chimney pipe; I kept half-waking up and saying to my sister, "What's that smell?" and she kept saying, "It's just roasting chestnuts." Finally we woke up and the kitchen ceiling was in flames.

Another time a couple my sister worked with at a chicken farm—my mother made her get a job when she was fourteen—came over on Christmas Eve and the adults got drunk and my father puked in the bathroom and my mother got furious because the couple, who weren't capable of having children, told her they'd be happy to adopt my sister, they thought of her as their kid anyway. My mother started ranting and raving about how you don't know it's your kid until you've changed its diapers, till you've gotten up at four o'clock in the morning when it has colic, and so forth. My sister and I lay in bed for hours listening to that. Much later they all got raucous and we heard the guy say, "Oops, I pissed my pants." I finally fell asleep with my fingers in my ears. I told Beaman those stories and even though we hadn't slept together yet, even though we weren't even letting on that we wanted to sleep together, he said, "Maybe we can spend Christmas together this year and I'll make it the best Christmas in the world for you."

But by the time Christmas rolled around all that optimism was gone. It was him who was making me miserable by that time, him who was the bad parent, the drunken stranger pissing his pants. And I was still the kid with her fingers in her ears. He knew it and I knew it but we didn't acknowledge it. We just went along, me trying to pretend it wasn't happening and Beaman feeling miserable, guilty about being the bad guy—not the rescuer but the person I needed to be rescued from—but doing it anyway, because he couldn't help it.

Four days before Christmas we got a tree, picked it from a batch in front of Kmart, drove it home, and left it overnight on the back of Jim's truck. He was supposed to help me put it up the next day but when I came home after doing an errand downtown I found it sitting on my porch. I waited and waited for him to turn up but he never did. In the end I dragged the tree into the house and set it up alone. I had to carry it by its prickly trunk through the kitchen and living room, lean it up against a wall while I spread a sheet on the floor and assembled the spider-legged metal stand, lift the tree half a foot in the air and position the bottom of its trunk in the tube inside the stand. Afterward there were pine needles everywhere. Jim showed up hours later, guilty and gray-faced, said he planned to return after dropping off the tree but got waylaid by a friend.

After an hour he said, "Let's give each other one of our Christmas presents." He went to his house to pick up mine but then he kept calling and saying, "I'm trying to wrap it, I'm having trouble wrapping it." I was suspicious even before I heard that scratchy raspy thing in his voice, the thing he always got when he'd been doing cocaine. Finally he brought the present down. It was a blue sweater. I gave him a black turtleneck.

Later on that night he says, "I've got to give this up but I can't do it, I can't do it tonight." So we make our peace with cocaine for that one night.

I say, "Okay, just don't abandon me." We go to his house and he sits at the desk and fiddles with the needles, ties off with a belt, tries to shoot up. But there's a problem, so he stands in the closet, saying, "Don't look, this is gross," and I think I hear him pulling down his pants. I can't imagine what he's doing; much later I learn he's shooting up in the thigh.

Then we go to my house. He's in my kitchen trying to shoot up again and I'm in the bedroom sitting in bed and we're chatting companionably, room to room. I can hear the effort of what he's doing in the little grunts and delays that punctuate his speaking, but otherwise he sounds normal, cheerful. We're talking about a couple he's acquainted with who know Steve, our mutual friend, speculating about whether they know I was dating Steve when Jim and I met. He's saying he doesn't mind if they do know, and I'm saying I sort of hope they don't. It's a cozy, intimate kind of conversation, the subtext all about us—we're closing ranks, reassuring each other that despite our obvious problems we'd rather be together than with anyone else. I sit in bed, smoking a cigarette; I feel safe, secure, and somehow oddly compelled by our situation, as if we're characters in a play; I'm kind of enjoying myself. But Jim's having trouble. He says, "I have to go home and get some more needles because these won't work," and he leaves and comes back with more but those don't work either. I don't know if they won't work because he can't get them into his veins or if he just can't seem to get high.

Finally he gives up and drinks a beer instead. He gets into bed and I doze for a while, and when I wake up he's sitting there leaning against the headboard looking down at me. He says, "Do you *know* how much I love you?"

The night before Christmas we called his sister—she asked him if he was happy and he said he was, and his neice got on the phone and asked him what he was doing for Christmas and he said, "I'm going to spend it with my lovely future wife," and I talked to both of them also—and then we went to my place. Jim brought the cat because he didn't want her to be alone on Christmas Eve; he carried her inside his coat on the walk from his house to my house. She'd only been out in the world four or five times in her life and I expected her to howl or try to jump down and run away, but she was perfectly still, her eyes gleaming inside of the cave of Jim's half-zipped jacket.

At my house we put a movie in the VCR at the foot of the bed and settled down on top of the covers with the cat. It seemed to make her happy to have us both so easily available; she kept ranging around on the bed, purring loudly, staring down into our faces. When she wasn't doing that she sat sphinxlike at the foot of the bed, her head blocking part of the

TV screen, ears sticking up like triangles, and Jim kept saying, "Will the lady with the funny hat on please get down in front?" He said she thought we were staring at her the whole time.

The next morning, Christmas Day, he went home to retrieve some things. He was gone longer than I expected and I felt twinges of anxiety, but it turned out he was just talking on the phone to his friend Robo. Up until then he'd been planning to visit Robo in San Diego for a few weeks in January, but when he came down after the phone call he said he'd decided not to go. While he was at his house the cat paced around my apartment meowing a loud, plaintive, terrified meow as if calling out for help, then went in the bedroom closet and hid behind some boxes. When Jim showed up she stepped out of the closet and ambled across the floor as if nothing had happened.

We opened our presents and I cooked a roast beef—I cooked it too long and it was dry, but that was okay—and after we ate I called my sister. My sister had sent a package from Massachusetts and Jim was surprised and touched that she'd included presents for him too, even though the main one was only a big pad of drawing paper that turned out to have a sketch my sister had drawn a long time ago on a page at the back. First I talked to her and then he talked to her. I remember he said something about how he never expected to find the right person and fall in love but he had, and he said how much he liked the outfit, which was what he kept calling a sexy white camisole she'd sent for me. I wore it to bed that night and he slept in one of his Stanley Kowalski undershirts, and it was the last happy night I had for a long, long time.

He went home the next morning but left his cat and his Christmas presents at my house; he said he was going to take his time bringing them home because after that it would seem like Christmas was over. He asked me if I wanted him to come to my house while I was at work and take down the Christmas tree so I wouldn't get depressed. I said, No, when Christmas was over I was ready for it to be over. But I had no idea what that would turn out to mean.

It was horrible getting rid of the Christmas tree afterward, but the presents were the hardest things to deal with. He gave me the blue sweater and that rose-colored silk coat and a pair of black leather gloves, which I exchanged because they didn't fit, and a twenty-five-dollar gift certificate to a bookstore which said "Omar Pignuts" on the line that tells you who it's from. I used the gift certificate later to buy some self-help books about grief. And I gave him a bunch of stuff: a watch and a model kit and the black turtleneck and some other things. One was a plaster cast of the end of my friend Robin Lillie's index finger. Robin works in the osteology department at the Office of the State Archaeologist, where they make casts of old dug-up bones. One day I was in her office and I saw one of those fingers, created to test the consistency of a batch of plaster; I begged her to make one of my finger so I could give it to Jim, but she didn't want to waste the plaster so she gave me the one that was already done.

I had to deal with all those Christmas presents after Jim died, his to me as well as mine to him. I hardly ever wore that rose silk coat because it made me sad, but I did wear it a little, especially in the beginning. Once in an elevator at the hospital, going up to see my therapist, someone said, "Oh what a beautiful coat, where did you get it," and I thought, If only you knew.

14

When I was a kid I was obsessed by the idea that a person could become someone else—someone evil, a kidnapper, a murderer—but still look the same. I suspected friends, babysitters—even my father, occasionally—of having been invaded, of literally not being themselves; I'd wait and watch for signs that betrayed them, but of course none ever came. I don't know what would give a child such strange thoughts—maybe it was my mother's mental illness or maybe it was something else—but they have a lot of resonance with what happened to Jim during his last week. Except that in my childhood fantasies the person looked and acted the same on the surface, whereas with Jim everything was different: Whoever or whatever was inside him showed; you couldn't miss it. It was as if someone else had literally taken over and inhabited his body, a man who was older, slower, stupider, meaner. There was an ugliness, a heaviness about him. Even his facial features seemed subtly altered: thicker, coarser, weighed down, full of lines and pouches.

Booze brought about the change.

December 26, the day of the launch of the fatal bender, he did a job with his friend Miller—pouring concrete in someone's sidewalk or hanging a door, something like that. In the afternoon it got too cold to work outside so they went to Miller's house and Miller broke out a bottle of scotch, which Jim hardly ever drank—even in his heyday he was strictly a beer and wine man—and Jim got very, very drunk. He called me at five o'clock and I said, "Put Miller on the phone," and I asked him to call a cab so Jim wouldn't drive home.

I met Miller for the first time at Jim's memorial service. When I was introduced to him he gave me a funny look I've always wondered about; it was kind of a defensive look and I used to have the idea it had something to do with money, that he owed Jim money or Jim owed him money, but now I think he probably felt like the suicide was his fault, or he thought I was going to accuse him of it being his fault, because he gave Jim that booze. One thing I discovered about suicide is that everybody—no matter how unlikely, no matter how distant their connection to the dead guy is—finds some way to think it was their fault, or at least that they could have prevented it.

Jim called me when he got home from Miller's house and said, "I'm back, why don't you come up." Then he called me back and said, "Don't come up, I'm really in bad shape, I'm no good to be around." Then he called me back again and said, "Would you do me a favor? Would you come up and check on me in half an hour?" I said okay. It was a bitterly cold night and I had a frozen chicken pot pie in the oven—I had some time left before I was supposed to check on Jim—and just when I took the pot pie out and was about to eat it I had a terrible thought. The thought was, what if he committed suicide. So I rushed up there in the frigid cold; I didn't even stop to get bundled up. I let myself in. Jim was lying on the bed passed out, and the shotgun was on the floor next to him.

Peggy wasn't home, and I went into the kitchen and looked under the sink until I found a shopping bag with a handle. I took it out and brought it into the bedroom. I picked up the gun—when I bent down to touch it it seemed alive, unpredictable, malevolent, but I picked it up very gingerly and wrapped it in my scarf and put it in the shopping bag. I closed and locked the front door behind me and carried the gun to my house. The sidewalks were icy and I was afraid of slipping and falling and the gun going off, but it didn't. I brought it into my house and put it into the cupboard above my refrigerator.

Jim woke up two hours later and called me and I went to his place. He was sitting up in bed and he didn't feel too good but he was cheerful enough. I didn't tell him I'd taken the gun away. He asked me about it a couple of days later and I told him and he chuckled, as if it pleased him that I didn't want him to kill himself, as if I was trying to keep him from catching a cold or from banging his thumb with a hammer. But we didn't talk about it that day—him sitting up in bed, me resting on the edge of the mattress beside him—we didn't talk about the gun or what you do with a gun or anything else about our actual, real-life situation; we just had sort of a silly conversation. Jim said Miller had asked him a favor and Jim had said no and Miller, who was a black guy, had said, "That's awfully white of you," which Jim thought was funny; and he said it turned out Miller was from the same region he was and Miller had seen him playing football once in high school—Miller was on the other team—and Jim asked him, "Was I good?" and Miller said, "No, you were average." And somehow, during that conversation, the subject of death must have come up, because I have a distinct memory of Jim sitting in bed saying somebody had weighed a body before and after death and determined the soul weighed however many ounces. It seems very odd to me now that we would have discussed that then, and so casually, so theoretically, that it didn't even occur to me to make the connection between the conversation and the gun lying on the floor by the bed just a couple of hours earlier. Surely I must have known on some level we weren't just talking about death in general but about Jim's death, his death that was soon to come.

But it seems to me I didn't know, despite the gun on the floor, despite the many warnings, spoken and unspoken, Jim had been giving me. I didn't know, at least, in the rational, waking part of my mind, the part that makes decisions, that interacts with the world. I see that part of me as possessing a certain innocence, like a character in a fairy tale, Little Red Riding Hood heading down the path to Grandma's house—being led by fate, inevitability, the necessities of the story, young, trusting, naive, never once suspecting despite all signs to the contrary that Grandma will be a wolf. She isn't supposed to suspect, to know what will be waiting for her inside the house, because then she might drag her feet, turn aside, decide to visit some other, friendlier place. And she's supposed to go, she has to go to Grandma's. It's part of the story.

After the day he got drunk on scotch with Miller, everything started sliding downhill, picking up momentum. In my imagination I see it as something like one of those cartoons—except it isn't funny—where a big pile of rocks looms precariously on a mountain peak in the distance and some little thing happens to snap the thread of whatever is holding the rocks in place and they start rolling down the mountain, falling, sliding, bouncing, picking up speed, kicking up all kinds of noise and dirt till they land in a broken heap at the bottom. And the thing that broke the thread, that made the rocks let go, that set gravity in motion, maybe, was the scotch Jim drank with Miller. The booze that opened the window to more booze, wine, beer, champagne on New Year's Eve, and on and on. Jim drank more or less nonstop for seven days. The whole time he didn't shave, and the stubble gave his face an angry, muddy, reddish-brownish aura. He was literally a different person. But every now and then and only for a moment he came to himself, the way you hear stories about patients in the late stages of Alzheimer's suddenly snapping out of it—people who can't even remember their own names or how to eat or use a toilet will suddenly look up from their bed or wheelchair and say something normal, "It's been a long time since you wore that turquoise blouse," or "How did your doctor's appointment go?" then lapse back into their previous state.

He had one of those moments one night about four days before he shot himself, just as he was leaving my house. Before that he'd been sitting at the kitchen table with his mean eyes and his three-day beard and his sullen, belligerent, drunken talk, but then as he got up to leave, standing in the open doorway, his face suddenly brightened, he grinned his usual generous, crooked grin, he kissed me on the mouth and said, "I love you, Punkin, see you tomorrow." And there was another moment like that one night when he was sitting on my bed eating chicken pie. He said, "This is so good," and I said, "It makes me happy to see you eat." And his face cleared all of a sudden, as if he remembered that I loved him, or as if he was surprised and pleased to learn that I did, still, love him.

I made that chicken pie from scratch. I boiled chicken and added potatoes and onions and carrots and stirred flour and salt and pepper into the broth and poured it all into a pie shell—two pie shells, I made two pies—put on the top pie crusts and baked them. I think I must've gotten the idea from that chicken pot pie I heated up but never ate the night I found the shotgun on the floor.

Those chicken pies keep coming up in all these memories. Jim really liked them, and at one point I remember him saying in his old, eager way, "I want you to make this every day when we're married." We'd both pretty much stopped talking about our engagement, about the future at all, in fact, though at one point, during another one of his lucid moments, he said, "Don't worry, all this will go away and things will get back to normal." I just said, "Yeah, right," and gave him a look like, Who are you kidding, or maybe I even said, "Things are not going to get better unless you get help," which was true enough. But later I regretted not being more positive at that moment because I felt like I cut off his hope for the future. He was trying to say, maybe as much to himself as to me, Things will get better, we'll still get married and things will be okay, but by then I didn't believe it anymore. I kept trying to talk him into going to a rehab program, attending twelve-step recovery meetings. I remember at one point I said, "You'd rather throw your life away than get help." And he gave me a certain look I've never forgotten. It was a look that seemed to say, Yeah, that's pretty smart, or, That's a pretty persuasive argument even though I'm not going to be persuaded, or maybe it said, I didn't know you knew I was throwing my life away. But he didn't get help; another time when I tried to talk to him about it he was merely surly. That was what I focused on afterward in my moments—hours, days, weeks—of rage, my terrible, thwarted, foot-stamping anger that was like someone trying over and over to start a car or somebody having dry heaves: that he wouldn't get help. Then one day it occurred to me that maybe by the time he shot himself he wasn't capable of the kind of optimism it takes to get help.

I remember he ate a piece of chicken pie at my kitchen table the night his face brightened as he was standing in the doorway saying good night, the night he was suddenly himself, but only for a moment. That night the chicken pie didn't please him at all—he only ate half of it and pushed the rest away. Of all the times during the last week when drinking made him ugly, that night was the worst. Except for that single moment in the doorway, the vibrations he gave off were uniformly coarse, dark, threatening. He sat glowering at the kitchen table; he mumbled something mean I didn't catch. I didn't like him at all; I was afraid of him; I was glad when he left. But after he left I started worrying about something he'd said a day or two earlier. We were sitting around in his living room and he said, "I'm afraid if Peggy comes home when I'm the way I've been these last few days and you're not here and she starts giving me a lot of shit, I'm afraid I might do something bad to her."

I couldn't stop worrying about that, and finally I called Peggy at work and said, "Jim is drinking, he's in a very bad mood, and if I were you, I'd steer clear of him." Peggy said, "Okay, I hear you," and hung up, and she did leave Jim alone. I didn't tell Jim I'd done that the next time I saw him—I guess I knew it wouldn't be a good idea to tell him. I wish I'd never told him, because if I hadn't there's a chance he might still be alive.

All this time, from Christmas Eve until the day he shot himself, the cat was at my house. She'd gotten used to being there alone with me and, at least as I remember it, we coexisted fairly peacefully. Her food was in a dish in the kitchen, and for a long time after Jim died, for a long time after the cat was dead herself, I kept finding those little Science Diet pellets on the floor against the refrigerator or by the kitchen sink. I kept finding needles from the Christmas tree, too. Even now, every now and then I find an old dried-up pine needle in the corner of my bedroom, against the wall where I can't get to it when I vacuum or sweep.

15

The day before Jim died I bought a pocketbook. It came from Younkers, in the Old Capitol Mall in downtown Iowa City, and it cost ninety-five dollars; it was a nice pocketbook and I had it for a long time. I also exchanged the pair of black leather gloves Jim had given me for Christmas for a smaller pair of gloves; I lost those after a month.

I spent a lot of time wandering around Younkers that day because I didn't want to deal with Jim. He'd said to call him when I got off work, but I was feeling nervous, reluctant to be around him, and anyway I figured he'd be sleeping. He'd gotten some Valium earlier in the day, which was a big relief because he needed it to be able to stop drinking and he hadn't been able to get any for about five days.

Finally I called him from a pay phone near the escalator in the mall and he said, "Where have you been? Come on over." His voice sounded clear and cheerful, like I hadn't heard it for a while. When I got to his apartment he was sitting on the edge of his bed in his underwear and a T-shirt and he looked and acted like himself again—boyish and handsome, the shadow of that other darker, coarser presence gone. He even said, half jokingly, "I bet you're glad I'm back," though I think that might have been later, when we were eating Chinese takeout from the Jade Garden. Beef with oyster sauce was what Jim got; I can't remember what I had but it wasn't as good as his, and I said, "Beef with oyster sauce is the ticket, now we know what to order." But I'm getting ahead of myself. Another thing he said, sitting there on his bed, was, "Tomorrow I'll start on the Hoover library," and he said, "Tonight we're going to make love," or maybe he said, "Tonight we're going to have sex." I can't remember exactly what he said, though I do know it wasn't, "Tonight we're going to roll around," which is what he would have said in other, happier moments. Mostly I remember the resoluteness in his voice and face; he was psyching himself up, throwing the engines into reverse to pull himself out of his tailspin, choosing life and love over drugs and death. Choosing work, too: All week long he'd been putting off several jobs, writing a proposal for restoring a historic barn, tuckpointing the basement walls in the Herbert Hoover Library.

We ordered Chinese food from Jade Garden and drove downtown to get it. There was one little moment when I realized he wasn't quite back to himself, when he bumped into a curb in the truck and that made him angry and he took on a certain look that I'd come to associate with alcohol. I'll bet anyone who lives with an alcoholic knows that look, or maybe not—maybe it was just Jim's particular alcohol-driven look; maybe all alcoholics have one uniquely their own. We set up the TV trays in the living room and started eating the Chinese food. That was when I said, "Beef with oyster sauce is the thing to get from now on," and when I recall saying it it comes back to me that I was trying to please him, I was walking on eggshells, still, even though he was back to himself, more or less. Then I thought I heard Peggy fumbling around with the key in the front door and I thought, I'd better tell him I called her, before she comes in and tells him herself. I think now it's unlikely she would have done that, but at the time I sort of panicked, and I said, "I have a confession to make, I called Peggy. . . ." And Jim just flew off the handle without any warning or buildup. One minute he was sitting there peacefully eating beef with oyster sauce and grinning and talking, and the next minute he was furious, his face full of cold hard rage. I can't remember exactly what he said, I've probably blocked it, but it was something like, "It's over, this relationship is over, get out now, just go," and there was a kind of urgency in the way he said it, as if I had to get out quickly because he was so angry. So I stood up, picked up my coat and my new purse, and left.

When I got home I called Kathy and told her what had happened. There wasn't anything she could say to make me feel better, but she tried. Then I watched a movie on the rented VCR, which was still at my house—the movie was *Blue Steel*, with Jamie Lee Curtis, about a woman cop—and then I took an over-the-counter pill that made me sleep. Jim called me three times that night, and each time he sounded more and more fucked up and nasty. Once he called to say, "I'm going to come down and pick up my cat tomorrow while you're at work." We had keys to each other's apartments, and he also said, "Leave my key out on the kitchen table and I'll leave your key there when I go." And once he called to say, "Do me a favor. Put all my stuff out on the kitchen table too. I'll pick it up when I get the cat tomorrow," and in the middle of the night he called, his speech very, very slurred, to say, "Have you been calling my house? Someone's been calling here and hanging up." He sounded very angry and threatening. And I said, "Nope, it wasn't me," just as cheerfully as anything, because I didn't know what else to say, and because I was detaching, pulling down the window shades, and because that's how I've learned to deal with men who are hurting me, to put on a cheerful face and act like it doesn't bother me, and he hung up.

That night I slept pretty well under the influence of the pill I'd taken, and I had two dreams. One was that I went to a bar and met some man who fell in love with me, but more important than that was the feeling I had in the dream, a light airy refreshing feeling, like a little gust of love and happiness. I thought about that later, thought it was as if for a minute somebody opened the door between this world and the next—the other world where the dead people live their happy, untroubled lives—and a little puff of wind came out. It might have been my grandfather and Hildegarde who opened the door. Because the other dream I had that night, the night before Jim died, was about them, Pop and Hildegarde; they weren't doing anything in particular, just hovering over me as I lay on my back in bed.

When I woke up in the morning the events of the previous night came rushing back and I felt awful. I went around the house gathering up all Jim's stuff—two clay chessmen he'd carved to look like little people, that white candleholder with the leaves, and some other things he'd given me to keep for him back in the summer when we were going to break up and he was planning to go somewhere—and put it all on the kitchen table. I should've remembered what he said—whenever I start giving my stuff away or taking it back you'll know I'm thinking about suicide—but I didn't. When I took those things of his off the shelf to put them on the kitchen table they left little dark places in the dust and those made me sad; I had an awful abandoned feeling. I didn't know whether I should put the gun on the table too. I called Kathy and asked her and she said, "Yes, give him back that gun, don't you have anything to do with it." So I did. I stood on a chair and took it down out of the cabinet above the refrigerator and put it on the table, partly because of what Kathy said but mostly because I couldn't figure out what else to do with it. It was like I was in sort of a trance; I didn't even really think about what might happen if I gave it back to him. It was almost as if some part of me knew what was going to happen if I put the gun out on the kitchen table for Jim to take but I did it anyway, as if somehow that was what I had to do. I wasn't operating from a place of rationality, in the clear bright light of day and reason, where you think things through, imagine the consequences, make reasonable, rational decisions, the sort of decisions afterward you kick yourself a thousand times for not making, such as, I won't give this gun back to Jim in the shape he's in, I'll take this gun down the street and bury it. It didn't seem possible, I didn't even have a shovel and there was nowhere to bury it anyway—there's nothing but lawns and yards and streets in my neighborhood— someone might see me. Of course, I could have hidden it in the house, but I couldn't think of anywhere to hide it—actually I did think of the back of my closet, but what stopped me, I guess, what stopped me, God help me, was the fear that Jim would get angry because I didn't give it back to him. And in a trance, I put it on the table.

A couple of months afterward, I told a friend of Jim's, Ace McDonald, a huge funny mild-mannered guy who was Jim's mechanic—he had a shop in his mother's garage down the street from us—the whole story of the fight Jim and I had the night before and about putting the gun on the table. I told Ace just to get it off my chest; it never occurred to me he'd say something that would make me feel worse about it. But he said, "Next time don't do that. You should have given it to me, you should have taken it down the road and buried it, you should have done anything with it except give it to him. Never, ever give somebody who's been on a bender a gun." Of course, Ace was just talking like that out of his own grief and regret, wishing time could stop and reverse itself and we could do it all over again, do it right this time, as if that would still be possible if only we had our intentions, our plan, right this time. If only we said, Okay, I didn't, I shouldn't, I won't give him back the gun. But still, it took me days to get over Ace saying that, just as it took me days to get over other innocent little remarks people made during those first few months. Like the time a friend of mine commented, "They say there's only a window of five minutes or so when someone will really kill themselves. If something comes along and distracts them it just passes and they don't do it." My friend was probably thinking of herself: Once, she had told me, when she was unhappily married, she put her head in the oven and turned on the gas. But it was just too nasty and smelly so she turned it off and forgot all about killing herself, then or ever. But it hurt me to think of Jim's life hanging in the balance of those five minutes—that it would have been so easy, so simple, to save his life, and yet nothing happened to save it, nothing came along to distract him during those five crucial minutes—and whatever delicate, precarious place I'd reached with the suicide collapsed out from under me and it took me days to get it back.

That morning, putting Jim's stuff out on the table, I thought about writing a note and leaving it there as well. In fact, I did write a note. I can't remember exactly what it said, but it was something contrite and full of love, something to let him know that I forgave him, and then I tore it up because I was too angry to leave a note like that; I thought it was his place to come to me. But I did leave a little note; it said, "Here's your stuff." Then I left. I went to a haircut appointment I'd had for weeks and then I spent some time hanging around in the public library, and when I got to work at twelve-thirty the secretary said, "You have a bunch of phone messages. Jim called three times." And it was a huge relief. I called him back and he said, "Let's not break up." I said, "Okay." He said, "I've been just sick all morning. I didn't know how much I loved you until I thought I was going to lose you," and he said, "I love you very very very very very much." Sometimes he would say that—keep stringing out the very's. He made some motions to talk about what had happened the night before, and I said,

"We'll talk about it tonight," and I made my voice sound a little threatening, as if maybe I was going to break up with him over what happened, because I was trying in a very mild, passive-aggressive way to threaten him into getting help, into stopping the booze and the drugs. Afterward I regretted that too, that little threatening passive-aggressive note in my voice; I wondered whether I should have handled that phone conversation differently, whether things might have gone another way if I had.

Jim said, "Are you going to work all day?" and I said, "Yes." He said, "Okay, then maybe I'll go out to the Hoover library and start setting up." When I looked back on that conversation it seemed to me there was something in his voice when he asked me, Are you going to work all day, a quiver, a little entreaty, a small extra charge as if it really mattered. I told his sister about it later and she thought he was asking me whether I was going to be at work all day because he didn't want me to come to his house, she thought he was making sure that I was going to be absent, that he set it up purposely so that I wouldn't find his body. She thought his asking for the key to his apartment back was also about that, which made sense. But mostly I thought—I still think, actually, though it isn't quite so painful now to think it—that he was asking me in some unspoken way to come over and spend the day with him because it was going to be a bad day, a terrible day, maybe it was like that time a few days earlier when he said, Will you do me a favor and come up and check on me in half an hour, like a kind of insurance policy against depression—he couldn't kill himself if I was there. But it was unspoken and I didn't catch on.

After he hung up I felt only relief that we had made up. I even called Kathy and said, "Everything's okay now, you can quit worrying about me." I even thought that at that point he'd be more receptive to getting help, treatment, that I would be able to talk him into it that night—hence, the little threat in my voice. "I can't take any more of this," I was going to say, "You've got to do something," and I was certain he would. In fact, as I was walking home that day, I was thinking and thinking about what I would say to him, talking to him in my head, lecturing him, being very persuasive. And then I saw a cop car parked across the street from his house.

16

I've wondered many times what happened to him that day.

When I talked to him on the phone, after we'd made up and he'd established that we weren't going to break up, he said, "Well, that's done," as if he were checking something off a list of things he needed to accomplish. He was in an accomplishing mood that day, and I don't think it was necessarily that he was trying to tie things up, get rid of loose ends before he killed himself, the way they say people do, that usually right before they kill themselves their mood lifts and they do the things that need to be done, say good-bye and so forth. I don't think he was necessarily doing that, because he also called his friend John Gray and asked for the phone number of the health club John belonged to, which Jim had been talking about joining for months. The brochure for the health club was on his bedside table as if he'd been looking at it, on that last day, weighing his options, considering how to solve his problems; we found it there when we went to his house to collect his things. And there are other indications he intended to get back on track that day. On the phone he'd said, "Maybe I'll go out to the Hoover library and start setting up." And he started another work project he'd been putting off and avoiding: writing a memo to the sheriff of Downey, who'd approached him about restoring an old barn. Above his suicide note, on the same piece of paper, it says in his handwriting, "Our recommendations consist of two major points. The first point is that the pavilion in its present condition is unsafe."

So what happened? Maybe his will simply flagged, maybe depression set in, his dopamine receptors started flapping in the wind, maybe the residual effects of the previous days simply reared their heads and he couldn't get past them. Or maybe he fell prey to some sudden temptation. Maybe someone called him and said, "I've got some cocaine, could you come over here and take it off my hands, could you do an errand for me?" Something like that. Peggy said he looked very disheveled and that he went somewhere for a while. I've always wondered where he went. Did he go out to buy wine? Or to do an "errand," to pick up some cocaine?

A "pillbottle w/ white powder," is item H, quantity 1, on the Iowa City Police Department Evidence Control Inventory, a copy of which I somehow ended up with; I keep it in a file along with the suicide note. I can't remember how I got the evidence report. Maybe I asked for it and they gave it to me at the police department when I picked up my copy of the note, or maybe Jim's sister Pat sent it to me in the mail. Item I is "five syringes," item K is "one spoon—bedroom." Item A is "one note found in bedroom," Item D is "two .410 casings taken from desktop in bedroom," Item N is "one work order w/ victim signature." Item Q, the last item, is "one .410 single shot shotgun w/ spent casing in chamber."

I've often wondered about that "pillbottle w/ white powder"—where he got it, what its role was on his final day. Was it that or was it booze—cheap white wine, probably—or was it both or something else that accounts for the state he was in during his last few minutes, which is manifested in the suicide note with its messy, wavy, scratched-out handwriting, its half-formed thoughts and distorted logic, like a message from a sleeping or a schizophrenic person, like a letter written in a dream.

"To my Catholic," it says, "I've no excuse—I know suicide is illegal in our"—the next word is illegible. "Cut me corner of slack and inside I'm a Lutheran. Mary I love you. With any luck someone will clean up the mess. Thanks for all Peggy. My all Mary wants please give to her."

And a last sentence, more illegible than the rest, which I think might say, "It's in Christ I see no choice."

Peggy found him. She was at home the whole afternoon, reading in her bedroom. She said at some point after he went out and came back he knocked on her door and asked if he could borrow her rosary beads. He apologized for being so hard to live with during the last couple of weeks and she said that was okay, she was a bitch too sometimes. She thought it was strange he wanted to borrow her rosary beads and later she said she must have known on some level what was going on but on another level she didn't even have a clue. She heard the shot but waited forty-five minutes to go into his bedroom. She heard it but didn't know what it was. It wasn't very loud and there was a large living room and a large kitchen between their two bedrooms, and maybe on some level she did know what it was, and that was another reason why she put off going into his bedroom.

He was covered with my green comforter when he shot himself. I asked the undertaker if he had a green comforter over him when they found him and he said he wasn't certain but he thought so. But I would've known that anyway, because by coincidence my green comforter was up there that day, and it was gone later. I had done a bunch of laundry; I had piles and piles of it and I did it all in one day, carting it down to the machines in an apartment complex two doors away. I felt rather pleased with myself for managing to get it all done and Jim said he was proud of me. Or maybe I just wanted him to be proud of me, or maybe I asked him whether he was proud of me and he said, yes, he was. The green comforter was still damp when I took it out of the dryer and I brought it over to his house instead of to mine—I can't remember why, maybe I simply picked it up on the way to his house or maybe I brought it over on purpose because his house was so hot in the winter and I thought the comforter would dry quicker there. It was a huge mint-green thing, and I draped one end of it over the radiator in his room by the window and the other end of it over his desk chair, a wooden framed chair with an orange leather seat. The cat used to lounge on top of that radiator, and once she was lying there scratching herself with one of her paws and another paw was making a thumping noise and Jim said she was sending Morse code to the universe saying, Help! I am a virgin, please send help before I die. Also, when I first met him, before we had slept together or maybe it was just after we'd slept together, Jim said he stood there by the radiator and looked out the window for a long time, waiting to see me to walk by.

I don't remember what day I did my laundry and brought over the green comforter but it was very close to the day he committed suicide, and it amazes me that things were still going on more or less normally: I was doing all my laundry and Jim was saying he was proud of me for doing all my laundry, although there was also this terrible, precarious feeling all the time, of things being just barely in control. I was very superstitious at that time. I remember I had an idea that if the toothbrushes—my blue one, Jim's pink one, which he kept at my house, of which he said when he bought it, This will be my lucky toothbrush—I had the idea that if the toothbrushes were facing toward each other in the toothbrush dispenser, if they were resting at an angle with the heads together or if the bristles were facing each other as if they were having a conversation, then it would be a good day and everything would go smoothly between me and Jim, with no drugs involved. And if one of them was facing forward—say, mine—and the other one was turned away, then one person would be in a good mood and okay, but the other one would be out of sorts. And if they were both facing away from each other, then it would be a day when we were on the outs with each other, when something bad was going to happen. Jim had given me some of those little cloth worry men made in Mexico and I carried them around with me everywhere I went. I had a sort of vague half-baked idea they were helping to keep us safe, and when Jim died I threw them away. I remember I broke a mirror a couple of days before he died—it was the mirror in a pretty cosmetic case someone gave me, the mirror I was always looking at myself in on the sly, to see if I was pretty enough. I was trying to look at the back of my head in the bathroom, doing that trick where you hold up one mirror and see the reflection of the back of your head in the dual reflection of another mirror, and it slipped out of my hand and broke and I knew it was a bad sign. I threw it away and tried not to think about it, but I knew it was bad, that it meant something very, very bad was going to happen.

I don't know whether my green comforter ended up on his bed by accident—something dirty got on his blanket and he threw it in the laundry basket and put my green comforter on the bed instead and it just happened to be there later, when he shot himself. Or whether he put it over him on purpose, at the last minute, because it was mine and he thought it would comfort him, because he wanted to go to the other world wrapped in a little part of me. I suppose it doesn't really matter—either way, the result was the same. He borrowed Peggy's rosary beads, and he smoked a couple of puffs off a last cigarette. I saw the butt in the ashtray, one long cigarette-shaped ash trailing off the filter, when we went into his room to collect his stuff. Kathy emptied it into the trashcan—she and my sister both came to Iowa after the death—and then I said, half hysterically, "I wanted that cigarette butt!" Because it had touched his lips.

And he took his pants off. He must've taken them off, because I found them in his laundry basket, the belt still threaded through the belt loops, my key to his house, which he took off my kitchen table that morning, still in the pocket. For a long time I used to lie awake at night and wonder why those jeans were in the laundry basket. Did he want to be more comfortable when he died? Did he only plan to take a nap, then change his mind? Those thoughts really bothered me. More than anything, though, it bothered me that he did it on the bed. That fact haunted me for a long, long time; it hung around in my mind like a little puff of evil left over from the event.

The bed was a single bed—a mattress on a bed frame—pushed up against the window, across from the desk. I used to stop by his apartment on my way home from work and sometimes I would find him napping, the late-afternoon sunlight sifting through the blinds onto his face or an empty part of the bed. Sometimes I would kiss him, or I would want to kiss him but wouldn't, afraid that it would disturb him. Once I left him a note on a scrap of paper that said, "I was here but couldn't bear to wake you." He saved that note along with every other note I ever wrote him; I found them all in his desk after he was dead. There was even a stamp torn off an envelope I'd sent; it was a Love stamp.

We took naps together there as well, on that bed. I remember lying on it beside him once. I was on the inside, next to the window; a blanket was pulled up to our waists and Jim was asleep and I was awake and the cat was awake too; she was nestled on his chest looking into his sleeping face. My hand was resting on his shoulder and the cat turned her head and stared long and hard at my hand on his shoulder and you could almost see her thinking her slow kitty thoughts, then she inserted her little head into the palm of one of his sleeping hands as if she was trying to get him to pet her, as if she was saying, You think he's yours? Well, he's not, he's mine.

It didn't even occur to me, in the beginning, that he might have shot himself on his bed. I kept picturing him doing it sitting up, in the chair at his desk. That's what you always see in the movies: guys sitting in cars, standing at windows, seated on benches or riverbanks. Never once have I seen an image of someone shooting themselves lying down on a bed. But of course that's not what it was about it that bothered me so much.

Jim was lying on a bed in the funeral home, too, a high raised narrow bed in the middle of an enormous empty room. I went there to look at his body because Mike Lensink, the funeral home director, said I should; he said seeing the body was important; according to research, people who don't view the body have trouble accepting the death. "You don't have to be afraid to see him," he said, almost tenderly, leading me into the room. "All the damage was internal." Jim was wearing a light cotton johnny, white with little blue flowers, the kind that ties in the back, that you wear in the hospital. There was a baby-blue blanket pulled up around his chest; his right arm was resting, elbow bent, outside of it. The left side of his face was slightly swollen, his eyes were closed, and his lips—the most beautiful lips in the world—were parted; he looked peaceful, in repose, he looked like he was napping.

So there I was, working all afternoon at the Office of the State Archaeologist, feeling perfectly content, thinking Jim and I had made up and the time was ripe to really work on him to get help for his problems, and there he was doing God knows what, thinking God knows what, getting hideously, unbearably depressed, then getting fucked up, or maybe it was the other way around, maybe he got fucked up first then got depressed about getting fucked up instead of doing all the things on his list, the things that were going to pull him out of it. Deciding today's the day. Today's the day I'm really going to do it. I can't know what he was thinking, what the process was that started off with "Our recommendations consist of two major points" and brought him all the way down to that bed with the shotgun in his mouth and my green comforter over him and the cigarette burning in the ashtray on the desk and the rosary beads on the bedside table and this time he pulled the trigger.

Afterward, I used to marvel at how one minute he was alive and the world was normal—even though he was lying on his bed with a shotgun in his mouth, even though he'd gotten fucked up and written that awful note and prayed and done and felt God knows what else, still he was alive, the world was still normal—and the next minute the whole world went out of whack, as if somebody turned a key and made everything go permanently, irreversibly strange. Strange like a circus with freaks in a sideshow—calves with extra heads, twisted pig fetuses floating in bottles, people with lizard skin and other deformities—the whole world was suddenly like that: off, weird, grotesque, distorted, because Jim had disappeared from it.

But I didn't know it yet. At that moment I was still in my office, I still thought the world was normal. And I still thought so as I was walking home in the early-winter twilight up the long, tedious, familiar slope of Washington Street, walking along planning what I was going to say to Jim, how I was going to convince him to get help for his substance abuse problems, lecturing him in my head, when I saw a cop car parked against the curb in front of his house. Or maybe there were two of them.

I walked past it, them, and to my house. I took my coat off, put my pocketbook on the couch and looked out the window. I was scared but not too scared. I tried to think up an explanation for why the cop cars were outside his house—I thought maybe it had something to do with a friend of his who was on parole and wasn't supposed to drink, the friend was there and the cops were coming to pick him up to take him back to the drunk tank; or I thought maybe even Jim himself had gotten into some kind of trouble but not very bad trouble; the cops would be about to leave, having straightened everything out. I imagined telling Jim about it later, how I felt when I saw the cop cars. I imagined saying, "I was scared to death when I saw those cop cars," and him smiling with pleasure that I had been concerned about him.

But I was still scared. I called his house and the phone rang and rang and nobody answered and the answering machine didn't go on. So I put my coat back on and walked to his house. As I approached a cop came out the front door and I heard him say something into his walkie-talkie about evacuation kits and I thought he was talking about Kitts, Jim's cat. I went up the walk toward the front steps and he came down the walk toward me and about halfway between the front door and the sidewalk we met and he said, "Who are you looking for?"

I said, "Jim Beaman, is he all right?"

The cop shook his head.

Something strange happened at that moment. It was as if the white sky contracted and a hole opened up and a large fist reached down from the clouds and clapped me—hard—on the back, forcing a scream from my lungs, my mouth, like air forced out of a horn, like a windy bloody piece of meat. I screamed and screamed and the sound was like the noise of the world halting, screeching, reversing its orbit, breaking apart.

I moved down the walk away from the house, still screaming, doubled over, the cop walking behind me.

But then for a moment I got distracted. For a split second I forgot that Jim was dead and I thought he'd heard me screaming and was going to come out of the house to see what was wrong, to try to help me. I stopped and turned around and looked at the front door, expecting to see him come out. Then of course he didn't come out and I remembered, the way in the beginning the information keeps going away and coming back, that he would never come out, and I screamed again and again, bending over the trunk of a car parked along the curb.

They say a place has a kind of memory, that whatever happens there is absorbed and retained, imprinted on the ether like a silent sound recorded on an invisible tape. Even the tiniest occurrence—a leaf falling, a bird resting on a telephone wire—gets recorded on the tape, but most strongly engraved are events involving shock, trauma, severe emotional pain. These days, walking by that house, that lawn, that stretch of sidewalk, I often think of it: me and the cop, the sky splitting open, my screams imprinted, still hanging around somehow, woven into the interstices of time and space, into the air.

Part Two

17

I have a friend who has two daughters, and when the older one was six and the younger one was a year and a half my friend and her husband took them to see *The Little Mermaid*. Mary Beth said they were worried about whether the younger girl, Celia, would be able to stay still long enough to watch a movie, but she sat through the whole thing very quietly, staring intently up at the screen, and afterward, when the movie was over and they took her out of the theater, she acted dazed and sad and disoriented. She kept blinking, looking around, staring into the air as if startled by the sudden absence of an entire, consuming reality, saying, "What happened Mermaid? What happened Mermaid?"

I know that feeling. I kept having it over and over after Jim died, during, say, the first six weeks.

Every morning when I woke up there'd be a tiny window of time when I'd feel good before I remembered he was dead. I kept having dreams in which I'd know I'd lost him for some reason; I'd think we'd broken up and I'd keep asking myself, How could that be? We never would have broken up. And then I'd think, Oh well, it can't be so impossible to get back together, I'll just go to his house and talk to him. Then I'd wake up and remember. It was weird and horrible, knowing that for once reality was worse than any nightmare. It was as if death doesn't exist in the world of sleep, of dreams—it only exists in the hard, bright, intractable everyday world I'd wake up to every morning like a traveler returning to some awful, familiar place.

I thought I saw Jim everywhere and I looked for him everywhere. Every time a brown pickup truck drove by I searched inside the cab for him, every time the phone rang I picked it up expecting to hear his voice on the other end. It wasn't that I really, consciously, thought it was going to be him; it was more some trick my mind kept playing on me, some combination of magical thinking and force of habit.

I remember watching the five o'clock news one day on my little black-and-white portable TV. Kathy was watching it too; she'd come to stay with me during the first weeks after the death; my sister came for a short while from Massachusetts, too. The Gulf War was about to start and the news was full of it—the deadline for Iraqi withdrawal approaching and spokespeople making announcements and politicians commenting and troops being sent over. The local news that day had interviews with families of soldiers: moms and dads seated on couches in living rooms, younger children standing around, photos of the soldiers in their dress uniforms. "I just hope and pray he comes home alive," one of the mothers said and it hurt me when she said it, reminding me as it did that in my case there was no use hoping and praying, Beaman wouldn't be coming home alive again. Everything hurt me back then— oatmeal cookies in the grocery store (Jim used to call them goatmeal cookies), KY Jelly (OK jelly) in the contraceptive aisle, the entire town of Solon, Iowa, which reminded me of beamonizing.

Kathy and I had the TV out on the kitchen table, and at some point during the news I stood up and looked out the front-door window, onto the street. It was cold and snowy, there was ice on the sidewalk, the scene was bathed in desolate, blue, late-afternoon winter light. Some guy came walking down the sidewalk wearing a winter coat and hat and for a split second I thought it was Jim, then I remembered it couldn't be him, it was never going to be him again. I sat back down in my chair and the phrase "Five o'clock, hour of loneliness and misery," came into my head and I repeated it silently again and again.

There was a set of footprints in the snow beside Jim's house. I must've seen them the day we went up there and picked up his stuff, or maybe I saw them on some other occasion. The footprints went down the steps and around the side of Beaman's house and they were men's footprints and I remember thinking they might have been Jim's, then realizing it was too late for them to be his because a little snow had fallen since his death. It really bothered me that even those footprints couldn't be his, as if there was any real comfort or pleasure or connection that could have been gotten out of a footprint. But at the time it seemed like there was.

Kathy and I took up playing solitaire a few days into her visit and I remember sitting on the living-room floor staring down at my cards. I was filled with pain as heavy and inert as lead, but at the same time I kept getting this magical feeling that if all the red cards would just line up right with the black cards so I could win the game, if only that one little good thing would happen, then some other good thing would follow. I'd only feel that way for an instant, then the big black immovable door of death would clang shut—I'd remember it was shut—again.

And I remember lying on the bed looking at the Christmas tree in my apartment the first time I was left alone. My sister and Kathy went somewhere together and before they left they kept asking me, "Are you sure you'll be all right?" They didn't say so but I think they were afraid I'd commit suicide myself. I said I'd be fine. After they left I lay down on the bed and smoked a cigarette. I noticed the tinsel on the Christmas tree was swaying slightly, and I remember lying there staring at it,

wishing as hard as you can wish—and at the same time knowing it was just my own wishful thinking—that Jim's ghost was
somehow there, moving the tinsel. Already he seemed more
like an absence than a presence. I remember looking at the
ceiling above the bed, thinking there was just empty space
there and wondering how a whole living person could become
nothing so quickly, in the time it takes to pull a trigger. That
absence, that blank space where Jim had been, was unbearable.
It filled me with an insatiable longing, a ceaseless nagging craving, and in the months to come I strained and strained to fill it.

Grief, I've observed through reading and talking to others and
through my own experience, affects different people differently. The sudden death of someone you love is like a violent
explosion; the force sends you flying and when you struggle to
your feet you find yourself turned around, far from where you
started, headed in some previously unforeseen direction. This
seems especially true when the death is caused by suicide. As a
survivor you find yourself at the head of a road that will take
you through and out the other end of grieving. Some people
go down one path, some go down another. Some people concentrate on figuring out what lay behind the suicide in order
to put their minds at rest; some change family patterns, end
unhealthy marriages, work with what they have left; some get
involved in research into social problems—drugs, the need for
gun control—for the benefit of other people, though it's too
late to save the dead person. I didn't do any of those things. I
went down the road marked life after death.

I could not let Jim go, for a variety of reasons: inability to
accept loss, an addictionlike attachment, unresolved issues
regarding his drug use and our relationship. But I like to think
it was more than just all that, more than just me being a codependent widow, as my friend JoAnn and I used to joke.

Although certainly that was a big part of it. But I like to think something larger was also driving me: I couldn't get over the fact that a whole human being—that *Jim Beaman*—could simply disappear, a door opens up and the universe swallows them without a trace, and I couldn't accept any of the usual explanations. No matter how hard I tried, I couldn't believe that a person is the result of biological processes in their body and their brain and when those stop the person stops as well: they simply cease to be, like a machine that's been turned off, permanently. Somehow I knew that a person, that *Jim Beaman*, was more than a complex bloody piece of machinery, reduced now to a pile of ashes in a cardboard box on my desk. I knew he had to be somewhere. And if he was, I wanted to know where. I wanted to know what condition he was in and what it was like in that place and what in the universe made it possible for him to be there. I wanted to know those things more than I've ever wanted to know anything, and I wasn't going to rest until I found them out.

Books that tell stories about people dying usually end with the death. Somebody's lover or mother, wife or child or brother dies of cerebral palsy, say, or fetal alcohol syndrome, or after a long fierce battle with cancer or AIDS, and that's it: The survivors fade off into grief and some unspecified means of coping. I used to pick up those books during a certain time in the months after Jim died, read a few pages, and toss them aside. They didn't have what I wanted. Neither did paperbacks about how to grieve or biographies of famous widows or psychology texts on suicide or self-help books for suicide survivors. But I read them all. I went to the library almost every day, walking down Washington Street past Jim's house with its blank, closed windows, past Ace McDonald's mother's house, where Ace, Jim's old mechanic, had his garage in the back, past the house where two scruffy orange cats sit on a retaining wall and meow and throw themselves to the ground, bellies exposed, and squint their eyes in kitty ecstasy when you pet them. I'd be carrying my white burlap sack bulging with yesterday's library books and I'd feel thin-skinned and vulnerable, shy and sad in the face of the bold, loud, colorful world.

When I got to the library I'd dump the books in the returns bin and go, not to the fiction shelves on the first floor where I'd headed automatically for years, but upstairs to the nonfiction section. Usually I'd stop at the computerized card catalogue and look up a certain book I'd heard or thought of, write down the call numbers, press the START OVER button on the computer, step away from the desk. Always, at that instant, crossing the floor to the stacks, my depression would lift and I'd have a momentary feeling of excitement; always, I'd think, just for an instant: Something good is about to happen.

I kept having that feeling, like a little light that goes on and off for no particular reason, throughout the first two months after Jim's death. It would come to me at odd moments: while I was playing solitaire, about to place the red ten on top of the black jack, or as I was bending over to pluck a dead leaf off a plant in my living room or standing in the bathroom staring at myself in the mirror. And it always happened in the library. The rest of the time I was utterly miserable, my heart shattered into a million pieces. I felt sick, injured, decrepit, hopeless. But there were those moments of excitement, of irrational expectation. When I traced the feeling down it always came to a dead-end of disappointment. What I wanted, of course, was Jim, to see his face, to hear his voice, to experience his living presence; I wanted him to be alive again or not be dead in the first place; I wanted the gun to have jammed; I wanted him to have changed his mind at the last minute. There was nothing in this world that could give me what I wanted. But still. I kept having those moments. Maybe it's just that hope dies hard, especially when the hoper is in the habit of denial; maybe it was just more love addiction and self-delusion. But it didn't feel like that. It felt sweeter, stranger, more disorienting, like seeing something good that disappeared so fast you didn't even know you'd seen it, or waking from a brief afternoon nap with the feeling that you'd just come back from someplace faraway you couldn't remember going to.

Mostly, when I had that feeling at the library, I was on the trail of another kind of book. Not narratives about someone's dying or comforting thoughts on suicide or biographies of famous widows or books of advice on grieving, but what my friend Patty and I called boojie books, the kind of book found in Prairie Lights bookstore in the nonordinary reality section. Nonordinary reality: A friend of mine told me he overheard a salesman and a bookstore employee making fun of that section—the place where they put books about near-death and out-of-body experiences, speculations on the afterlife, messages from the dead that came through famous mediums—and I understand the impulse. I used to feel the same way, too, and I still do occasionally, when I borrow someone else's pair of glasses to see the world through. But mostly I love that part of the bookstore. After Jim died I used to stand in front of it with a feeling of excitement, of expectation, as if, even though part of me knew I wouldn't, part of me thought I was going to find the secret to life, death, where Beaman went, maybe even Jim Beaman himself in those books. Of course I didn't, but in a strange way the looking, the half expecting to find him—to find *something*, at least—gave me a little of the same satisfaction.

And in the end I came up with some theories about life, death, where Beaman went. Enough to put my mind at rest. I don't really know, of course; I don't claim to have the answers.

But one thing I know for sure: Death is not the end of the story.

18

The other day in my apartment I came across two large shoe boxes full of paper covered with strange squiggly writing. I was rearranging some of the furniture and found the boxes under my bed, covered with dust—they'd been sitting there since June of 1991, the year of Beaman's death. I found my Ouija board under the bed as well, also covered with dust. My first impulse was to jettison the writing into the trash and never think about it again. Then I cracked open one of the boxes and looked inside and decided I'd hold on to it for a while. So I dusted off both boxes, then squeezed them onto a shelf in my closet and put some other, normal stuff on top of them—a puzzle my sister gave me for Christmas, a pair of curtains that came with the apartment—so that anybody who happened to look in the closet—a visitor searching for a dish towel, my landlord in the middle of some repair—would be less likely to encounter them.

I felt as if anyone who saw what was in those boxes would know the worst about me: that I was—not that I am now, because I know I'm not now—but that I was, at one time, crazy. That for about two months, starting at the end of March of the year of Jim Beaman's death, I sat at my kitchen table covering page after page with meaningless squiggles. At least, what appear now to be meaningless squiggles. At the time they weren't meaningless. At the time they made perfect sense, what I was doing didn't seem crazy at all. I'm still not sure whether it was actually, totally crazy.

But to get to the writing—automatic writing, it is called—I have to start with the Ouija board. What I'm embarrassed by about the Ouija board is the box, which at one point I wrote all over with a black ballpoint pen, made little *y*'s and *n*'s that look like birds, or rather that *looked* like birds, because they don't look like birds to me now. That's what happened then: Things looked different, they looked like what I thought they were instead of having objective reality. I could make a squiggle and it would turn into something else, an idea it represented. That's the way things always are, I guess—isn't any, regular writing, for example, just a bunch of squiggles transformed by ideas into something else?—but maybe not quite so much. Or maybe it's that what was in my head was so different from what's in there now, from what's in most people's heads. What was in there, mostly, was Jim, a dead but still somehow living Jim, which was how I ended up being drawn into that place where everything looked so different from the way it should look, from the way it looks now.

So there's the Ouija board, with little *y*'s and *n*'s written all over the box, which stood for "yes" and "no" and which also looked like birds. You can imagine it, can't you? The two little humps on the *n*'s were wings, and the tail on the *y*—I can't remember any more what the tail on the *y* was supposed to represent. They were written in small handwriting that looked just like Beaman's—it still looks like Beaman's handwriting, that at least is true—and as well as birds they were the answers to questions. The questions were mine and the answers were Jim's—the dead-guy version of him.

At some point later on I painted white-out over the *y*'s and *n*'s, so that now the picture on the box—eerily lit forearms of a man and woman, the rest of their bodies shrouded in darkness, their fingertips poised on the little plastic heart-shaped thing that goes around the board, indicating messages from spirits—that picture on my box is now covered with little blobs of white paint I daubed on it at some point later on, when I found the Ouija board under the bed and didn't want to throw it away, didn't want to take the trouble to get another box for it, but didn't want anyone to see, didn't even want to see myself, that evidence—those little *y*'s and *n*'s all over the box—of my craziness. Of that world I lived in for a while with different rules and conventions and altered possibilities, which is maybe what being crazy is.

I didn't start out in that other world or go there all at once. I went slowly, gradually, like a person being drawn inch by inch through a crack or a keyhole, her parts subtly rearranged over time so she can fit. And the Ouija board was the tool that did the rearranging, the key that disengaged the lock, the vehicle that took me from one world into another, in the beginning at least. But it didn't start out as a key or a vehicle. It started out as just an ordinary object, at least as ordinary as an object that's meant to be used for contacting spirits can be.

And when I say it took me there, I don't mean to imply it tricked me into going, transported me against my will. I went willingly, eagerly; I would have gone more quickly and directly if I could. The only thing is, the world I got wasn't exactly the one I wanted. It was a different world than the one I thought I was going to get.

The Ouija board has a smooth glossy surface printed with the alphabet, a row of numbers, and, at the bottom, the word GOOD-BYE. It also says OUIJA, MYSTIFYING ORACLE at the top and in the upper left-hand corner is a spooky-looking sun next to the word YES; in the upper right-hand corner is a similar-looking moon and the word NO. A tan plastic heart-shaped thing comes in the box as well—this is called a planchette.

There's a little graphic in the lower left- and right-hand corners of the board, the same picture but reversed in either corner so the two are facing each other. It's drawn with rough, simple lines like an old-fashioned block print, and it shows a woman with her hands hovering over the planchette, a thick lock of hair hanging down beside her face. In the space behind her head as if speaking to her, through her, communicating a message, is another, disembodied, head: a young, male, not-bad-looking head with eyes and a nose and lips, short hair neatly parted and brushed away from the forehead. I used to think, during a certain point after Beaman's death, that that was a picture of him and me.

Ouija boards are a strange phenomenon, when you think about it. They're made by a toy company but they're not exactly toys, but they aren't straightforward tools, either, or anything else that fits into the ordinary, rational, no-nonsense world. Everybody knows about them, almost everyone has had some experience with one at some time or another, you can buy them in stores like Wal-Mart or Kmart. We take their existence for granted and yet their purpose—to allow the living to receive messages from the dead—implies all kinds of possibilities almost nobody really believes in. Even people who do believe in spiritual stuff scoff at the idea of making real contact with actual dead people through the use of a Ouija board. I've heard people say that what you get through the Ouija board is the work of the devil: The spirits of the dead exist, isolated, in heaven; they do not talk to the living. And I've heard other people say that Ouija boards are dangerous and you should use them cautiously or not at all, because bad or stupid spirits can take control and send you harmful, misleading messages. But I've almost never heard anybody say they used the

Ouija board to try to get a genuine communication from someone they loved who was dead. But that's what I did. Not because I thought it was a good idea, not because I had any confidence it would work, but because it was the only available method.

Jim and I bought my Ouija board together at Kmart—back when he was still alive, before he became one of those amorphous spirits you can only talk to through such a silly clunky vehicle. It was his idea to get it. During our couch days he said some friends of his used to receive messages on one from a spirit named Tim. He, Beaman, was over at their house one night and got really involved in using it, something kind of strange happened to him, he couldn't stop asking it questions and the people who owned the Ouija board finally said, "What's *wrong* with you?" I'm not sure whether it was that experience or something else that made him say a few weeks after we got together that we should get one. It seemed like a fun, cheerful thing to do, so we went to the store and bought one from the toy department and brought it back to my house and set it up on my bed.

We did not get many results. After we'd set up the board and gone through a few preliminaries, he asked it if my engagement ring had anything to do with Colonel Davenport and the Davenport house—later he said he didn't know what prompted him to ask that—and the Ouija board said yes, and he asked whether his Grandma Beaman was mad at him because he didn't go to her funeral—he was drinking at the time—and it said no. Then he asked me if I wanted to ask it any questions and I said yes, but then I couldn't think of anything. After that the whole project deteriorated; Jim started making jokes and finally he said, "Suck my dick, Ouija," which I said was very bad for karma, so we stopped. We put the board away and never got it out again, though every now and then Jim would talk about using it.

The first encounter I had with the Ouija board after Jim's death came a week after the suicide. It wasn't my idea to do it; up till then the thought of the Ouija board was the furthest thing from my head. It was Kathy who brought it up. I can't remember what she said; I only remember it was after dinner and she and my sister and I were in the kitchen. Kathy was putting things away in the refrigerator and my sister was standing at the sink emptying dishes from the dish drainer. I was sitting at the table, too debilitated by grief to do much of anything. But the thought of the Ouija board cheered me up. I felt a sudden small wave of optimism, not about anything offered by life or the future, but at the thought that there might be some tiny little opening, a minuscule lighted doorway set into the bottom of the big black permanently closed door of death, through which I could still have contact with Jim.

Kathy and I didn't do the Ouija board that night and we didn't do it the next night. On the third night we were talking about it again after dinner when we heard something fall in the other room. My bedroom was full of boxes and garbage bags overflowing with Jim's stuff, which we'd retrieved from his apartment a few days earlier. I went in there and picked my way across the floor, searching for an item that might have fallen over or out of something. What I found was something of mine on the floor beside the open closet door—the oblong cardboard box my telephone came in, which had been sitting on the top shelf of the closet for months between a stack of files and a jigsaw puzzle. Jim had given me the phone in July as a late birthday present. I looked in the closet. Nothing else was disturbed, nothing new had been put in there recently to disturb it. The phone box had apparently fallen out on its own. I picked it up and brought it in the kitchen and told my sister and Kathy.

My sister widened her eyes. "E.T., phone home," she said.

We decided it was a sign from Jim telling us to do the Ouija board. Part of me believed this, another part of me thought it was nothing, just a coincidence that the phone box had fallen off the shelf, and another part of me let myself believe Jim had knocked it off whether it was true or not, like an actor giving herself over entirely to a part. I felt the same uneasy mixture of believing and not believing and letting myself believe during everything—all the boojie stuff—that happened later.

Only two people can participate in using the Ouija board and it was decided that Kathy and I would do it in my bedroom while my sister took a nap on the couch. Kathy took a bottle of wine from the refrigerator and I turned the heat up to eighty. Kathy and I went to my room and closed the door and sat opposite each other on my bed with our legs crossed and the board between us, wine and wineglasses and my cigarettes on the night table. We rested our fingers lightly on either side of the plastic planchette. I asked whether Jim was there and the pointer glided over to YES; then we asked a few more questions and the thing moved slowly around the board to a bunch of letters that couldn't possibly be interpreted as making sense. Then it came to a stop. "Hmm," Kathy said. I asked several more questions and the same thing happened: The planchette floated aimlessly around the board. Sometimes it would seem to be spelling out something that made a little bit of sense if we stretched it, but it was generally very unsatisfying. I kept having an empty, painful feeling, a feeling of straining after an absence, looking at the board and thinking how futile it was to imagine you could get something authentic, even a tiny taste of a real, living person, from a plastic heart and a piece of laminated cardboard.

Kathy said, "I have an idea. I think we should ask it only yes-or-no questions."

Kathy is slightly psychic. She'll hear her brother's voice saying her name as she's going to sleep and the next day he'll call from Seattle; she'll be thinking about an old movie and ten minutes later it'll come on television. Once when we were roller-skating she turned around to look just as I was falling; later she said she looked because she'd seen a picture in her head of me with my feet sliding out from under me.

And when she said we should ask the Ouija board yes-or-no questions, I felt like she knew what she was talking about. I took a swallow of wine and a question popped into my head. I put my fingertips back on the plastic heart, closed my eyes and said, "Are you glad you did it?" For some reason, maybe because of all those accounts of near-death experiences where death is peaceful and blissful, or maybe because I thought Jim had found a way to solve his problems as much as I hated the solution, I was expecting the pointer to float over to YES. But instead it seemed to pick up energy and went directly, emphatically to NO. "Oh," I said. "I wasn't expecting that." Kathy said she wasn't either. We took our hands off the planchette, sat back and talked about it, how strongly the pointer went to NO and what it possibly meant, how it really did seem like a genuine message.

I think that was the moment I got sucked into the idea of using the Ouija board and other means to try to contact Jim, the idea that maybe I didn't have to let him go completely, after all. With that one little word, like one of those monkeys that presses the bar twelve thousand times for a single dose of cocaine, I got a hit of Jim. I could press the bar of the Ouija board hundreds, thousands, of times and not get a thing, but that one little word that night with Kathy gave me the feeling that if I pressed it long enough, often enough, something might come out.

19

The next encounter I had with the Ouija board happened when my friend Patty came to visit from San Diego.

Patty and I have been friends since 1983, when we shared an apartment in Cambridge. We always call each other Miz Mary and Miz Patty and often talk to each other in silly, nasal, high-pitched voices. When Jim died Patty was in the Marshall Islands doing research for a book she was writing. I called her there at a number her roommate in San Diego gave me. I remember Patty's voice echoing over the line, all those miles of land and ocean stretching out between us. She'd never met Jim but she was shocked and saddened by his death; her mother had died just four months earlier. When Patty got back from the Marshall Islands she called again and we decided she'd come and stay with me for a week when I got back from North Carolina. I spent the second half of January and the first half of February there in Wrightsville Beach with Kathy and her boyfriend, Micah. They were living there temporarily while Micah worked as a soundman on a movie being made by Carolco Studios. Patty's flight arrived from San Diego forty-five minutes after mine got in from Raleigh. I met her at the gate and we took the limo home together from the airport. I didn't have to spend any time at all by myself in my apartment, which was what I wanted. I wasn't ready to be alone.

The day after Patty arrived I came down with the flu, and for the first three days of her visit I stayed in bed with a cough and congestion and a fever of 102. She had brought me back some gifts from the Marshall Islands: a crown made of palm fibers and tiny shells shaped like teeth; a small shell called a cat's eye with a flat back and a front that looks like an orange-and-white, brown-irised eye. I remember lying in bed crying a little, the cat's eye on the sheet beside my pillow. Patty put it there, saying it had magical comforting powers. Then she went into the kitchen and brought me back a cup of hot Theraflu and left it on the night table, saying, "Here you go, your assholishness."

After my flu got better we went to the library and returned with a bunch of books about life after death and related topics: boojie books, we started calling them. Patty had as much at stake as I did in the whole subject—she was still grieving fiercely over her mother—and I think we were both determined to figure out some way of getting around death, both stuck in the denial stage of grief. I can't remember exactly when we started using the word "boojie" to describe all that stuff. It was Patty's word to begin with, something her brother used to call ghosts and spooky things, but it quickly became an expression that belonged to both of us.

We spent hours and hours during that visit talking about grief and death and life after death and reading our library books. The first book Patty read was called *Love, Karen*, about a seventeen-year-old girl who died of leukemia and as a "spirit" communicated a bunch of messages to her mother through a famous medium in Southern California. The messages appeared to be genuine; they contained information only Karen, the spirit, could have known from when she was alive, and according to her mother they sounded like her as well. Patty was fascinated by that book, but at first I thought it looked kind of silly, just some dumpy old library book with a torn plastic dust jacket and a bad picture on the cover, and I kept trying to get her to stop reading and talk to me instead. But she wouldn't—she'd look up, nod distractedly, say a few words and return to reading, which is very unlike her. Patty is tall, willowy, and restless; some boyfriend once described her as a nervous bird. She fidgets and paces, cracks her knuckles, performs all kinds of small abrupt motions; she never just sits there and quietly reads. But this time she did, and eventually I was forced to read a book myself. Mine was called *Afterlife*, by a guy named Colin Wilson. Patty had picked it out at the library, along with *Love, Karen* and *Seth Speaks*. *Seth Speaks* is the first in a series of dense, tough-going treatises on the nature of reality and the universe, supposedly channeled through Jane Roberts by an advanced spirit named Seth. Jane Roberts herself is now dead but she used to be married to a guy named Robert Butts, and while Patty and I were reading the chapter on death—that chapter was the reason we took out the book— we kept saying, "Seth speaks through Jane's butts," not because we thought the book was too silly to deserve respect but because that was the sort of silly thing we always said. I remember what it felt like to do that at that moment, the two of us sitting on my bed laughing our heads off; I remember feeling a little ashamed of laughing at something so stupid, and relieved to be laughing at all, and miserable underneath— always miserable—because Jim was dead and I was never going to see him again.

Afterlife is a history of recorded cases and other information relating to the possibility of life after death: the British Society for Psychical Research investigating reports of psychic experiences and finding some airtight cases; famous mediums producing "evidential" messages, where the information communicated is true and only the dead person could know it; hundreds of thousands of people reporting the same set of experiences after they "died" and before they were resuscitated. I loved that book. I loved the historical perspective it gave and Colin Wilson's writing style and his cheerful, impartial, inquiring attitude. But most of all I loved it because it made me feel as if Jim really was somewhere and someday I might see him again. All the rest of the time, even during all the stuff that happened later, even when I thought I was in contact with Jim himself, I had nagging doubts; there was always a part of me that felt uneasy. But when I was reading those books—I went from Colin Wilson to *Love, Karen*, which I exchanged for *Afterlife* with Patty, to *Seth Speaks* to *Life After Life* by Raymond Moody to (after Patty left) other accounts of near-death experiences, biographies of famous mediums, speculations by various people on why life after death might be feasible—when I was reading those books I felt calm and assured.

Those books became a kind of addiction for me. After Patty left I went to the library and took out some more and when I had read all those and every other boojie book they had I scoured the bookstores and went to the university library for more. I read those books compulsively, somewhat furtively, the way some people read pornography; I read them on park benches and in the aisles of bookstores and late at night in bed. I sampled books on other, more traditional subjects as well: *How to Survive the Suicide of a Loved One*, and *When Bad Things Happen to Good People*, and *Widow* by Dr. Joyce Brothers, and a book called *Coming Back*, about people who survived and overcame various disasters in their lives. But those things didn't do it for me, as Patty and I would have said. I longed for something that spoke to me of my own experience, and my own experience was all wrapped up in my quest to know what had happened to Jim, to understand where he'd gone and what death really meant. All the advice about moving on, the stories about healing, didn't interest me. I couldn't be interested in life until I had figured out death.

The Rooms of Heaven

. . .

Patty and I retrieved the Ouija board from under the bed during her visit and used it as well—"did" it, as we would say, the way you'd say "we did it" about sex. We did it four or five days in a row, taking it out and setting it up in the late afternoon or evening, trying for protracted periods to get it to speak. Patty kept wanting to ask it about her former lives but I was only interested in receiving messages from Jim and we kept arguing about who got to spend how much time on what questions, but it didn't really matter anyway because none of the answers we got were even remotely informative or satisfying. Mostly the plastic heart went around and around in circles or slid off the board or spelled out half-gibberish things that we would try to interpret as having meaning.

But then, on the last night of Patty's visit, when we were doing it in the kitchen with the light out and some candles lit, Patty got what she thought was a real message from her mother: The plastic pointer picked up energy beneath our fingertips and for once it spelled out words. I can't remember what was communicated except for one little thing that was kind of funny: Patty asked it a question she had already gotten an answer for and the plastic heart spelled out "Are you deaf?" which Patty said was exactly like something her mother would have said. That message meant a lot to her; she wrote it down and afterward she talked and talked about it. A few things seemed to come through from Jim that night, too—a couple of words and some sentence fragments that might have meant something—and I felt sort of half pleased, half appeased, and at the same time dissatisfied. It wasn't just the fragmentary aspect of the messages that didn't satisfy me, it was the entire experience, the idea of Jim as some invisible energy floating around the kitchen spelling out little half-nonsense messages through some unimaginable mechanism. Even though I wanted to, I couldn't quite believe it.

But I couldn't stop trying to find Jim—to talk to him—either, so I regretted it when Patty left and I no longer had a partner to do the Ouija board with. I tried and tried to find some other method of contacting Beaman. I took a book out of the library about how to meditate in a certain way to reach the dead. The book said to meditate at the same time every day and to hold a picture of the dead person in your mind. It also said to make a little altar with white flowers and candles in a room all its own, but that seemed too difficult: I only had a three-room apartment, so there was no possibility of dedicating a room to it or even finding an unused space, and the white candles and the flowers and the altar all seemed like too much trouble as well. I just wanted to get on with it. I remember sitting in my pink armchair with my eyes closed trying to hold an image in my mind of Jim, but that also proved impossible. I couldn't concentrate because of all the misery and rage and grief and frustration boiling around inside me, and I couldn't see Beaman. I didn't know it at the time but I'm sure that was at least partly because I had so many negative pictures of him in my mind that I didn't want to see: him at my kitchen table drunk with his three-day beard, him sitting at his desk weighing baggies filled with cocaine. It was years before I could let myself see those pictures and so it was years before I could picture him at all, and even then I couldn't get him to come in very clearly.

Anyway, I sat in that chair straining and straining to conjure up an image of his face and I couldn't do it. Then I opened my eyes and looked down at the front of my shirt and there, like an escapee from another dimension, a little tiny exception to the laws of nature, was one of his hairs. The shirt I was wearing was Jim's, one of those thick cotton polo shirts I admired so much when we first met, and probably the hair had been riding around, as Beaman would have said, on the front all along. Probably it came loose and fell out of his head and landed on the shirt at some point before he was dead, sat in a drawer at his house and survived the trip to my house and the shirt getting unpacked and put in the closet and taken out and pulled on over my head. But at that moment, I felt like it was a little miracle, that hair. Not that it brought me any pleasure or relief. I plucked it off the shirt and held it up between my fingers and stared at it and cried and cried. Then I taped it to a piece of paper and put it in Jim's trunk. It's still in there now, reminding me of the strangeness, the nuttiness of that part of my life—a short brown hair taped to a blank sheet of typing paper.

I did a bunch of other things as well to try to contact Jim. I was willing to try anything. I read in another book that to speak to the dead you need to open your throat chakra and to do that you should chant "thooo" over and over, and so I would lie on my bed at night before I went to sleep and chant "thooo" in a very quiet voice so my upstairs neighbor wouldn't hear me. The chanting must've had some effect, because once after doing it as I was falling asleep I had a beautiful little vision. I was lying on my back in bed facing the ceiling and a rectangle of celestial blue opened up before me, like an outdoor movie screen filled with a little piece of heaven. I got scared and woke myself up.

And I would go downtown and visit John Birkbeck, a friend of Jim's I'd gotten to know at the memorial service. John's an artist, a goofy crazy imaginative guy of about sixty-five. He has a studio on the second floor of an old brick building that looks out over the pedestrian mall; downstairs is a store called the Soap Opera and his studio always smells like soap and incense and candles. Someone once commissioned him to do a depiction of the universe and he spent six whole months working on various ideas involving a black gesso background and circles, triangles, and squares. In the end it was too hard and he gave up.

John has a talent for lucid dreaming, dreams in which everything is as clear and real as in real life except that you can fly. Once during a lucid dream he saw a young couple sitting on a window ledge; he was flying around trying to impress them with his daring and prowess and then he started to wake up and the couple screamed in dismay and horror, the way we scream here when somebody suddenly passes over into the other world. Occasionally in his lucid dreams John visits his dead mother. Once he found her in a plain little room in heaven and he said, "I have to tell Dad about this!" and she said, "No, don't bother him, he'll be here soon enough." And sure enough, his father died soon after that, and then John had a dream about him. I loved those stories; I couldn't get enough of them; I thought they were like tiny windows into the place—the invisible, inaccessible country—where Jim Beaman lived.

Then one day I went down and visited John in his studio and he said, holding his index finger up as if pointing at the ceiling, "Oh say. I had a dream about Jim." And then he told me how he saw Jim in one of those lucid, absolutely vivid, lifelike dreams. Jim had no shirt on and he was sitting on top of a pyramidlike sculpture that he, Jim, had made, and he said to John, one artist to another, "This is how it's done, John!" meaning, this is how art is really created. I loved hearing about that dream. I thought and thought about it, whether John had had a real encounter with Jim in another dimension, what the thing Jim said might mean, why no shirt and why a sculpture shaped like a pyramid. I would have done anything to have had a dream like that. I told John so the next time I visited him and he said, "Well, you know what you could do then? Buy a bottle of Richard's Wild Irish Rose. There's something a little bit otherworldly about Richard's Wild Irish Rose. Buy a bottle and drink a glass at night staring at a lighted candle, and when you go to bed you'll have strange dreams." So that's what I did. I ate a banana because I had read that bananas make you have vivid dreams, and I drank a bunch of that cheap rosé wine, staring at a candle. I was only planning on drinking a glass but I ended up drinking the whole bottle. I got drunk and very sad and very frustrated; I felt everything I was feeling at other times only more so, and then I shuffled into the bedroom and passed out and woke up in the morning with a hangover without having had one single dream.

Then one day I was sitting around and it came to me that I should try to do the Ouija board by myself. I don't know why it took me so long to think of it. A lot of the books I was reading talked about automatic writing, a practice where someone holds a pen loosely in her hand and the pen seems to take on energy of its own and writes what may be interpreted as messages from spirits. It's similar to the Ouija board but it only requires a pen and one person to do it. A long illustrious history exists of people receiving serious, cogent, apparently legitimate communications through automatic writing— William Butler Yeats's wife did it, for example, and Yeats wrote a book about the messages. As I read those books I was filled with longing and envy. I wanted to do automatic writing more than I've ever wanted to do anything and I'd pick up a pen and hold it loosely but nothing would happen and I'd put it back down, feeling silly and frustrated.

Then one day it came to me that the Ouija board was essentially the same vehicle and might be easier to use; I'd used it before, at least, and it had worked at least once with one little word. So I got it out and sat on my bed and rested my fingertips on the plastic planchette. The thing didn't move, and after a while I put the board back in the box and returned it under the bed. But I couldn't leave it alone, once I had gotten the idea to do it. So a few days later I took it out and set it up again. Again nothing happened. Then, just as I was about to give up, the planchette began to move ever so slightly under my fingertips. I couldn't really tell whether I was pushing it myself. In a way it felt like I was, but when I raised my fingertips until they were just barely touching it the thing continued moving. It went off the board and I put it back on and it started going around very slowly in circles. And then, agonizingly slowly, it spelled out a word. The word was W-A-S-T-E-D.

I want to say here, before going on, that I don't know where this stuff comes from—what you get on the Ouija board and through other, similar methods. I have a friend who thinks it comes from the devil. He thinks there's a dark force as well as a light force in the universe and the dark force is the devil but the devil isn't very smart, and if you invite spirits to talk to you via the Ouija board and other ways, what you'll get is that dumb old faker the devil. This, from a perfectly normal person whom you'd never suspect would have such opinions. Another more common, mainstream theory is that writing on the Ouija board comes from your own subconscious, which has a kind of mind of its own and will do what you want it to. I used to get impatient with that theory and think, How could your own subconscious be smart enough to write those things without your knowing it? But lately I've been reading a lot of books about how your subconscious carries out the orders you give it and so you have to train it to bring you positive rather than negative results, and now I think it *is* possible that it was my own subconscious doing that writing all along—the Ouija board writing and then the automatic writing—because I wanted it so much. That doesn't mean I see life through the other pair of glasses, that I believe a person is a machine and when the machine stops functioning that's it, no more person. I know—somehow I *know*—that's not the way life is. And I know Jim Beaman and all the other dead people are still around somewhere. But I'm not sure whether they can communicate through Ouija boards and automatic writing. But still, every once in a while something would come through the Ouija board, the automatic writing, that would be so surprising, so much what I never could have, would have, thought of myself, that I wonder. Maybe most of it was just stuff my subconscious obligingly generated, but maybe some of it, a little bit of it, was real.

And maybe when the board spelled out W-A-S-T-E-D, that was one of those times.

I had no idea what it was talking about and I asked, "What do you mean? You mean you wasted your chance to send me a message or what?" And the thing spelled out, again agonizingly slowly, M-Y-L-I-F-E. I took my fingers off the planchette and sat back, staring at the board. I'm not sure why I should have been shocked, because it seems perfectly logical now that if Jim Beaman's spirit were around he would have thought he had wasted his life, but at the time it was the last thing I anticipated. It was just such a bald, devastating statement, a statement so full of misery and despair. We don't expect dead people to be full of misery and despair. And maybe I was shocked that the Ouija board actually spelled out something I wasn't expecting, the way you'd be shocked if a real rabbit turned up in a hat during a magic act, even though you'd been pretending all along you could make one.

After a minute or two I put my hands back on the planchette and the thing slowly spelled out, U-S-E-A-P-E-N. Now I'm not sure whether it really spelled that out on its own or whether on a subconscious level I made it do it because I wanted it to, because I wanted to believe I could do automatic writing. I think it's possible, even likely, that the latter was true, but I think it's possible that when it spelled out the other thing, when it spelled out WASTED MY LIFE, that was real.

Anyway, I got a pen and held it loosely over a piece of paper just like I'd read about in all those books, and it spelled out in large shaky handwriting, "Hello." Then it spelled out "Soon," whatever that was supposed to mean, and then "enough, tomorrow." The next day I tried again and it spelled out a couple of sentence fragments and the following day it wrote some more and this time it picked up a little speed and the handwriting looked a little more normal, and so on and so forth, on and on from there.

And that was how I got drawn into that other, parallel world.

I was still in my apartment, sitting at the kitchen table, at my desk, on my bed. I was there, but at the same time I was somewhere else. It wasn't a concrete place with a landscape and details, it was a blank white sort of place, something like a sheet of paper; I could write anything I wanted on it. Nobody could have figured out where I was by looking at me through the window. They would have seen me seated at my kitchen table, pen in hand, cigarette burning in an ashtray and a glass of water on the table. But I wasn't really there. I was . . . where?

I was with Jim and we were talking.

20

It wouldn't be possible to re-create all those conversations. Now when I look at all that scribbling on all those pieces of paper I have no idea what it says. I didn't cross the *t*'s or use punctuation and the words and letters all run together because I didn't lift the pen off the paper. You can pick out a few phrases here and there—on some pages less, on some pages more, but for the most part, it's unreadable. But even if that weren't the case, it would be an insurmountable task to translate and put together all that material, like John Birkbeck trying to portray the universe. But I do remember some of the highlights, some of the events that took place in that strange interior world where I lived for a while, the second time around, with Jim Beaman.

What comes to mind immediately are the little blue dreams. I had two of them. One took place in the context of an automatic writing message. I had a book out of the library that was sitting on my coffee table. The book was about cocaine addiction. I was reading it partly because I felt, belatedly, that I needed to inform myself about what Beaman was going through when he was alive, and partly because in the writing he asked me to.

I don't know what to call him, it—that little voice I heard in my head, that invisible being I imagined on the other end of the writing. "Jim" in quotes is too sarcastic; it adds a note of

detraction I don't want to add. But if I call him Jim that con-
fuses him with the real-life Beaman and the Jim of the writing
wasn't at all the same as the real-life Beaman. And if I call him
the spirit of Jim that sounds too unearthly, too idealized and
heavenly. So I don't know what to call him. Maybe I should call
him X, the way Richard Ford calls the wife X in *The Sports-
writer*. Or maybe since that's been done I should call him Y—
call him some letter anyway, because a letter is a symbol that
represents a mystery, a component of a unit of language or a
mathematical unknown. So okay, let's call him Y.

Anyway, Y said—if by "said" you understand I mean I held a
pen in my hand and wrote it down myself, though that wasn't
how I experienced it, and how I experienced it has a kind of
reality of its own; it was like a dream and like most dreams,
when you try to describe it in the clear bright rational daylight
of the next morning, it doesn't make much sense—Y "said":
"Would you do me a favor? Would you get some books about
cocaine and read them and tell me what they say?" And so I
did: I went to the library and took out a book about cocaine
addiction, so the spirit of my dead boyfriend could find out
about it. The book was resting on my coffee table, and one
night while I was sitting at the kitchen table writing my messy,
illegible, unreadable-to-anyone-but-me messages, which I
thought came from Jim, he, Y, said, "I'll try to show you how
I'm sick in a dream." We had been "talking" about how *I* was
sick. Most of what went on between us took place silently; it
wasn't like I sat there and wrote down those messages from
Jim—from Y—then replied to them out loud, as if he could
only hear with his ears. He didn't even *have* ears. I took it
for granted that he could communicate telepathically; that's
what people do in that strange, interior world where I was living then. I also believed he knew what was in my mind,
whether or not I intended to pass it along, and that made me

very self-conscious. Maybe if you trust someone perfectly or there's nothing you're ashamed of it wouldn't be a problem, but neither was the case for me, and sometimes I would freak out at the idea that he had access to whatever was in my mind and I would picture gross, weird, embarrassing things simply because I *didn't* want him to see them. I was doing it the night I had the dream and we were talking and joking about how sick I was, and then Y said, "If you take a nap, I'll try to show you in a dream how *I'm* sick." And so I went and lay down on my bed and took a twenty-minute nap, and something woke me up: a knocking, a tapping in a dream, and the tapping was the sound of a finger pointing at something, and what it was pointing at was the book about cocaine addiction on my coffee table. All in a little blue dream with the fizzy crackly feeling of fluorescent light. The fizziness of that dream didn't feel very good; it gave me a slightly unpleasant sensation, like a tiny, low-level shock.

I still remember waking up with that sound of tapping in my head, lying on the bed for a few seconds remembering what Y had said—I'll show you how I'm sick in a dream—registering what the dream must have meant. Then I jumped off the bed and ran into the kitchen and took up my pen and Y confirmed it: He didn't know how or why but he was still addicted to cocaine. He said the craving was worse than it had been when he was alive, it was like wanting something more than you've ever wanted anything and having no hope of getting it. I tried to figure out ways to help him and he tried to figure out ways I *could* help him, but we couldn't come up with any.

Whenever I tell people the story of what happened to me after Jim's death—the automatic writing and all that—their eyes sort of glaze over when I get to this part, as if cocaine addiction after death is impossible to conceive of, even for believers. I know how they feel. I don't know what to make of it either. Somehow it just doesn't seem possible that dead people would continue to have such problems. But Y—the dead Jim

Beaman I was in touch with—*did* have problems; he was addicted and sad and vulnerable, he was ashamed of having been a drug addict, he needed help from me. But maybe that was just the way I wanted him to be.

I'm sitting here at my desk with the two large shoe boxes filled with automatic writing on the table beside me. There are three spiral notebooks of it as well, which I dug up recently out of a file cabinet. I've been sitting here for days. I'm stuck, I can't figure out how to write about the automatic writing. Every time I open one of the boxes or flip through one of the notebooks and stare at the squiggles on all those pages, every time I try to paraphrase some of what I remember Y saying, a kind of malaise comes over me, I feel slightly queasy, I want to fall asleep. I just cannot seem to find the right way to approach it. Part of the problem, I'm sure, is that I'm ashamed of it. It isn't easy to admit that you spent days, weeks, months in your apartment talking to your dead boyfriend, not about anything important but just about this and that, asking him questions in your head and writing the answers with your own hand. It's even harder when you can't quite bring yourself to discount the whole experience, even now—can't quite make yourself say it was all just crazy, all just in your head, you made up every bit of it out of need and grief and unresolved feelings, you weren't really talking to anybody dead. And it's especially hard to say *what* was said: It's one thing to talk about doing it in the abstract; in the abstract it can exist in a way that's ambiguous, metaphysical. But when it comes right down to pinpointing exactly what your dead boyfriend said—he said this, he said that—it shrinks to something small and literal, something less than it was, like an organism that needs to live in water exposed and shriveled in the air.

But the problem I have with the writing goes beyond even

that. It's almost as if I'm afraid of it. Whenever I'm about to open one of the boxes I feel as if something scary might come rushing out, some ugly spider that's been hiding in there all this time the way spiders hide in dusty corners, musty boxes, unopened things. Or maybe what I'm really scared of is of getting it all back—of having a little piece of that time, those ideas, that state of mind come swooping up out of the box and land in my head, take root in my consciousness once again.

But what comes rushing out at me when I open the box and look inside, try to puzzle out some of the squiggles, is neither of those things. What I see so rawly, so painfully, what radiates off the pages, making me want to close the box and put it back in the closet and forget about it, maybe even throw it away for good, is the pain of Beaman's death.

It makes me feel a little sick, all that pain.

21

Recently I tried as an experiment to do automatic writing. I held a black ballpoint pen loosely in my hand, the point resting lightly against a piece of paper. I felt a little apprehensive at the thought that it might work—the pen might acquire energy of its own and start moving across the paper—but that didn't happen and I didn't really expect it to. I've changed a lot since those days when I sat at my kitchen table talking endlessly to Y; I'm in a whole different state of mind than I was back then, and state of mind seems to have been an important factor in having it work. I think partly it *was* a matter of what I expected to happen when I held the pen over the paper. It was my expectation, my willingness, my desire that made the writing possible. And it was something else too: a kind of opening inside my head, a subtle shift in consciousness, a small but definite movement from one mental place to another that occurred whenever I picked up the pen.

I'm not in that place anymore, the place in which it was possible, even natural to do automatic writing. I'm not even close to it. I couldn't go there if I tried.

I remember one night when I was doing automatic writing in bed. I had pajamas on and I was sitting under the covers. In the past I would have been reading, but this time I was writing. Only it wasn't just that I was writing. It was like I was having a conversation, but the conversation was silent and it was between me and the pen moving across the paper. Except that it wasn't between me and an inanimate object, two inanimate objects, a pen and a piece of paper. It was between me and an invisible being and the invisible being was Y, the dead-guy version of Jim Beaman. I was no more aware of the pen and the paper than I was of the matches I was using to light my cigarettes. And it wasn't like I was making up what was being said; at least, if I was I didn't know I was making it up. Because when I asked questions and the pen wrote down the answers, those answers surprised me. I was totally, completely absorbed in what was being said.

So there I was sitting on my bed in my pajamas, talking to an invisible dead guy. We weren't talking about anything special, just sort of yacking about this and that. Then I looked up out the back window of my apartment—the window I once saw Beaman through, wearing a long-sleeved shirt—I glanced out that window and saw a blinking light out there. I said to Y, in my head, "Oh no! What's that? Extraterrestrials? I hope not. Because that's where I draw the line."

I was thinking of being beamed up onto spaceships, anal probes, all that.

"It's Martians," the automatic writing said. Then it said, "Only joking. It's a police car on Iowa Avenue."

And sure enough, that's what it must've been. I never actually verified it, but it made sense, once Y said it; the light I saw was a flashing blue light and from that window, through the alleyway and between two houses, you can see a piece of Iowa Avenue. But I didn't know that until then, didn't make the connection, when I looked out the back window of my apartment, that Iowa Avenue was what I was seeing.

That was early on, when the writing made me really happy, when the messages were at their best. I remember walking downtown during that time and running into an acquaintance, a woman who was the librarian at the Office of the State

Archaeologist. I remember stopping on the pedestrian mall and having a little chat with her, feeling so happy, bursting with a secret, with knowing that even though I might look alone I really wasn't, my dead boyfriend was with me. When I got home I would talk to him.

Another time, also taking place on my bed. It was late at night, I had been writing and writing, which is to say, talking and talking, for hours, with Y. I said there was no good word for the state he was in because he didn't seem "dead" and he said, "Let me think about it for a minute." The automatic writing stopped and then came back after a couple of minutes and he, Y, said, "How about 'undressed'?"

"The soul steps out of the body like a set of clothes," I had read in some boojie book, and "undressed" pleased me as a word for dead, the way "rolling around" had pleased me as an expression for sex back when it was still possible to have sex, when life was still normal and it wasn't necessary to sit around trying to come up with acceptable ways to conceive of death. But I liked the word "undressed." It was neutral and kind of elegant, without connotations of gore or nothingness or pious religiosity or vague, fake-profound mysticism. It had no connotations at all. So after that, whenever anything came up in the writing about being dead that's what we said—"undressed."

It might have been the same night or another night—all those nights blend together in my head—that Y said, "I am always with you in a way you wouldn't understand." And once I asked him, "Are you what is known as earthbound?"—"earthbound" is an occult word for spirits stuck to the earth, who can't make it into the light—and he said, "No, I'm Marybound."

Another time he said, "Death is like hypnosis only you can't stop." And one night, when I was sitting at my kitchen table he said, "I don't know how to work."

"What do you mean?" I said.

The Rooms of Heaven

He said it was hard to explain. It wasn't the kind of work we do in this world, laying bricks or pounding nails or designing computer programs or writing books. Though the latter two, designing computer programs and writing books, were closer than the other things. He said that I *did* know how to work— he'd been told so in the other world—and from that I drew the conclusion that he was talking about psychological work, work you do with your mind, at any rate. When I was reading all my boojie books I read something that used the word "work" in a similar way. It was in one of those books containing messages channeled by spirits; there was a part where the spirits were showing the living people how work gets done on the spirit plane; it was all a matter of using your thoughts to make something, the way you'd create a mental picture with your imagination. Except that it wasn't just in your imagination. Once I said to Y, "So, thoughts are like things?" And he said, "No. Thoughts *are* things." Which I had also read in boojie books.

Anyway, Y didn't know how to work. Part of the problem was, he hadn't learned how to work during his life—instead he mostly checked out on alcohol and drugs—and part of the problem was, a lot of his mental energy was still being taken up with craving cocaine. This was right around the time when Y said, I'll try to show you how I'm sick in a dream, and the finger tapping on the library book about cocaine addiction woke me up from a little blue dream. In fact, it might have been that dream that brought on the whole I-can't-work conversation. Not being able to work appeared to be fairly devastating in the world he was in; he was more or less paralyzed, and it caused him a lot of pain. So I tried to show him how I worked. I did it by forming pictures in my mind that he could see and then changing them.

It seems to me now that this was the pinnacle of the automatic writing. I felt sharp, the messages were clear, Y seemed real and very much there. I was able to concentrate for unlimited periods and my concentration had a different, somewhat improved quality than it had had earlier, as if a lens in my mind had been adjusted slightly, focusing the picture. I was extraordinarily attuned to Y, or so it seemed to me. In addition to the writing we found new ways to communicate. There was the dream, in which Y managed to tell me something while I was asleep. And I started smelling odors and tasting tastes and having other bodily sensations as part of the communication. Once, for example, when Y was talking about craving cocaine I tasted novocaine, bitter and numbing on the back of my tongue, and Y said, "That's the closest to cocaine you can come because you've never done it but you have had novocaine."

It was right after this time that things started getting weird, and it seems to me that the weirdness grew out of that very focus and clarity, that improved ability to concentrate. It was as if I was narrowing my view, my focus, down and down and down and finally it got so small it slipped through a crack in the door, through the keyhole into another room. And it wasn't a good room, either.

Not that things weren't already weird, of course. All along, it was an odd thing to be doing—sitting at your kitchen table, talking to your dead boyfriend—a thing without context or precedent, a thing you couldn't go out and tell people you were doing. And maybe that in itself constitutes a kind of insanity, a precondition to insanity, at least. But so far, up until then, there was a logic, a reasonableness to the messages. The whole experience didn't necessarily sound crazy if you were predisposed to believing in boojie stuff; I can report what the writing said without feeling overly embarrassed. Still, that thing was happening in my head, that thing that had to happen in order for the writing to come. Some little muscle in my mind was stretching, opening up; I had to go—not exactly inside myself, but to some other mental place or state in order to receive the writing.

And that in itself was a little bit weird.

One day I picked up the pen and the energy seemed different, and when the writing came it was smaller and more cramped. I said, "Who is this? Is this Jim?" And the writing said—I actually found this on a piece of paper among those piles of squiggle-covered pages—"Just a spirit who wants to talk to a woman who talks to spirits like equals." I was horrified; I felt the way you'd feel if a spider opened its mouth and said something to you from a corner of the room. But I was also intrigued. I wanted to know what this spirit had to say. So I talked to him. He said his name was Robert and he had known me in a past life. He said I had been married to Jim then but Jim had been killed in World War I. I'd gone on to marry someone else I didn't love—a guy I'd dated in this life as well; I didn't love him this time around, either. I'd been a housewife the other time and had many children, had wanted to write but couldn't and shot myself in the end, leaving behind all those kids.

I have a feeling that when I was talking to Robert, the place that was opening in my head, letting in the writing, was opening wider. I was no longer just receiving messages from my dead boyfriend, I was in contact with an unknown quantity. If I had just stuck with Jim, I think I might have been okay. Maybe it wouldn't have been normal, me sitting at my kitchen table day after day, holding silent conversations with my dead boyfriend. Eventually I would have had to quit and return to normal life again. But I think if it had only been Jim I probably wouldn't have gotten so crazy. Or maybe it was the presence of other spirits—Robert, and then some others—their showing up that was the signpost, the indicator that I was going crazy.

Somehow, I became afraid of Robert. I got the idea that he was a malevolent spirit, not just some neutral guy who had known me in a past life and wanted to talk to me because I talked to spirits like equals. I don't know how the idea came to me, but once it arrived I grabbed it and ran. That was easy to do in the world I was in then, where thoughts grew out of silent conversations with the invisible dead, where there were no boundaries, no limits, where there was nothing to tell you, This is happening but this isn't, this is all just some goofy thing you're coming up with yourself. Any idea you had could be real; it turned real, took on weight and reality, grew and changed and evolved all on its own, just because you had it. Because there was nothing to tell you it was all in your imagination, it was all a crock of shit.

I think more than anything it was that absence of any standard of measurement, of any way to distinguish between real, legitimate psychic experiences and what was merely coming out of me and my unconscious, that caused me, allowed me, to go off the deep end.

I became actively afraid of Robert. I thought Robert was in my house—at one point I looked over at my closet and thought I saw a flash of light and I thought that was Robert, making that happen. I was very very spooked. I didn't really think Robert could do anything to me, he was just a spirit after all, he had no physical powers, but I didn't like the idea of him hanging around my house. Then I got the idea that if I fell asleep, that would give Robert an opening, an entryway to do something harmful to me, so I stayed awake all night. I sat up in bed with the light on all night long writing messages from Jim. Jim was afraid of Robert too. We were both terrified of Robert, the way we'd been scared of those imaginary guys from Muscatine who were ripping people off back when Jim was alive.

The Rooms of Heaven

In the end, Jim got rid of Robert. I stood outside the house while Jim dealt in some way with Robert and Robert went away and I forgot about him. I forgot about him and went on to the next weird thing.

All this time I was attending a suicide survivors group at the Crisis Center. I didn't get much out of the meetings because at that point I wasn't really grieving, but I didn't act inappropriately either. You had to tell your story as part of the healing process and I did; I remember sitting in a gray chair in the dingy little room where we met, telling the other suicide survivors every detail I could remember about the events leading up to Jim's death. The other people in the group told their stories too. There was a woman who had four sons and one of them, an eighteen-year-old, had killed himself—went down to the basement one evening and shot himself with a revolver. The mother found him with his mouth open and one of his eyes popping out of his head, blood dripping all over the place. It was a terrible image, and the story of what led up to the suicide was a terrible story: Some older man had taken him on an outing and given him wine and made him drunk and then raped him. The family reported it to the police and the man was arrested but he was quickly released. In the meantime, the kid's fellow students had found out about the rape and were calling the boy a fag and stuff like that. When the kid found out how easily the rapist had gotten off he threw a brick through the rapist's car window and then he was arrested and spent longer in jail than the rapist had. The kid wrote letters to his congressman, the whole family took actions to try to get justice, but there was no justice to be had and so the kid went down to the basement and shot himself. And the thing is, he was the most beautiful boy in the world. His mother talked about how smart and funny and special he was and she showed me a picture of him and you could tell it was true. The picture showed him grinning and leaning against a tree, arms folded, hank of blond hair falling over his forehead, intelligent blue eyes smiling straight into the camera. His name was Rex, and he became part of my weirdness—my boojie freak-out—too.

But before I get to Rex, I want to talk about Emmett. Emmett was another spirit who found his way into my boojie freak-out, my crazy pie, as a friend of mine calls it. I can't remember when or how I first encountered Emmett. He just sort of came to me, one day as I was sitting at my desk doing automatic writing. Emmett was a bumbling, absentminded, bureaucratic spirit; he was the sort of spirit who would shamble around in a seedy cardigan sweater. But he was also powerful, way up there in the hierarchy of spirits. I think I got the idea for him from the movie *Made in Heaven*, which I watched with Kathy in North Carolina. In the movie Timothy Hutton drowns and goes to heaven and falls in love with a woman who reincarnates and Timothy Hutton follows her back to earth. God is the only one who gets to smoke in heaven and God's name is Emmett. Emmett is a very flawed and human God in the movie, and Emmett in my boojie freak-out was very flawed and human too. No exalted, perfect Gods for me. I think by the time Emmett came along I was running pretty much on imagination; the opening in my mind had opened so wide just about anything could get in and out, there was no thought too strange, too wacky for me to come up with and then believe. So for a while, instead of talking to Jim I talked to Emmett. Emmett was sad, a little muddled, he could never find his glasses, and he told me things about the way the natural order worked. Miracles, Emmett said, came in twos. If one miracle happened, another one had to happen too, otherwise the proper order of things would get confused. In fact, everything came in twos, for every one thing that took place there had to be another to balance it out. If something good occurred somewhere in the world, something bad had to happen somewhere else. It was partly Emmett's job to keep track of it all, to make the whole system of checks and balances work, which made him very anxious, very nervous. And furthermore, now that I knew about it, the situation was even more precarious. Because when it was just Emmett doing it, everything pretty much ran along on its own steam, but now that I, with my clunky conscious mind and my fears, had been brought into the picture, we had to be extra careful. It was partly the fear of fucking up the natural order that got me into trouble in the end.

I'm not sure whether Rex or Emmett came first. I have a feeling it was Rex, because there was something more plausible about the psychic experiences I had involving Rex. He was closer to the earth, to reality, whereas Emmett was vaguer, more a product of fantasy, of me getting farther and farther out in space.

Rex's mother used to give me a ride home from the suicide survivors meeting, and a few times afterward we went to a bar called the Mill or had peppermint tea at my house. She was in tremendous pain—not for her the relief of escaping through a doorway into the other world—and I wanted very much to help her. So I told her about the automatic writing. I said I knew Jim was nearby and fine and I was sure Rex was, too, and it made me feel a lot better to do automatic writing. She said she was willing to try it. So we sat at my kitchen table and she picked up a pen and after a minute the pen started moving very slowly along the paper. Earlier she'd been talking about how she had a feeling that Rex was mad at her for some reason, and the pen wrote, "I'm not angry I'm happy." Then it said, "Let me go," and then it stopped. She asked it—him—whether he knew Jim Beaman and he said, "Yes. We are friends." And he said, about me: "She has nice hair." The mother said that sounded like him; he had a girlfriend with blond hair and he liked blondes.

I remember feeling it was a little hard-hearted of Rex to say, Let me go. It was my worst fear that Jim would say that to me. Every book I read about life after death had that phrase in it, the spirit saying, Let me go or the living person saying, I knew I had to let him go. And for that matter, books about grieving, advice for widows, self-help books for suicide survivors are full of it too: this idea that you have to, sooner or later and preferably sooner, if you know what's good for you—good for them, the dead people, too—let them go. I didn't want to let Jim Beaman go, and I didn't want him to want me to let him go. And he never did give me any indication, this invisible dead boyfriend of mine, that he wanted to be let go. But Rex said that to his mom right off the bat. I remember sitting there watching the pen move, ever so slowly, across the paper, large shaky letters forming: Let me go. I felt sorry for her to have gotten that message and I felt a little self-satisfied, a little luckier, more loved than she; after she was finished with her messages from Rex I got some from Jim and his seemed to me much friendlier. But it didn't appear to bother her much, she didn't seem as hung up on whether Rex wanted to be let go as I was with Jim. Her pain seemed more generalized than mine, more unassuageable. I had the feeling there was nothing Rex could have said that would have made her feel any worse or better. I didn't really understand that either, didn't understand why the automatic writing, the thought of Rex hanging around nearby, invisible but present, didn't help her as much as it helped me. But now I think what she was going through was probably a lot more normal than what I was going through, if there is such a thing as a normal way to be. She was grieving, she was here in this world dealing with what had happened. Whereas in some gradual way I wasn't aware of, I was breaking down, being reduced to molecules, atoms, being reassembled piece by piece in some lighter, airier, happier place.

I thought and thought about those messages from Rex. I thought about them for days, in the particular way I thought about boojie things then: grasped ahold of them, analyzed them, tried to figure out what they meant. More than anything I wanted to know what it was like where Beaman was. And I was very, very interested in the fact that Rex had said that he and Jim were friends. I kept thinking about what that meant, what did they do together, what was life like when you were dead? I had read in some boojie book a channeled account of some little dead boy playing with other dead children, being happy, having fun, and I'd mentioned that to Rex's mom when she was visiting me. She said, "Yes, I'm sure Rex is up on some cloud having the time of his life." But that didn't seem to make her happy. It didn't make me happy, either, though probably for a different reason: I didn't want to think life after death was like that, sweet angelic spirits sitting on clouds, and other clichés. But I couldn't imagine what else it was, either. Every now and then Y would give me a hint—once he told me about meeting some other guy who'd committed suicide, running into him in a swimming pool in some celestial gym—but there was something about those details that didn't ring true to me and I always felt uneasy with them. I felt the same way whenever I tried to picture Jim in the afterlife, when I tried to picture Y himself—where was he in the room? Was he opposite me at the table, sitting beside me on the bed? I couldn't get over the feeling there was something wrong with that kind of thinking, but I couldn't figure out what, and I couldn't figure out what to think instead. I kept having the feeling that there was some mystery at the heart of the whole thing, something I could almost but not quite get.

It was that mystery and my constant straining after it, straining after Jim, anyway, and the place, the state, he was in, that kept pulling me along. And part of the straining was that whenever I was given one little detail I'd take it like a ball and run. Rex became one of those details. He, I knew, was friends with Jim, and pretty soon I thought he and Jim were living together on the other side, they were roommates and would continue to be roommates until I came along and Jim and I could be together again—until I died, in other words. All of which seems totally silly now, too embarrassing even to admit. Even at the time I knew there was something wrong with it; it was too literal, too something else—that thing at the heart of the mystery.

One day, when I was taking a nap, I had a little vision concerning Rex. I was lying on my back, three quarters of the way asleep, and I had a dream that someone who was sort of Rex and sort of Jesus Christ came and hovered above me. He had been raped—sodomized—this visitor, when he was alive. I could feel the sadness and humiliation of that, I could even feel the physical pain of it—literally, my rectum hurt—and I was given, in a certain way I can't describe, the information that this was Rex but it was also Jesus and also every gay man who was dying or had died of AIDS, that all gay men in some way had a little bit of Jesus Christ in them. Then I woke up.

I don't know what to make of this now, don't know what it means. But I do know it happened. I know it in a way I don't actually *know* I did the automatic writing, because there's a chance I could have been making that up, tailoring it to what I wanted to believe. But I know I didn't make up that dream. I don't think it's possible to make up a dream.

Again, I took that dream about Rex, about Christ, about all gay men and ran with it. I started thinking that in some cosmic, larger-than-life, spiritual way, Rex was linked with Jesus Christ. I thought there was even symbolism in his name, Rex, that he ended up with that name because Rex means "king," as in King of the Jews. I had read in some channeled book what I think of now as the bathtub theory of reincarnation. The spirit in the book said there isn't actually reincarnation, wherein a whole spirit steps into a new body, then leaves that body behind and steps into another whole body in another life. It's more complicated than that. It's like whenever somebody dies all their experiences and attributes go into a big bathtub and whenever a baby is born, their soul gets a dipperful of water from the bathtub. They could end up with a whole lot of one person and a little bit of some others, or they could end up with a single drop from a million people or nearly all of their water from one person. Jesus and Mary and Joseph and Pontius Pilate are in the bathtub along with everybody else, so it's possible for one person or a bunch of people to have a little bit of any one of them. And so I thought Rex had a bunch of Jesus Christ in him. Then it came to me that I probably had at least a few drops of the Virgin Mary. I didn't know who Jim Beaman had water from. I thought maybe it was Judas.

My thinking, my fantasies, my whatever just went on from there. There were no limits in the world I was in. You could be Jesus and the Virgin Mary and yourself all rolled into one, invisible people could talk to you, anything you came in contact with could be symbolic of something else. Songs had messages about the future; photographs could tell you about your role in the universe. I remember poring over a series of pictures of Jim Beaman, having insights—what I thought were insights—about his past lives. There was one picture in which he looked kind of green and sick and his head was tilted strangely to one side and I thought that depicted a lifetime in which he was hung for being a thief or a murderer. And there was another that showed him standing in a living room with Peggy, his old roommate, dressed up in a suit and looking very wholesome, and I thought that was about a life in which he and Peggy were married and he was a minister. That would have been typical of Beaman, to have been a murderer in one life and a minister in another. He was like both in this life, plus a lot of other things; he was everything you could imagine all rolled into one, and back then—during my boojie freak-out—I thought that was because his past lives bled through into this life more than other people's do.

But my insights weren't confined to Beaman. I remember listening to "What's Going On" by Marvin Gaye and thinking it was not just an old song about the Vietnam War, it was about AIDS and drug abuse and suicide and the ruin of the environment, and that one of the mothers crying in the song was Rex's mother, and that Rex and Jim were two of the brothers dying in the song. At some point it came to me that Rex had killed himself not only because he'd been raped but because he'd been given AIDS by the guy who raped him. I told his poor mother that when she was visiting me one afternoon, and I played the Marvin Gaye album for her and told her how all the problems in the world were going to be solved soon. Another day, in the Mill, I got messages from Rex through automatic writing and passed them along to her. Rex said that he was always with her, if she wanted to have a dream about him she should look at a picture of him every night before she went to sleep, and in general, for his sake, she should fix up his old room so it was a place he wanted to spend time in, and he also said that if she didn't quit smoking she was going to be where he was soon. I thought I was going to be where he was soon—reunited with Jim—whether I quit smoking or not, and I was looking forward to it. I might have passed that along to her too. I can't remember whether I did or not but I probably did; I wasn't holding anything back. I lost contact with her after the suicide survivors group ended, she never called me and I never called her, and maybe it had nothing to do with all those things I said about Rex and Beaman living together in heaven and Marvin Gaye songs being about solutions to world problems and Rex having AIDS, but part of me can't get over the suspicion that it did. I cringe when I think of those times in the Mill, at my house, me blissfully doing automatic writing, saying the things I said, completely unaware that something was going wrong inside my head. There were very few people I told what I was thinking then, and I squirm whenever I remember telling the people I did. One of them was my next-door neighbor, Martha, a graduate student in the English department at the University of Iowa.

One night I woke up in the night and I didn't even have to reach for the pen and paper, I could hear the voice inside my head. The quality of the voice was subtly different from the voice of Y as I heard it—felt it—in the automatic writing or even the voice of Robert or Emmett. It was closer to some place inside me and at the same time more impersonal, and it wasn't entirely friendly, either; there was something unpleasant about it that wasn't so much attached to what it said as to a feeling that seemed to mingle with it, as if the feeling was part of the voice and the voice was part of the feeling. Also, it wouldn't stop talking; I couldn't shut it up. Some of what it said was just basic commentary: I was walking along the sidewalk one day and the voice said, "There's John," and I looked around and saw John Birkbeck, my friend who had the lucid dream about Beaman, on the opposite side of the street. But the voice said a lot of other things as well, mostly predictions; at one point, I remember, it made a list of bad things that would happen to my friends: Such-and-such was going to die of cancer and so-and-so's husband was going to be killed in a car crash and so forth. I got scared and stopped doing any automatic writing for six days and the voice went away. But I couldn't leave it alone, couldn't give up on the idea of making contact with Jim. One day I thought, I'll just try to get one little message from him, and I picked up the pen and held it to the paper.

22

The night before I got committed I did my laundry but I didn't fold it; I left it lying all over the couch. I went to a bar named Jirsa's with Martha, my next-door neighbor, and a friend of hers, a male graduate student.

Jirsa's is a little bar on First Avenue, on the east side of town. It's in a strip mall next to a laundromat and not many people know about it, so it isn't very smoky or crowded. Martha and I used to say there was something special about the air in there, it was strangely clean and pleasant—almost crackly; we thought it must be filtered through an ionizer or something. The winter before Jim and I got together, she and I used to do our laundry in the laundromat and play pool in Jirsa's while our clothes were in the dryer. Then she went to California for the summer and I met Jim.

Martha had an old blue Chevy truck, which she left in our driveway while she was away during the summer. She gave me the keys and told me to use it whenever I wanted, but I almost never did. It was almost impossible to drive; it didn't have power steering and it was hard to shift; you were supposed to double clutch it but I didn't know what that meant so I just jammed it into gear the best I could. Jim was even worse at it than I was. He saw driving it as a kind of challenge, something he should be good at because he was a man. He took it once or twice to the grocery store in August, and he drove it to the airport the day Martha came back from California. We were supposed to take his truck but at the last minute its water pump blew so we ended up going in Martha's vehicle instead. Jim was in a bad mood because of the water pump and was having a bad day in general, and on the way to the airport he stopped and bought a sixpack. I think he was nervous about meeting Martha, wanting to make a good impression because she was my friend and at the same time getting geared up for the fact they probably wouldn't get along. She was a feminist, politically correct and unbending in what she considered right and wrong. And Beaman was, if not exactly politically conservative, at the very least quirky; he liked to make up his mind on each issue, he didn't think liberal views were any more correct than any other views, and he liked to shock people, especially if he thought they had an ax to grind. Anyway, I think all that made him apprehensive about meeting Martha. Also, I suspect, though it didn't occur to me at the time, he was afraid she'd take one look at him and see something about him he thought I didn't see—that he was an alcoholic, a drug abuser, someone who wasn't worthy of me who I shouldn't be going out with. I think he was afraid she'd know that about him and tell me and then I would know it about him too. But instead of making him act on his best behavior, all those fears brought out the worst in him and he behaved just the way he was probably afraid Martha would see him as being.

We had some time before Martha's flight arrived and he drove past the airport, then took a right onto a smaller road, parked the truck on a turn-off and drank three beers in rapid succession, one after the other, the way people who are addicted to alcohol drink. At one point a police car came along and Jim grabbed me and started kissing me, not because he loved me but because he had an idea the cop would stop and hassle us for being there without a good reason, and if we were kissing that would be a good reason; as soon as the cop car drove past he straightened up and turned to face the windshield. When Martha's plane finally arrived she was in a bad mood. Her flight had been delayed for four hours, she hadn't eaten and she was exhausted, and she wasn't the sort of person to pander to men in any case, let alone alcoholic men. So the night was perfectly set up for disaster. When I introduced them at the gate, Jim smiled, held out his hand, and said, "I'm wearing my Oliver North belt buckle, I hope we can agree to disagree." I think he was trying to be charming, to diffuse potential tension around their differences, but Martha just glared at him and said nothing. Jim insisted on driving and then got lost, and Martha got mad and made him pull over so she could drive, and they argued and finally Jim insulted her. The three of us were squeezed into the cab of the truck and he said something about the stick shift between her legs.

After that Jim and Martha hated each other and Martha and I stopped hanging around together. I was in denial about Jim's problems and it was painful to me to be around someone who was in the opposite of denial about him. Martha probably felt abandoned and concerned about whether Beaman was an appropriate partner for me. I don't think she knew he was an alcoholic and God knows I didn't tell her about his drug problem, but I'm sure she must've picked up some clues that all was far from right with him, with us. After he died I made some overtures to be friends with her again but I was too preoccupied to do much normal socializing. At one point she started a bridge club and invited me over to play bridge with her and some other graduate students, but I just wasn't in a state of mind where I could sit around making small talk and laughing at jokes and learning a complicated card game and caring whether or not I won. I was over in my apartment, smoking cigarettes, reading books about life after death, talking to my dead boyfriend.

I can't remember why I went to Jirsa's with Martha and her friend the night before I got committed to the psych ward—to the bin, as I always think of it. Maybe we were doing our laundry next door and she invited her friend to join us, or maybe he was doing his laundry too, or maybe I had done my laundry earlier and gone to Jirsa's with them afterward. All I know is that that night I did my laundry but I didn't fold it, and I was at Jirsa's with Martha and her friend.

I remember I was very tired. I had not been sleeping well for a few days—I actually seemed to have lost the ability to sleep. I was taking antidepressants and up until then those always guaranteed a full, deep, forgetful night's sleep. But the night before the night we went to Jirsa's, even the antidepressant didn't make me sleep. Instead I lay on my bed all night in a kind of semi-waking state. It was as if I couldn't achieve the proper brain wave for sleep, all my brain waves were jumbled together or I was on some wave that doesn't normally exist, a wave like a wire that got stretched too far and then sprang back, full of crimps and twists. In my half-waking, half-sleeping state I could hear crackly sounds like static and terrifying thoughts would come to me like information revealed by an angry, malevolent voice: You have AIDS and this is a symptom, was one thing it said. I'm a hypochondriac and AIDS is the most terrifying thing I can imagine, so it makes sense that if my brain was going haywire, the unconscious spitting out fears like a transmitter shooting out sparks, that's the fear that would come to me. But of course at the time I didn't interpret it in any way nearly so rational. I simply felt afraid. I thought it was the truth, that the voice that told me I had AIDS must know I had AIDS. But I made myself forget it, suppress it, when morning rolled around.

I remember standing around in Jirsa's while Martha was

taking her shot at pool, her friend and I talking about Beaman's suicide. The friend had a sympathetic look on his face and I remember also thinking that he looked impressed by me. Maybe that was delusional on my part or maybe it was his way of hiding what he really felt or maybe he truly was impressed by God knows what; some people are impressed by anyone who's been in the Writers' Workshop. I can't remember what I said to him but I think I behaved in a way that was normal.

It amazes me now that all that was going on in the same time period. It's as if I have two simultaneous memories, a normal memory of a normal evening, playing pool, making conversation, and a memory of all the rest—the semi-waking state, the bad thoughts and crackling voices, all the strange places I was going in my head. It's like the trip to the bar is a little window of one kind of experience, one mental state, plopped down in the middle of an entirely different mental state.

When I got home I put my purse down, took off my jacket, and went straight to the kitchen table. I picked up the pen and started writing, and the voice, the presence, the whatever that sprang to life on the other end was Y, was Jim. I hadn't been getting him much lately; I'd been getting other spirits: Emmett, the bumbling, seedy God who kept track of the checks and balances in the universe, and some other nameless spirit who told me about history and the Bible. But Jim was mostly absent. I missed him, and I was grateful when I got home from Jirsa's, sat down at my kitchen table, picked up the pen and there he was. I can't remember what we talked about, but I don't think it was anything important—just this and that, stuff about the bar, about Martha and her friend.

I stayed up all night talking, that is, writing. I wrote and wrote, covering page after page with squiggles. At some point I moved from the kitchen table to my bed, and at some point I stopped talking to the spirit of Jim and started talking to the spirit who knew about history and the Bible, who knew about everything, or so I thought—but it was a seamless transition from Jim to him; I didn't even notice. I just sat there, following the conversation from one thought to another, completely absorbed, not questioning anything—questioning is something you do in the clear, bright everyday world, the world of boundaries and edges, right and wrong, sane and crazy. It wouldn't even occur to you to question in the world where I was then. I sat on my bed all night long, smoking cigarettes, filling sheet after sheet of paper.

I'm tempted to say I don't remember what the writing was saying, but that wouldn't be true, or it would only be partly true. It isn't so much that I don't remember, it's that the quality of the memory is dim, chaotic, patchy. I remember there were a lot of lists. There was a comparison of major events in Jim's life and major events in my life: totting them up like figures on a ledger sheet. I thought—or rather I was told by a spirit, or maybe it was both; there wasn't much difference between the two at that point—I thought all the major events in our lives would balance out perfectly in terms of the suffering we'd caused others and the suffering we'd done ourselves, and I covered sheet after sheet of paper with two rows of lists, one for him, one for me. He had an affair with a married woman, I had one with a married man. Mine lasted a couple of months and hurt the wife but was insignificant to me, his lasted years and didn't matter to the husband but caused Jim tremendous pain. Then there was something else that balanced that out, some other pair of relationships in which his lasted a couple of months and was insignificant, mine lasted years and was significant, and on and on.

Jim—Y—wasn't around for this reckoning. The voice inside my head belonged to the nameless spirit who knew about everything, who'd told me earlier and would continue to tell me that night and part of the following day about history and the Bible. He said the apple in Genesis wasn't a symbol for knowledge but for shame and that was why Adam and Eve covered their nakedness after they ate it. He said shame had done more harm than anything over the centuries; it was at the bottom of all the wars and other problems. And he said that all the major disasters in history had been planned in a certain way by the gods, the higher-up spirits in heaven, to try to teach us something, to bring us to a place where human beings love each other and have a conscience. But none of it worked, and it was terrible, just terrible, when those things happened. I remember him saying, "You can't imagine what it was like for us, hearing all the Jews in Nazi concentration camps praying so desperately, crying out for help." And then the spirit drew a picture of a wall with a roll of barbed wire on top—drew it with my hand, by way of automatic writing. I remember sitting there on my couch holding the pen and the pen moving up and down on the paper, drawing the wall and then the barbed wire circles, me watching it happen, being surprised as it came out.

I had the idea—I don't remember when or how it came to me, whether it came from the nameless spirit or in some other way—that everything was going to work out. Not on a small scale, but on a large scale: There were going to be cures for AIDS and war and other problems, people were going to start believing—*knowing*—there was life after death and this would bring about a general healing of fear and shame because everyone would know that God exists and life has meaning. God was working on it all, and I had a pivotal part. There were big plans going on all around the world; in this country there was the Massachusetts plan, and the Montana plan, and the Iowa plan. My part was the Iowa plan. The Iowa plan was that God was going to prove once and for all that life was eternal. He was going to do it by bringing some people back to life, restoring them to their original bodies. One of the people he was going to bring back to life was—you guessed it—Jim Beaman.

Sometime during the night, the night I went to Jirsa's with Martha and her friend, I got the idea that the Iowa plan was going to start the following day: That is, Jim Beaman was going to come back in his body, and this was going to set in motion a kind of global cleansing and reordering, putting to rest a number of problems, misunderstandings, and this would usher in the New Age.

In the morning I pulled some clothes out of the pile of laundry on the couch and got dressed. I remember I put on a T-shirt and a pair of green shorts. I never liked those shorts. They made me feel fat because the waistband was too tight and the pale-celery color didn't look good on me either. But that morning it wasn't a problem. I didn't take a shower either and I didn't shave my legs; I hadn't shaved my legs for days and I remember looking down at them—my white legs emerging beyond the pale-celery shorts, the paper-white skin covered with brown, quarter-inch-long hairs—but for once in my life the sight didn't bother me. I had God by my side, the universe at my fingertips—what did I care about hairy legs. The truth is I did care, still, a little, which is either a testimony to how powerful those messages are about women having to look good, or a statement about the nature of mental illness—maybe you never get completely ungrounded from "reality"; all mental states simply coexist together—or both.

I thought there was a committee of people, of spirits, working on the Iowa plan, and on the committee was Rex, Beaman, me, and the nameless spirit who for lack of any other designation I will refer to as God. I thought the committee was going to be materializing at around ten A.M., and I went down to Mighty Shop and bought four packs of cigarettes, one for each of them and one for me. I bought Marlboros for Rex, Old Gold Lights 100s for Jim, which had really been his brand, Lucky

Strikes for God—who as Emmett was the only one who got to smoke in heaven—and some low-tar kind for me, whatever I was smoking at the time. I walked down Washington Street to Burlington Street and went to the store and then I walked home again and sat in my apartment getting messages.

I thought Rex and God and Beaman were going to be my new family. I thought Rex was going to stay with God in heaven—or wherever it is the dead people go—and Beaman was going to be on earth with me, but the barriers, the distinctions between heaven and earth were going to get a lot weaker, a lot less important, so it wouldn't matter where they were: They could still be my family. I would be able to be talk to Rex even though he was in heaven and I was going to get to spend some time with God every so often, just me and him sitting around visiting, and that was nice. I was happy because finally I had a normal, supportive family.

But I also thought all this happening was contingent on a series of actions that I was supposed to take, things I had to do. Not important, significant actions, actions that would alter the world in any way to make all that possible, or actions that would change my thinking, prepare me for all that big change. They were actions that had symbolic meaning—uses that I didn't understand but that I accepted because I was told—I thought I was told—that I had to do them. I thought I had to do them because if I didn't there was a chance things would not work out. Jim wouldn't come back to life, there wouldn't be a cure for AIDS, the New Age wouldn't be ushered in, even the existing natural order could go haywire. All that, I thought, was riding on whether or not I did everything God told me to.

I don't remember all the little actions God told me to do. I remember one of them involved lighting matches and blowing them out. One of them was brushing my teeth, another was combing my hair, and so forth. Then there were some others

I'm more embarrassed to admit. At one point God told me to flush my ring—my pink coral cameo engagement ring that Jim had given me—down the toilet. I was about to do it, I actually had my engagement ring off and was holding it over the water, when God said, via automatic writing—by that time I could hear the messages in my head, I didn't have to write them out but I still sometimes did—God said, "I can't believe you think we would ask you to destroy the thing you care about the most in the world." So I didn't flush my ring down the toilet. God told me to do some other things, which even I knew were crazy. I remember saying, "If anyone knew I was doing this they would think I was crazy," and God said, "Yup, you're going to have to go through that too." God told me to call Martha and tell her the house was going to blow up. So I did. When she came over God told me to empty an ashtray into the waste basket and lick it and I did. I still remember what that was like, the bitterness of the ashes, and the feeling of dismay at tasting something you know you're not supposed to taste. Martha suggested we go to her house and we did. I remember standing inside her living room near the front door getting messages without a pen and paper, just writing in the air with my finger, which I sometimes did. Martha called some friends and asked them to come over—one was the guy who'd played pool with us the previous evening, another was Jackie, my other, upstairs neighbor. We sat on Martha's back porch and I told them how important things were changing, there was going to be a new world order and all that—then I got a bunch of messages. I took them down like dictation without a pen and a paper and Martha and her friends thought I was chanting. I know that's what they thought because that's what Martha told the staff in the emergency room. In the psych ward the doctors kept saying, discussing what was wrong with me: "I understand you were chanting." "I wasn't chanting," I'd say, "I was doing automatic writing." But the doctors just shrugged and looked away. To them it's all the same. And maybe they're right, maybe it is all the same.

Martha and her friends kept trying to interrupt me but I wouldn't let them, just talked right over them, because I thought I had to hear it all out at that moment. I have no memory whatsoever of what those messages were; all I remember is that at the time I thought they were very serious and momentous, all about what needed to be done in order to change the world and bring in a new order, find a cure for AIDS and so forth. I sat there on that porch holding my index finger out, reading the messages, feeling full of significance, absolutely certain something of utmost importance was happening, while they sat there and watched me—Martha and my upstairs neighbor, Jackie, and that guy who played pool with us the previous evening and maybe one or two other people. Martha kept leaving, then coming back. I didn't know it but she was making phone calls, trying to get ahold of my therapist, who didn't answer, calling the psych ward at the hospital. The psych ward told her it takes two people in Iowa to have someone committed and they should bring me up.

I remember sitting with Martha and Jackie at a round white metal table in the courtyard outside the hospital because I refused to go in. The courtyard's surrounded by tall brick hospital buildings; the buildings are full of little windows that look down onto the courtyard and the whole scene is reminiscent of a prison or a landscape in a futuristic movie, *Fahrenheit 451* or some movie like that. There's a heliport on top of the tallest building and helicopters carrying emergency patients—couples who've had terrible car wrecks out on the highway, farmers who've had heart attacks in rural areas—fly in and land on top of the building. Maybe the helicopters carry in hearts on buckets of ice, too, and kidneys and other organs for transplants.

The courtyard has a brick floor and the tables have umbrellas over them to keep you from getting too much sun. It was cold and cloudy that day so there wasn't much sun to be protected from. I remember sitting at one of those tables with Martha and Jackie, sitting outside the hospital because I refused to go in, and hearing the sound of a helicopter overhead going *whop-whop-whop-whop*, the whole courtyard filling up like a glass with that enormous sound coming closer and closer, getting louder and louder, and in my head I asked the spirit who was talking to me, who I thought was telling me about history and what it was all about, what "they" tried to teach us with it and how the lessons failed and how terribly sad and guilty they felt about all the slaughter and pain, I said to that voice in my head, "What's that for," meaning the helicopter, and it said, "Vietnam."

I thought I was reliving some past-life moment, perhaps my own, perhaps somebody else's, everybody else's—it didn't really matter whose or whether it was a genuine past-life experience—I just thought I was connecting with history, and that God, the spirit, the godlike being, the whoever I was talking to was telling me something about it. I thought I was something like a concentration camp victim, and I thought Jackie, who was very thin and had dark hair and an infinitely sad face, was a Jew killed in a concentration camp in her last life, and I thought Martha was like the Germans who lived next door to the concentration camps who claimed to be righteous and innocent but in fact were secret collaborators: Without their silent consent the whole thing wouldn't have been able to happen.

After I'd been in the hospital for a week another patient, a young woman I talked to many times in the smoking room, said, "Yeah, when they were bringing me in I thought they were taking me to a concentration camp too." And we laughed and laughed.

But I was in a different place then, not just literally—inside versus outside the hospital—but in some other, profounder sense as well. Sitting in the smoking room, laughing with another patient, I was in a tamer, more solid, more limited world than the wild, windy world I was in while I was sitting in the courtyard, talking to that guy inside my head. In the safer, tamer world inside the psych ward a hospital is only a hospital and overtones of concentration camps are all in your imagination, but in the world I was in out in the courtyard there are no such distinctions; thoughts can be as real—*more* real—than tables, windows, hospitals; there's no such thing as crazy.

The doctor on call at the psych ward, a pretty woman with floppy blond hair, kept coming out and trying to talk me into going inside, and I kept saying, "Nope, I'm not going to. Once you go in those places they don't let you out. They did that to my mother but they're not going to do it to me." The doctor kept asking me, saying, "It'll be easier for you if you come in on your own," and I kept refusing. I felt powerful, righteous, I felt that I was acting on principle, that I was making a point. I saw the mental hospital people as my persecutors but I thought I was more powerful than they were, I did not think they could make me give in. Finally the doctor came back out with two big orderlies and they picked me up in my chair and carried me in. When they picked me up I let out an enormous scream that bellowed through the courtyard; I screamed as loud as I could. I'm sure it disturbed some of the patients in the hospital, a lot more than Kathy's metal roller skates had disturbed them all those months ago.

23

I slept in two different rooms during my stay in the psych ward. The first was a single room at the end of a long corridor. Down the hall was a man who produced an endless stream of incoherent, distressed noises: moaning and crying, murmuring, yelling. He was old and I think he had some kind of senile dementia. In the middle of the night, my first night there, I got up and tiptoed down the hall to go to the bathroom and just as I was opposite his doorway I thought I heard him say, stuck in the middle of a bunch of raving, my name: Mary Allen! I hurried back to bed without going to the bathroom.

The second room I had was down another corridor. I moved to it after I'd been in the psych ward four or five days. Someone else checked out and the nurse said I could transfer there. Three other women, all around my age, shared that room. One was a young mother with two small children who was diagnosed, as I was, with bipolar illness. Another was a woman in her early thirties with long black hair and recent slash marks on her wrists, who'd tried to kill herself over a man. And the third was a big friendly retarded girl with straight brown bangs. I didn't understand what the retarded girl was doing in the psych ward until one day she said, "At home when my roommate makes me mad I hit her—hard!" That gave me pause for a moment. But for the most part I felt safer, happier in the second room with those women. It seemed like a little haven—cleaner and more brightly lit, more normal than other parts of the ward. One of the women in the second room, the mother of two children, used to sit on her bed and read and write. Everybody else, including me, would be down in the smoking room, smoking and talking endlessly, obsessively, about the things they talked about: The woman with the long black hair and scars on her wrists would talk about the man she was in love with, and I would talk about how I wasn't crazy but I couldn't get out—Beaman's suicide was still too raw for me to talk about—and the retarded girl talked about what good friends she was with her roommate at home. But the mother of the children stayed in the room and quietly and with dignity, worked. That's what I think of when I think of that room: her, propped against a pillow on her bed across from mine, reading, writing. It was inspiring to me and I asked my upstairs neighbor, Jackie, to bring up some of my books when she visited and I asked the nurses to give me a pen and some paper and I tried to read and write, too, but I was much too distracted, so I went back down to the smoking room and sat there and smoked. But every so often in my room I'd pick up a book and read a paragraph, and I had been reminded that I did, in fact, sometimes read and write. I was starting to heal a bit, to come back up from the underworld into the normal, everyday world of lamplight, books, reading, writing.

When I think of the other room, the first room I stayed in, I think of lying there in the dark on my first night—lying there hour after hour on a sprung saggy unfamiliar mattress, the white sheets smelling of bleach. I hardly slept at all but I must've dozed at one point, because I remember startling awake in terror when someone opened the door. For a moment I thought it was another patient, some madwoman in a nighty with long gray hair come to murder me in my sleep, start my bed on fire, like Rochester's wife in *Jane Eyre*. Then I saw that it was a young man dressed in white—an orderly. He shone a flashlight on me, then went away, leaving the door open behind him. He was merely doing a routine check, but at the time I didn't know that.

I was in an odd state of mind, that first night in the psych ward. It was as if I was in two mental places simultaneously, like two quilts, one lying on top of the other, except the quilts were made of thought instead of fabric. The top quilt was the world I was in when they brought me there, the world where anything is possible and everything is meaningful, where powerful spirits can and will help you if you need it. But the top quilt was starting to get thin, acquire holes, like a cloud cover breaking up, and the other world was starting to show through underneath.

I remember walking around earlier in the day thinking my circumstances were going to change at any moment, playing ping-pong in the smoking room with another patient, laughing, bouncing the ball off the ceiling. I remember eating dinner next to a handsome white-haired seventyish man who began telling me his story the minute I sat down. It took me a while to figure out he was repeating the same phrases over and over, like a needle stuck in a groove on a record: worked on a farm in Minnesota, strong healthy man, too much drinking, manic depression, awful bad thing, twenty-three courses of shock treatment, never been the same. He had a vacant, ravaged look and I remember sitting there with tears in my eyes, giving him my full attention, though later I avoided him like everybody else did, because he was so hard to listen to, so insistent on talking. But that first night in the psych ward I found him completely engaging. I thought he was some kind of physical manifestation, some analogue, some whatever of the farmworker in *Noon Wine* by Katherine Anne Porter, that story about the Norwegian hired hand who saves a white-trash family with his hard work and industry, who plays sweet sad songs on the harmonica and turns out to be crazy, who killed a guy before and kills another guy when the guy comes to the farm to take him away, back to the nuthouse. I thought this man was that man. I didn't wonder how a person could be a character in a book. I was still in the world without boundaries, limits. I remember sitting at the table in the white institutional dining room eating meatloaf and mashed potatoes, carrots and peas, listening to that man, thinking this was all just part of a story that was being made up for me, that I was going to be rescued from it by my spirit friends at any moment, saved and proved right and those other people—the doctors, the nurses, Martha—proved wrong.

But as the night wore on, lying there in the dark in an unfamiliar bed, I was beginning to see—to consider at least—that this wasn't an accurate view of the situation. I still thought I was going to be rescued, but I was starting to get impatient. I kept saying, Okay, this has gone far enough, come and get me now. But nothing happened. Finally I dozed a little and when I woke up it was very late and silent in the hospital and I realized I wasn't going to be saved: I was really there and I was going to have to stay, I had gotten myself into this terrible situation and nobody was going to get me out, and I lay there and cried and cried.

When I fell asleep again I had a horrible dream. It was very vivid and had a crackly, staticky, too-much-electricity quality, as if there were a lot of interference coming in over the wires. In the dream there was going to be a birthday party for Jim and a roomful of people were assembled but the party was canceled. All my notes to him that had been floating up to the sky were torn to pieces by an angry, malevolent presence and came raining back down like snow or confetti. Then I saw Jim's body—small, as if in the distance—being picked up and swung from side to side by invisible beings, one at the head, one at the feet. In the background was the open furnace of the cremato-

rium—I could see the yellow spears of flame leaping and flickering—and the invisible beings swung the body back and forth
and cast it into the fire.

That was the start of my return to the everyday world—to sanity, as most people would say. I can't remember how I com-
pleted the transition. All I know is that by the end of my first
few days in the psych ward, I was back in normal reality. I don't
know what did it, either—whether it was the lithium they
made me take or simply me no longer being isolated or the
shock of being in the bin and my fear of being crazy. Whatever
it was, something closed the little door that had opened in my
brain—the door through which the automatic writing and all
that followed it came—and it has never been open again.

In a way, it was like waking up from a nap. I take a lot of
short afternoon naps and often when I wake up I feel disoriented. Then I look around the room and it all comes back—I
remember who I am, where I am, what I was thinking before I
went to sleep—and a pang of dread arrives along with those
realizations: Whatever problem or fear was weighing on me
before I dozed off leaps back into my head and I feel like, Oh
no, here it is again. And when I came to in the psych ward,
woke up in a way—though the transition was a lot more gradual and the change less dramatic—it was also like coming back
to an unpleasant reality, to a place full of misery and problems.
The main misery wasn't Beaman's death, as you might expect it
to be. I hadn't even gotten to that yet; it took me a lot longer to
wake up to that one. The main problem was being locked up in
the psych ward and the whole attendant issue of insanity.

There was a little sunporch in one corner of the ward. It was a
small room with a door that closed, windows on two walls, and

a bank of three pay telephones where patients made and received calls. If you happened to walk past while one of the phones was ringing you'd answer it, put the caller on hold and go all around the floor, into the bathroom even, asking have you seen so and so, until you found the person it was for. I remember how strange it was to pick up that phone and say, "Psych ward," like a regular person in the regular world—a nursing attendant, a receptionist in an office—forgetting for an instant, then remembering, that I, like the receiver of the call, was a patient.

I spent large parts of my first days in the ward down in the phone room talking to various people about my situation: Kathy, who was now in New York, and Patty in San Diego, and my sister in Massachusetts, and various others. Nobody could believe I was there, and neither could I. My sister and I talked about how much it mirrored our mother's fate, how terrified we'd always been of this very thing. Patty and I talked about how nobody understands automatic writing, how scary it is that you can be locked up for doing it. Kathy and I talked about how everyone claims to believe in God, even an afterlife, but if you *really* believe in it you end up in the bin.

I didn't tell any of them the whole story of what I had done to get there: telling Martha the house was going to blow up, licking the ashtray, sitting on Martha's porch "writing" in front of everyone. Already I had become ashamed of those things. I was afraid that if I described them to my friends they'd say, "Oh! You really *did* have a problem," and that would mean that everything that was being done to me now was justified, was okay. It would mean that I really was crazy. But it wasn't as if I felt that fear and then consciously withheld the information. I withheld the information from myself as well. I "forgot" it, suppressed it, and I continued to suppress it for a long time. It wasn't until very recently that I allowed myself—*made* myself—remember. Up until then, whenever anyone asked me what I did to get locked up in the bin I waved my hand and said something vague. Either that or I implied it was because I was involved with the occult, which people don't understand so they interpret what you're doing as crazy. And that wasn't just something I told people. It was what I believed myself. But it wasn't exactly that I *believed* it either, that in my mind in place of the truth was a different story. In my mind in place of the truth was a blank space.

There are few things in life more humbling than being forced to enter a mental hospital against your will. Forced to enter and then to stay there. They take away your personal items when you arrive. Your clothes, your money, your keys, your dental floss. Then gradually, after you've proved you're capable of behaving, they give them back. They gave me back my clothes on the third day; before that I had to wear green pajamas and paper slippers. They gave me back my purse, my keys, my money after I'd been in there for a week. They never gave me back my dental floss, though I can't imagine why, what they think you could possibly do to yourself with a piece of dental floss.

Once you're in you're a prisoner. There are bars on all the windows and there's a sign outside the exit, which is locked, of course—I saw the sign coming back from outings, which I was allowed to go on after five days—which says ELOPEMENT PRECAUTIONS. It seems an odd choice of words, as if escaping from the bin would be like running off and getting married.

One night we had a tornado warning. We have those a lot in Iowa. It gets very hot and still and the sky goes all green and yellow followed by tremendous thunder and lightning and rain, and some meteorologist spots a tornado funnel on a radar screen and a whistle goes off in the park and they announce it on TV and everybody gets nervous and tries to figure out what to do. In the psych ward they lined us all up and herded us downstairs into a long, wide corridor in the basement. A window was open on the landing in the stairway and I put my face up to it and breathed in deeply, sucked into my nose and mouth and lungs the fresh wet green spring air, the first fresh air I'd breathed in days. It was sweet and at the same time painful; it reminded me of the existence of a whole other world: the bright colorful specific world of houses and sidewalks and cars and trees, which it seemed as if I'd forgotten for a long time, though on some important level I'd missed it painfully.

Down in the basement it felt like an air-raid shelter, everyone crowded into a hallway, staring at each other. I was anxious and claustrophobic, and a moment came when I felt unbearably alone, unbearably abandoned. I asked if anyone had a pen and someone gave me one and I held it over the copyright page of a book I'd brought with me and it wrote a few squiggles but nothing intelligible. Later on when I got back upstairs to my room I tried again on a piece of paper and I got a message that said, No writing, and that was the last time I was ever able to do automatic writing.

Every hour and a half in the psych ward the orderlies do "checks." They circulate throughout the floor observing your behavior and noting it down on a clipboard and in the night they come into your room and shine a flashlight on you in bed. They even go around at eight o'clock every night and ask you whether you've had a bowel movement that day. It's called the "eight o'clock question." It isn't really the orderlies' fault; they let us know they didn't especially enjoy invading our privacy that way, they'd make a little face when they asked you the question. I used to say, "Yes, and if I didn't I'd lie."

There's almost nothing you can do in the psych ward just

because you want to. If you like you can stay awake all night and no one will force you to sleep, but otherwise there is no leeway: You can't go for a walk or hop in the car and drive to the store, you can't even open a window and breathe some fresh air; you can't shave your legs without supervision or light your cigarettes with your own matches or take your own vitamin C. It was the vitamin C that really got to me. I've taken 1,000 milligrams every day since 1983 and I'm convinced that if I don't I'll get a cold. After I'd been in the psych ward for a day my upstairs neighbor, Jackie, called and asked if I wanted her to bring me anything and I said my vitamin C and some other things. When she came the nurses went through the paper bag and removed the vitamins. I asked them to give them to me or at least let me take two 500-milligram pills a day, and they said, "We'll have to ask your doctor first." It took a couple of days for the doctor to get back to them and then the doctor said, "She can take *one* 500-milligram pill a day." I was furious. I felt incredibly trapped, incredibly powerless. I had fantasies about taking the vitamin C by force—breaking into the nursing station, twisting the nurse's arm, and grabbing the bottle away—but even in fantasy I knew the satisfaction wouldn't be worth the repercussions. I would be thrown into the quiet room, given more drugs, made to stay in the bin for months or years instead of weeks or days. All I could do was sit in the smoking room and smoke.

I remember lying on my bed at three in the afternoon, my second day in the psych ward, thinking that I'd stepped onto a kind of wheel, a treadmill from which it could be difficult to get off: I had been labeled mentally ill and from then on whatever I did could be interpreted that way; I'd been dragged in there once against my will and it would be even easier for me to be dragged in again, because now I had a history of mental illness. And I pictured a life in which that was the case: I didn't have to go through this once, I had to go through it over and over with no hope of getting off the treadmill. I couldn't imagine anything bleaker and I thought, for the first time in my life, if that happened to me I would almost certainly kill myself. But I knew on some level that wasn't going to happen to me; I don't know how I knew that but I did. But it *was* what happened to my mother. And lying there on my bed in the psych ward, I saw my mother in a whole new light; I understood for the first time what it must've been like, felt like, to live her life, all those years in and out of state hospitals, shock treatments, everyone discounting her because she was crazy—I saw the ways in which I had discounted her. And I thought that it was like karma, my being in the psych ward as my mother had been in psych wards. It was too late to do anything about it—my mother's been dead since 1981; I can't talk to her, can't give her sympathy now in any actual, face-to-face way, but I can still sympathize with her, I can understand what she went through. And even then, lying there trapped and miserable in the psych ward, that seemed to me a valuable thing.

Every patient in the psych ward has a staffing, which is a meeting attended by all the doctors, a handful of medical students, and for part of the meeting by you. At the staffing they decide whether you can be released or whether you should stay. If you're going to stay you have to commit yourself or be committed by a judge after a hearing. They can only keep you against your will for forty-eight hours, according to Iowa law. But my forty-eight hours didn't start until I'd been there three days. I arrived on Saturday of Memorial Day weekend and the doctors were gone except for one doctor on call and the doctors have to be there, I was told sometime over the weekend, for the forty-eight hours to count. So I had my staffing on Wednesday afternoon, when I'd been in the hospital five days. I remember sitting in a conference room under fluorescent lights next to Dr. Railsback, the head resident, a tableful of others seated opposite and to my right.

Dr. Railsback had diagnosed me: came to my bed at seven in the morning on Tuesday trailed by a retinue of medical students, woke me up and had a little conversation with me, then said he thought I had bipolar illness. That's how I remember it, at least. The strange thing is, I can't place the bed I was in. In the memory it seems to me I'm in a large room with lots of people, like the room on the ward where the nonsmokers sat around doing puzzles or watching TV, but I'm lying in a bed. It's like one of those dreams where you're sort of in one place and sort of in another, where identities are blended but it doesn't matter because that's the natural state of the dream. Try as hard as I might, I can't pull this memory up out of the lake of consciousness and see it any other way.

But I do remember the conversation, or at least I think I do. He said, "How are you feeling?" and I said, "Fine." He said, "I understand you've been depressed over a suicide," and I said, "I haven't been depressed. I've been grieving." And he said, "Oh yes, technically you're quite right. There is a difference." Then he said, "I think you're suffering from bipolar illness, also known as manic depression." I was a little relieved because I was afraid they were going to say I was schizophrenic.

At the staffing they gave me a chance to talk and I tried to explain what I thought had happened to me, how I got involved with automatic writing and so forth. I tried to say a little about the background of automatic writing, how it was really a legitimate occult practice, W. B. Yeats's wife did it and all that, but Dr. Railsback cut me off. He said, "You've been acting very rational since you've been here, maybe being here *is* doing you some good." Then they told me I could leave the room. Awhile later, Dr. Koval came out and said, "We want you to commit yourself." Dr. Koval was the resident who happened to be working the day they brought me in and was therefore assigned to be my doctor on the ward. She was a pretty young woman with puffy blond hair, probably in her middle thirties. Whenever she talked to me something stubborn and slightly frightened passed across her eyes, as if she was gearing up to defend her authority. I couldn't stand her, because of that very authority, because of the power she had over me.

I said I didn't want to commit myself, that I was good at taking care of myself and I would be fine on my own, I would do whatever it took to solve my problems, but I would be better off at home. Dr. Koval hardly listened. She just said again, "We'd like you to commit yourself," and when I refused again she said she was going to send my papers to the courthouse, which meant there would be a little trial and the judge would get to decide whether I got committed. I wasn't sure I wanted that, either. If the judge gets to commit you, as Dr. Koval informed me, you may have to stay longer than if you commit yourself, because the judge and not you determines how long you will stay. So that just seemed like another way of handing over control to an authority figure. On the other hand, if I committed myself, it seemed like giving up, admitting they were right and I was wrong, and it made me feel better to think of going to court and fighting for myself. So I said I needed time to think about it. It was 3:10 and Dr. Koval, pink with annoyance, said the messenger to take the papers to the courthouse came at 3:30 and I would have to make a decision by then. I paced the hallway, went into the phone room and tried to call my sister, Kathy, Patty for help in making the decision. Nobody was home. I felt incredibly anxious, incredibly trapped. In the end I just didn't have the nerve to put my fate in the hands of a judge. I signed the paper to commit myself, went down to the smoking room and smoked.

It was a bad moment, one of the worst of my life. Up until then I'd had hope that I could easily get out. Not hope like I'd had at the beginning that God would wave a wand and I'd be saved by some supernatural event. I'd figured out that wasn't going to happen, had transferred my hope to earthly agencies. Though I did still have a recurring fantasy that Beaman would come riding through the door on a motorcycle, stop while I jumped on, and roar away with me behind him. I was certain if he were alive he would have gotten me out somehow, though at God knows what cost to both of us, and that thought led to the thought that he wasn't alive, I had been there for him when he was in the hospital but he wasn't here for me now, at least not in any form with earthly power; he was gone, dead, I was abandoned. Not him or anyone else was going to save me from the bin. But up until the moment I signed myself in I still had hope that I could save myself—find some way to convince the doctors to let me out, contact a patient advocate and get them to help me, plead my case to Senator Tom Harkin, who was supposed to be sympathetic to mental patients' rights—at the very least hope that I would not have to stay much longer because the doctors would see that I was sane and simply let me out. But at the moment I signed the paper to commit myself I gave up. And that felt terrible, just terrible.

In the smoking room I sat in a chair and cried. A patient I was friends with, Joe, who'd been picked up by the cops for fighting and given a choice between the psych ward and jail— he had a history of suicide attempts as well—came and sat beside me and asked what was wrong. I told him and he said, "That really sucks." Another patient, Barbara, approached and asked what happened. Barbara used to bum cigarettes from me in the smoking room and sit and talk. She told me she'd been quite successful when she was younger, went to junior college, even wrote some poems and had them published. "What happened?" I asked. "I don't know," she said shrugging, "I just went schizy," and the way she said it made us laugh and laugh. Joe told Barbara they made me commit myself, and she sat down on the other side of me and patted my arm. Then Martin came along—Martin was a young guy who thought he was Jesus—and we all sat there together smoking, hating the doctors, hating our lives.

In the psych ward every minute feels like an hour, every hour like an entire day. Time drags by at an agonizingly slow pace. I was only there for eleven days in all, but it seemed like a year, a decade, an era, an infinity in which regular ways of measuring time are meaningless. My release kept getting pushed back for one reason or another. There were the three days at the beginning because I checked in on Memorial Day weekend. On Tuesday, after Dr. Railsback diagnosed me, I started taking lithium; then I had to wait 24 hours for my lithium levels to rise so they could be tested. I had the blood test on Wednesday, then I had to wait 24 hours for the results to come in. When they got the results they said my lithium levels weren't high enough so I had to take more pills and go through the whole procedure again. So that was another 48 hours, which brings us up to seven days, or 168 hours. Then there were four more days when I was simply waiting for the doctor to say I could leave. I don't know what they were waiting for at that point. When I think of all that time—all those minutes that were hours, hours that were days—I think of sitting in the smoking room, sitting there endlessly, smoking, smoking.

The smoking room was a large rectangular room with chairs lining all four walls, like chairs pushed against the walls at a dance. There was a TV at one end and a big green ping-pong table at the other. On the ceiling was a device that made a zapping sound every five minutes, like those things people have in suburban backyards that supposedly kill bugs. At first I hardly noticed it; it just seemed like a natural aspect, another slightly sinister part of the place. Then after I'd been in for five days somebody told me it was a smoke eater.

At eye level behind the ping-pong table was another device related to smoking: an electric cigarette lighter, mounted on the wall. It consisted of an iron grid and a black, pill-shaped button; you'd put the tip of your cigarette on the grid and push the button and the grid would heat up to a glow and finally get hot enough to light a cigarette, though it took awhile. There were two of them, I suppose in case two people wanted to light their cigarettes at the same time. Those cigarette lighters were old, they probably dated back to World War II, and there was something about them that resonated with gas chambers, with shock treatments and electric chairs. Nobody wanted to use them, mostly because they took so long. Usually we lit our cigarettes off each other's. The reason they kept those things on the wall, of course, was that we weren't allowed to have our own lighters or matches in case we burned the place down. Once in the smoking room an orderly handed me his matches to light my own cigarette. He did it as if it was no big deal, like he hadn't given it any thought at all, but for a strange moment I actually felt—the way I sometimes feel in department stores when someone's watching me suspiciously, that I might somehow shoplift something in spite of myself: Are you really sure you want to trust me with these things?

The orderly who gave me his matches was a guy everybody liked named Jim. I didn't get to know him till after I'd been in the bin for several days so it didn't seem like a coincidence, didn't carry any special weight or meaning that his name was Jim the way it probably would have if I'd met him when I first got in. He worked four days a week from two until midnight and would often sit and smoke with us in the smoking room before dinner. He treated everybody like equals and friends and everybody trusted him, even a patient named Madeline, who was so paranoid she would say to us, her fellow inmates, "I know you don't want to be here because I'm here." When we were sitting around before dinner smoking with Jim, Madeline would say to him, "How much longer do I have to live, Jim?" meaning how much longer before they give me shock treatments. She was terrified of shock treatments and I was with her on that one. Jim would say, "Don't worry, Madeline! You're not getting those. They're only for depression." And Madeline would shrug and look at the floor.

I remember walking down the hall with Jim on the way to dinner, him singing, "I fee-eel *good*, da, da, da, da, da, da, *da*"—that song by James Brown. I didn't feel particularly good at the moment and I doubt that he did either, though he probably didn't feel as bad as me—he hated his job, hated the psych ward, but working there wasn't the same as being there, locked up because you were crazy. But at that moment, joining him in James Brown, stepping along quickly beside him—this tall stocky white guy with a wife and a ponytail and a mortgage and a kid—I did feel, briefly, a little bit good.

All the patients in the psych ward had an easy, natural belief in life after death, an openness to spiritual notions, but none of the doctors did. If you talked to the doctors about God or souls or anything occult, anything that can't be tested and measured and comprehended with the physical senses, they frowned and looked away impatiently, and you got the feeling they were mentally noting it down, adding it to your ledger sheet of psychiatric symptoms. But in the smoking room the talk often went to spiritual matters. A woman named Harriet whose uncle had died in a motorcycle accident and whose daughter had recently died of leukemia said her dead uncle once appeared to her mother in a dream and said, "You've got to let me go." Harriet hadn't been contacted by her daughter yet but she said somebody told her, "Well, at least now you'll have somebody waiting for you on the other side when you go." My roommate with the broken heart and slashed wrists said she could sense spirits around me. Once I even asked Madeline, when she was in one of her better, more talkative moods, if she believed in life after death and she said, "Of course, everybody believes that."

One night my friend Joe and I were sitting in the smoking room, complaining our usual psych ward complaints—we used to say it's like the roach motel, you can check in but you can't check out; Joe, who'd chosen it over a night in the county jail, was on his fourth day—when we noticed the people across the room, Harriet and some others, staring at the floor. They were watching a big black ant crawl around and calling it the Wanderer, making up a whole story about it, how the Wanderer happened to stray into this place and now he was going around investigating, trying to figure out what to make of it. They were following the ant's every movement, saying, the Wanderer's crawling up the leg of the chair, now he's hesitating, he can't make up his mind what to do, he's turning around and going back down. Then somebody came along and stomped on him. Harriet was really upset, she actually started crying. I said, "Oh that's terrible, somebody stepped on the Wanderer," and Joe said, "Oh Mary, you're just as nuts as they are." Because our basic premise was that he and I weren't nuts, we were just trapped like innocent prisoners, held against our wills.

The people on the other end of the room felt really bad about the Wanderer but after a few minutes somebody said, "Well, his little spirit is rising out of his body, now he's going down a long tunnel, pretty soon he'll see a bright light," and that made everyone laugh.

There were two Jesuses in the psych ward when I was there. One of them I only saw twice, once when the orderlies brought him down to the smoking room and once through the window of the quiet room. The quiet room was a cell with padded walls and a tiny square window in the door; they put you there if you were acting out of control. I was never in the quiet room but one of my roommates was—the woman with the two young children who'd inspired me by reading and writing. She said she was in the quiet room for twenty-four hours when they brought her in, she got through it by singing and counting over and over to one thousand.

I don't know why the first Jesus had to spend all his time in the quiet room. He seemed like a mild-mannered, childlike, sweet and innocent person. No more violent than Jesus himself would have been. Whenever someone was in there two orderlies would sit outside the door, and once I went over to talk to the orderlies and saw the round moonface of that guy— that poor little Jesus—appear in the window, and then I heard him begging to get out, his voice muffled by the glass. Finally, on some other occasion, the orderlies took him down to the smoking room to have a cigarette and that was the second time I saw him. I was sitting there with some people when the orderlies brought him in. Fred, a young guy who'd flipped out on drugs, was sitting next to the door, and when the orderlies brought in Jesus they asked him if he could spare a cigarette. Fred took one out of his pack and gave it to them and Jesus grabbed his hand, raised it to his lips and kissed it. Then the orderlies whisked him back to the quiet room.

My friend Martin was the other Jesus. He thought I was the Virgin Mary; he said he could tell right away because I looked like his mother. The cops brought him in one night at two in the morning and put him in the room that Fred and Joe shared. Joe told me the next day he and Fred were scared shitless of their new roommate, who was really nuts and violent. He kept threatening them with punishment from God, saying, "My father's going to smite you if you do such and such, He'll reach out his long arm and strike you dead." I caught a glimpse of him in the hallway later that day, wearing those loose green pajamas, hair sticking out all over his head. The next time I saw him, in the smoking room a day or so later, he had on jeans and a maroon alligator shirt and his hair was neatly combed. It was the middle of the afternoon, there was almost no one down there, I felt a little wary around him. But all he did was smoke and read—the Bible, it turned out—and tap his ashes into the ashtray. Somehow, later, we got to be friendly. If I saw him at night before I went to bed he'd say, "I'll pray for you," and I'd say, "Yeah, put in a good word for me, I need all the help I can get." He'd talk about God in personal terms as if God was really his father in the normal, everyday sense, and if someone did something he didn't like he'd say, "My father will get back at him, He'll make him burn in hell forever." One day I said, "Why would God want to make people suffer in hell forever instead of giving them a chance to change and act better?" and he said, "Oh!" as if that was a groundbreaking thought. That might have been the day he decided I was the Virgin Mary. He told all the other people in the room, smiling at me proudly.

Most of us who'd been in the bin more than forty-eight hours had voluntarily committed ourselves and supposedly we were also free to let ourselves out again, but the rumor was that if you did the doctors would be waiting on the other side of the door, and the fact that you'd checked yourself out AMA—against medical advice—would be enough ammunition for them to get you committed. But Martin checked out and got away with it. One day he was sitting in the smoking room talking about doing it and the next day he was gone. Evidently nobody was standing on the other side of the door waiting to catch him like a fish in a net and bring him back in. Maybe it was just a rumor that they would, or maybe, as I sometimes suspect, the doctors were simply so fed up with Martin and his Jesus talk they let him go. Because he didn't come back and I never saw him again. Sometimes I wonder what became of him. I try to picture him out in the world, fighting the good fight, relying on God for protection. But I know he didn't last long out there, that he's probably sitting in some other psych ward, smoking and reading his Bible.

There was a rating system in the bin: Levels I through IV.

When you were at Level I you couldn't go anywhere, just had to stay inside the locked ward and do nothing, sit in the smoking room and smoke. At Level II you could leave and go to the rec room two floors below, in a group, with supervision. There were pinball machines down there and a pool table, and sometimes the recreational therapist would organize little craft events—making boxes with popsicle sticks, stuff like that. Once, down in the recreation room, I saw a guy in a green hospital uniform playing pinball and grunting, shouting when he got it wrong, rocking back and forth in front of the machine. He wasn't on our ward and I thought he was some kind of orderly and I kept saying, possibly within his hearing, to Peter, who was another friend of mine: "Why isn't he in the bin? Why isn't he in the bin?" That was my constant theme, the whole time I was there. It seemed to me that everyone was crazy, but only we were unlucky enough to get caught. Once, watching TV in the smoking room, I saw in a news report a bunch of young people with green and red mohawk haircuts, wearing goofy costumes, marching in a parade, and I said several times to whoever was sitting next to me, maybe it was Peter again, "Why aren't they in the bin?" I had the same idea about that guy playing pinball down in the rec room.

Peter had been an accountant and was taking drugs for schizophrenia. He said when he flipped out, before he got brought in, he thought he was Norman Schwartzkopf's adviser, thought he'd pushed the button by accident to drop the

atom bomb and his mother's and sister's dead bodies were outside the house in the garbage cans—he was afraid to open the
lids and look in. Once in the smoking room I said something
to Peter to the effect that I, unlike some of our fellow patients,
wasn't really crazy when they brought me in—something
resentful about being there—and Peter laughed and said, "Oh
really? You think you weren't crazy?" And then he laughed
again.

That time, down in the rec room, he and I were playing
pool. I remember standing there getting ready to take a shot,
glancing over at the guy in the hospital outfit, saying again,
"Why isn't he in the bin?" And Peter saying, "Mary. Be quiet.
He is in the bin." It turned out there was another ward, an east
wing I didn't know about with patients who were even crazier
than those of us in the west wing, and that guy was in the east
wing.

When you were designated Level III you could go on outings. I went on three or four of those, not because I especially
wanted to play miniature golf or go for a walk on a trail in the
woods but because, having been locked up for days without a
single breath of fresh air, there was nothing I wouldn't do to
get outdoors. But it was almost worse, being out in the world
but not being part of it, during those outings. What I remember most is riding in the van with the other patients, being
afraid someone I knew from the outside, the real world, would
see me there. And it didn't get any better when we arrived at
our destination. I remember playing miniature golf in the
warm, humid evening air. I remember hitting the ball with the
fake golf club and watching the ball roll along the little fake
green, trying over and over to get the ball past a turning windmill, then marking the score on a card. A young woman with
dark hair who'd had many shock treatments won the game.
Afterward we stood in line and ordered ice cream cones from
Dairy Queen.

Another outing took place earlier in the day. It was very hot and the recreational therapist drove us to a field beside a building, short grass turning brown in the sun. We were supposed to throw a Frisbee from one goalpost to another and some people did, but Peter and I didn't play. Instead we sat at a picnic table in the shade and sipped sodas. At one point we stood up to take a little walk and the recreational therapist hurried over and told us we weren't allowed to go anywhere. So we sat back down. I remember seeing some guy ride by on a Harley Davidson, wondering if it was someone who had known Jim Beaman, and I remember making snide remarks with Peter about the day and the activity and the recreational therapist, who Peter said was a real no-brainer.

On another day we went for a hike on a nature trail. I remember crossing a wooden bridge over a brook, walking along a path through the woods, sunlight filtering through the leaves, signs with pictures of local birds—red-headed woodpecker, blue jay, tufted titmouse—nailed to the trees. The scenery was pretty but I wasn't able to enjoy it; I couldn't get out of the psych ward in my head. The psych ward was a state of mind, a mental landscape; I knew I had to return there and in some way just as real as the trees, the brook, the sunlight—maybe *more* real—I'd never really left it. That was the last outing I went on. There was a trip to the mall I didn't sign up for and a couple of other things. Partly it was just too painful, going on those outings. But also I got upgraded to Level IV.

Level IV meant you could leave the hospital on your own with a pass, be gone for a couple of hours, and then come back. I had Level IV status during my last two days. By then I didn't mind being in the psych ward quite so much. Not that I ever got to like it, not that I ever came to think of the quiet room or shock treatments or involuntary commitment as good wholesome therapeutic things, but I sort of got used to the place. It came to seem ordinary in a certain way. Familiar. Everyday.

Whereas when I was first in there it seemed threatening, evil, sinister, alien. It had overtones of Buchenwald and Auschwitz, the Soviet Union, *One Flew over the Cuckoo's Nest.* I wasn't angry anymore, either, during my last few days, or maybe it wasn't so much that I wasn't angry as that I'd put my anger away. I just didn't have enough energy left to fight, even in my imagination. Also, I'd figured out that the way to get released was to stop resisting and accept the whole program, or at least act like you did. I talked politely about my illness with the doctors and nurses, took my lithium without complaining, said that I would continue to take it. The nurses were pleased with how well I was doing, the doctors said my recovery was amazing.

What I did with my pass was go home to my apartment. I took the Cambus—part of the free bus system the university offers; the psych ward was part of the university hospital complex—from the hospital to downtown, then walked the rest of the way. When I was getting ready to leave, one of the nurses asked me where I was going and when I told her she said, voice full of concern, "Do you think you'll be all right taking the bus?" That was a strange moment, a moment I never would have anticipated in my life up until then: someone seriously asking me whether I was capable of getting on a bus. Of course I can, I felt like saying, I have a master's degree! I'm an adult, I'm competent, all my life I've taken care of myself. But at the same time a tiny shred of doubt *did* pop into my head, a doubt planted, I suppose, by the nurse's anxiety, by having spent a week and a half with people taking care of me—people thinking that they *had* to take care of me; I couldn't do it myself.

But I *was* capable of taking the bus, of course. I left the hospital, my pass in my wallet, sat outside on a bench and waited for the bus and when it came I got on and sat in one of the hard plastic seats and stared out the window while the bus chugged and puffed, stopped and started down the hill to downtown.

And then I walked the rest of the way to my house. I remember letting myself in, looking around my apartment. It seemed strange and peaceful, a little shabbier, a little smaller than the way I remembered it. It was also neater than when I had left it. Someone—Martha, I found out later—had gone in and emptied the ashtrays, made the bed, gotten rid of a bunch of papers covered with automatic writing, folded the laundry I'd left all over the couch. Martha herself was gone; she'd moved away to Colorado. She was getting her Ph.D., had had a job lined up for months. I'd known she was leaving. Her leaving just happened to coincide with my being in the pysch ward, but I was sort of glad about the coincidence. I was relieved I didn't have to face her.

I stayed in my apartment for an hour. I remember sitting in the pink chair in the living room, staring at myself in the bathroom mirror, keeping an eye on the clock.

The next day they let me out and I made the same trip again, only this time I didn't have to go back.

Part Three

24

A few years ago I was having breakfast with my friend Rudy in Micky's in downtown Iowa City. Two women, a couple, were sitting near us; one of them knew Rudy and on their way out they stopped by our table. Rudy started talking to his friend, and I started talking to her friend. She said she might go to a twelve-step meeting with me and we exchanged phone numbers. She asked whether I had a work number as well as a home number and I said I didn't because I worked at home and she said, "Oh really? What do you do?" So I told her I was a writer and she asked me what I was writing and I said a memoir about a particular incident and she asked what the incident was. I didn't know how to describe it, so I said, "Well, did you ever know Jim Beaman?" The woman got an odd look on her face and said, "I only knew him in this one strange way. I was driving down his street the day he killed himself, my son was home from college and he was with me, and as we were going by Jim Beaman's house we saw his girlfriend crying on the lawn."

I was stunned.

I said, "That was me."

The woman was totally taken aback; she couldn't stop saying how awful she felt. I said it was fine; I was reminded of what happened all the time; it didn't bother me to hear her say that. And it didn't, really, but it was awfully strange. It gave me the weirdest feeling and I walked around in a kind of daze for the rest of the day. I've heard humor described as the convergence of two normally unrelated trains of thought, the collision of two opposing ideas, creating a small explosion. And that woman's comment—I saw his girlfriend crying on the lawn—was something like that for me. I couldn't get over it; every time I thought of it I felt an odd little jolt of surprise. It was like the momentary eclipse of one view by another, the convergence of two separate lines of perspective, hers and mine, a brief telescopic vision of myself through someone else's eyes during the most amazing moment of my life. "Amazing" isn't an adequate word to describe it, of course—that moment when the cop shook his head on Jim Beaman's lawn—but no other, better adjective comes to mind. There is no word to describe the pain and shock of it, but what I seem to remember when I look back isn't pain or shock but—somehow—a great white burst of energy.

But she had it wrong, that woman, she had one thing wrong, at least. When she saw me on Jim Beaman's lawn all those years ago, I wasn't crying. I was screaming. When that cop shook his head I opened my mouth and screams came out and those screams seemed like wind that merged with some wind that was all around me, wind and light like the effects of a nuclear blast, enough to light up or destroy an entire city. No wonder that woman got a funny look on her face when she remembered seeing me.

And it occurs to me now that I got something wrong, too. It wasn't me she saw on that lawn. It was, but in a way it wasn't. Because the me I am now is a very different person than the me I was then.

Somebody told me the story of Jim and me was like the myth of Orpheus and Euridice. So I went to the library and got out *Mythology* by Edith Hamilton and read about Orpheus and Euridice. They're madly in love, but right after their wedding

Euridice dies and Orpheus can't get over it. So he goes down to the world of death and appeals to the god who rules it to let her out so she can be with him again. He plays his lyre, and his music charms Pluto, the Lord of the Dead, and Pluto says, "Okay, but there's one thing. You can't look at her till you get out into the upper world. You can't look back at her as she's following you out of Hades. If you do, all will be lost." Orpheus agrees, and he finds Euridice and she's following him out of the underworld and they're almost out, almost into the daylight, and Orpheus just cannot help himself, he's simply got to make sure she's there, so he turns around and looks. And then—*poof*—she's gone, back down into the depths of Hades, never to be seen again.

Which I suppose is something like my story. Beaman dies, I go to the underworld to try to find him and maybe I do for a little while, but in the end he has to stay and I have to go back alone without him. But here's where Orpheus and I part company. He and I are both crushed, but Orpheus doesn't recover. He wanders around alone and miserable for a while and then he's torn to pieces by a band of mythological women who run through the woods frenzied from drinking wine, which I interpret to mean he dies of alcoholism. But that didn't happen to me. I didn't die, of grief or alcoholism or by any other means, though there were times I was so miserable I wished I would. But I didn't. Somehow, I ended up stronger, clearer, happier after my trip to the underworld. It wasn't apparent immediately, it was a long time before I could actually *feel* any of those things, but in the end that's what happened. And if I were to take this whole story-to-myth comparison further, I'd say that when I came back up from the underworld, I had something with me: a new pair of glasses—a new set of lenses to see the world through. These glasses are something like the rose-colored spectacles Dorothy and her crew looked at the Emerald City through. They make the world appear more real, deeper, more three-dimensional, more colorful, somehow. When I looked through the old glasses, the old perspective I used to wear, the world looked flatter, shallower, dingier, grayer. Something like a British mining town in a D. H. Lawrence novel, or Kansas before the tornado. All misery and limitations and shades of black and white and gray.

What it comes down to is what I think is possible, what I think the world—the universe, everything—is, and what I used to think they were, back before my trip to the underworld, before I met Jim Beaman. I used to think the universe was absolutely devoid of magic.

I've changed in other, practical ways too. I don't smoke cigarettes anymore. I gave those up through a long frustrating difficult process involving several go-rounds with the American Lung Association, nicotine gum, quitting, bumming cigarettes, inching my way into smoking again. Then one day I just quit altogether; I don't remember when. I didn't write it down and I don't think about it much. I just don't smoke. I don't even have the urge to smoke. It's as if it's been taken away from me, the way alcoholics in twelve-step programs talk about having their character defects taken away.

I don't get involved—enmeshed, entangled—with alcoholics and drug addicts. That sounds so bald, so psychological; it makes Jim Beaman sound like a symptom, it makes what happened between us sound like a weakness, an illness, an aberration. And I don't think of it like that. But it's true. I don't get entangled with alcoholics and drug addicts anymore. That went the same way as cigarettes, through a similar, sort of mysterious, process. I just don't do it anymore. It simply wouldn't fit with who I am. And there are other changes in me as well.

It occurs to me that some of the ways I've changed are similar to transformations in people who've had near-death experiences, those little forays into the world of death I read about in boojie books: *Life After Life* by Raymond Moody, and *Embraced by the Light* by Betty Eadie, and many others. First there were the books that chronicled the near-death experiences themselves. Then came a spate of books about the effects of near-death experiences on the people who had them. The people all had a fairly predictable set of after-effects: They believed in life after death, and they started taking care of themselves, and they were more capable of unconditional love and forgiveness, and they had a burning desire to learn more about the universe. I remember thinking that was kind of like how I've changed, except without the near-death experience.

I used to long for one of those near-death experiences, after Jim died. I'd read all those books about people having heart attacks or almost drowning or getting hit by lightning, how they hovered above their bodies, went down tunnels, saw dead loved ones, met with a being of light, had a life review. It was the meeting with dead loved ones that interested me, that and what the being of light had to say. I remember in one account it laughed—when a woman said she had to return to life because she hadn't danced enough—and once it told a nearly dead minister who tried to talk about theology, "That doesn't matter here; the only thing that matters is the way you think." Of course, in those books about NDEs, the person who had one usually had to go through some terrible health crisis involving great fear and physical suffering before they got to the death. That didn't sound desirable to me. But the actual near-death experience sounded great. I wanted really bad to have one—to find out for myself whether the afterlife was real, to get a little taste of heaven, a little bit of extra time with Jim Beaman. But all I could do was read about other people's. But now, it seems, in a certain way that can't be explained, I did have one. Or at least I seem to have gotten the benefits of having one even if I didn't have one.

The Rooms of Heaven

When it comes right down to it, it's mysterious, how I've changed, the ways in which I'm not my old self anymore. Sure, I don't smoke cigarettes, I don't get involved with addicts, I don't eat food that's bad for me or beat up on myself in other ways. And I have a new pair of glasses to look at the world through. I have this feeling that won't go away that everything happens for a reason, that there's some lovely gracious intelligence that overlooks the universe, that everything is not just random, not just material, that people are more than bodies that turn into buckets of slop in the end. But still, the change in me feels like more than that. It feels like something essentially mysterious, the way life and death and near-death experiences are essentially mysterious. All I know is that I'm not the same person I was that day on Beaman's lawn. Although I suppose that person is still part of me, inside of me, like one of those dolls inside a larger doll in those Russian nests of dolls.

In a way it seems like the change happened gradually, over time, slowly, painfully. It happened while I was grieving, making mistakes and learning from them, going to my therapist, attending twelve-step meetings. It's still happening. But in another way it seems as though it took place all at once. In a way it seems as though it happened that day on Beaman's lawn, as if the moment the cop shook his head an atom bomb really did go off, shattering my old self, breaking me down into a million zillion subatomic, microscopic pieces.

Then I had to put myself together again.

25

The first thing I had to do was grieve.

When I got home from the hospital I still hadn't given up on the notion that I could somehow, through some act of will, bring Jim Beaman back to land of the living. I just could not make my peace with the idea that I was never going to see him again. I thought I could bring him back through automatic writing, but the writing was, is, no longer available to me. Now I'm grateful I stopped being able to get those messages from dead people, or stopped being able to split myself in half, one half giving the other half messages, if that's what was happening. But at the time, in those first days out of the hospital, I wanted desperately to do it. I kept picking up a pen and holding it to paper, even though I knew I shouldn't, it had driven me crazy once and it could do it again. But it didn't matter anyway because nothing happened; the pen just sat there, lifeless in my hand. I felt abandoned, frustrated. I was like someone trying over and over to start a car, turning the key in the ignition—*urrrr-urrr-urr*—but the engine wouldn't get going, the automatic writing wouldn't happen, and Jim Beaman was, once and for all, dead.

So. I cried, and I beat a pillow with a hammer, and I read detective novels by women authors: Sue Grafton, Sarah Peretsky, Marcia Muller. I cried every night for about forty-five minutes before I went to sleep; I cried so much my pillow would actually get wet. For years afterward, until I bought a new pillow, whenever I took the pillow case off the old one I'd see large tan stains on it like water stains on wallpaper, and I'd wonder, Are those really tear stains? Did I really cry that much? After I cried I'd fall into an exhausted sleep and feel a little better in the morning, as if crying had released some poison. Then as the day wore on the poison would build up again, and by bedtime I'd have to discharge it with more crying. I never cried during the day.

It took me a while to get to the pillow beating. I had always heard it was good to get rage out of your system by hitting inanimate objects or screaming. My friend Patty used to punch her pillow when we were roommates in Cambridge, and once another friend said, "I have to go upstairs and get some of this anger out," and I heard her up there shrieking. But I'd never been able to bring myself to do anything like that. I felt too self-conscious, too uptight, too held in to do it. But then, one day during my grieving period, I came home from a walk and I just *had* to do it, I had to do something to get out that rage and frustration: rage at Beaman for killing himself and abandoning me, frustration at the fact that there was nothing, absolutely nothing that would change the situation. So I went to the closet and got out one of those gray reading pillows he and I had bought together, for reading in bed and for rolling around—I'd put them away because I couldn't bring myself to look at them. I brought one of them out and turned it upside down so the bottom of the pillow was sticking up, and I went into the kitchen and took a little hammer out of a drawer by the sink and I whacked that pillow with it as hard as I could. Every couple of minutes I had to stop to let my arm rest, then I whacked the pillow again.

I beat that pillow over and over and every time after a while I'd feel an ugly little snarl come over my face, and all the old stale left-over rage of my life—rage at my mother, my father, whomever—would come seething up from where it had settled at the bottom of the pot and join the new, fierce, hot, bubbling, boiling rage at Beaman, for killing himself and leaving me, and then I'd gag. I'd gag once or twice, sometimes three times. Once I even ran into the bathroom and bent over the toilet, thinking I was going to vomit but I didn't, I just stood there, feeling empty, all the anger settling back down to the bottom of the pot again. I'd stop when the gagging happened, put the hammer and pillow away until the next day. This, the pillow-beating part of grieving, lasted for about a month. I could have, probably should have, done it longer, but I stopped as soon as the worst of the rage was skimmed off the top of the pot. I left some in there, I know: It was just so unpleasant, all that gagging, all that dredging up.

The reading took place at the same time as the crying and the pillow beating. Earlier I'd read boojie books obsessively and I would still pick up anything new I came across on the subject, but there weren't many books I hadn't already read, and in any case I'd had most of the stuffing knocked out of me, as my father used to say, as far as boojie went. So instead I read murder mysteries by women authors. Not Agatha Christie novels or anything like that, but a certain type of contemporary novel with young, tough, capable, cynical female protagonists. The protagonists were always single, too—that was another important aspect; I couldn't read anything involving married women, anything with romance. But I loved those books about single women scoping out murders, driving around in beat-up cars stalking perpetrators, creeping through the bushes wearing black jeans and turtlenecks. There was something about them that soothed and lulled me, that made the pain of grief a little bit more bearable. I suppose it was the suspense, and maybe there was also something about the idea of a single woman solving death that appealed to me. In any case, all I did for about two months—all I wanted to do—was sit around and read those books. I read them lying on my couch and eating at my kitchen table and sitting up at night in bed, smoking cigarettes all the time, tapping the ashes into ashtrays that Jim and I had used together. If I felt the need to get out of the house I'd take my book to the park and read it on a bench, then I'd take it home and read it on the couch again. When I finished one book I'd close it and open another.

At the end of July, just when my savings were running out, I got a job in the physics department at the university. The job was working for a journal, sending manuscripts written by physicists to other physicists known as referees, who would tell us in written reports whether the manuscripts were any good. We had no idea ourselves whether or not they were any good. They might as well have been written by aliens, for all we understood them. My friend JoAnn and I, that is. I'm sure Chris Goertz, our boss, who was a theoretical physicist, knew exactly what they meant. But JoAnn and I didn't. All we knew how to do—all we had to do—was photocopy and type and file and call up referees and tell them their reports were late. JoAnn had had the job alone for years, but she was going back to school and needed someone to share it so she could work part time. That's why I was hired.

I remember the day I went for the interview. I needed the job desperately because I was running out of money, but I was feeling very shaky, literally as well as otherwise. Literally because of the post–psych ward drug I was taking. Lithium made me shake; it was as if something was frozen somewhere in my nervous system and whenever I put a small amount of pressure on my arm muscles, lifting a cup of coffee, say, the stiffness of my muscles would make my hands tremble noticeably. After two months my doctor at the psych ward lowered my dosage and the shaking stopped, but I was still shaking the day I went to my interview in the physics department.

I'm not on lithium anymore, needless to say; I went off it after a year. The doctors predicted I would have another "episode" when I quit, but I didn't. I haven't had any problems with mental illness since my trip to the psych ward, but for a long time afterward I continued to follow up with a psychiatrist, just to be safe. I switched from the outpatient clinic at the psych ward to a community mental health place, and a few years ago a doctor there said she believed I had been misdiagnosed: I probably never had bipolar illness; I probably had brief psychotic disorder, a one-time only, stress-related thing. I liked the idea; a short, temporary illness seemed less horrible than a chronic long-term disease. But I don't think that was right, either; I don't think brief psychotic disorder or any other existing psychiatric diagnosis explains what happened to me. I think what happened was all bound up with automatic writing, with doing it for hours and hours, for days on end, with throwing open the door to the spirit world and inviting it in, with the little hole that had to open in my head to let the writing in.

I was very self-conscious about my lithium shaking. It contributed to a feeling I had that summer of being weak, pale, brittle, crazy. I simply could not imagine presenting myself confidently during an interview. But I got dressed in my interview outfit, a cream-colored knit suit that smelled stale from hanging unworn for years in the closet, and I put on a pair of modest black high heels with straps going over the arches. I hadn't worn the shoes for years either, and in the interim my feet had grown by a size or two. That happens when you get older, your feet grow; somebody told me it's from standing on them all that time. But I didn't know my feet had grown and I walked all the way to the interview and back wearing shoes that were at least a size too small. When I got home and took them off there were deep imprints on my feet where the straps had been. But I'm getting ahead of myself.

After I put on my interview clothes I tried to psyche myself up for the interview. I lay down on my couch and tried to hypnotize myself. I do that sometimes and it works. I get into a little trance by counting backward, imagining myself going down a set of stairs, and when I get to the bottom of the stairs I picture myself confidently performing the thing I'm afraid of performing. So I was lying on my couch doing that, but not very successfully. I couldn't manage to get into the little trance; I couldn't get past the fear when I thought about being interviewed, and I kept getting distracted from the entire process. Then something happened that allowed me to make it through the interview. I did more than make it through—I performed calmly, successfully, confidently, according to JoAnn, who became my good friend after we'd worked together a week. The thing that happened was: When I closed my eyes one last time, when I'd almost given up on getting hypnotized, a little picture of Jim Beaman's truck popped into my mind. Which might not have been such a big deal to another person but *was* a big deal to me, because I interpreted it as a sign from Jim Beaman. I was always on the lookout for him, always vigilant for some hint, some word, some indication of his presence. And when that picture of the truck popped into my head, that's how I took it, as a little message that was sent to me by Jim. As his way of saying, "If I were there I'd give you a ride to the interview. And this little picture is here to help you get through it." And it worked. I went downtown to Van Allen Hall wearing my too-small shoes and my old stale interview outfit and I had a great interview with JoAnn and Chris Goertz and they picked me out of fifteen candidates. That job was really important, in some way that's hard to put my finger on, to my recovery from grief.

Partly, I suppose, it was just being out of the house, having something to occupy me, being in daily contact with other human beings. But it also had a lot to do, specifically, with working with JoAnn. I remember my first day on the job. In a way it was like a repeat of the day of the interview. I had a lot of the same fears. I was afraid I'd shake when I was typing, afraid I'd say or do something that would give away my mental hospital background. I was even self-conscious about smoking, afraid they'd smell cigarettes on me and think something along the lines of what they'd think if they saw me shaking. So I went off to work on my first day with all those fears, and this time I didn't have any little vision of Jim Beaman's truck.

Our office was a big room with a desk in front of the windows, a large table sitting in the middle of the floor, a photo-copying machine, and a huge blackboard on one wall. The blackboard was for the physicists, in case they wanted to write down a couple of formulas while they were communicating. Later on, after we became friends, JoAnn and I drew pictures on the blackboard with colored chalk and left them there for months—pictures that had meaning only for us, pictures that were symbolic of, say, something we wanted to accomplish emotionally. For example, there was a picture of a potato with a chunk being gouged out with a potato peeler. Then there was a picture of the chunk, all green and black to indicate rot, sitting inside a kryptonite box. Those two pictures were for JoAnn. They were visual depictions of what we called the potato plan. JoAnn, like me, had a broken heart. Hers had been broken by her husband, who had left her and gotten together with another woman. Mine had been broken, of course, by Jim Beaman's suicide. The potato plan came into being when I told JoAnn one day that once a long time ago, when some boyfriend abandoned me for another woman, I cut him out of my heart like a bad spot out of a potato. The next day JoAnn came in and said, "Today I start the potato plan." The picture appeared on the board a couple of days later. There were pictures for me up there too. There was a drawing of a green box and a little key, which related to a vision I'd once had a long time ago in hypnosis, and there was a picture of me in a wedding dress, big fat tears flying out of my head.

I remember sitting at the long table in the middle of the room on my first day at the job, JoAnn sitting at the desk describing my tasks, me nodding, trying to look like I was paying attention. At ten o'clock JoAnn stood up and said, a little defensively, "I'm going down to the break room to smoke a cigarette." I said, "You smoke? So do I!" So JoAnn sat back down, found me an ashtray, and we took out our packs of cigarettes and our lighters and lit up. While we were smoking JoAnn said, "I'm having a crisis." I said, "So am I! Tell me about yours first." So JoAnn told me about her husband and her divorce, and then I told her about Jim Beaman and his suicide, and we've been friends ever since.

We processed our broken hearts together, and we were angry together about our abandonment, and we were ironic together about ourselves and our situations. Our worktimes only overlapped a couple of hours a week and during those hours we never got anything done; before every task we'd say, "Let's smoke a cigarette first," and end up sitting around talking and smoking. Most of the time we worked separately. Our computer had a function whereby the first piece of paper of the day would come out of the printer with a short quote on it, sometimes by famous writers or public figures and sometimes by regular people. And we would draw a picture that seemed to go with the quote and color it in with magic markers and leave it in the drawer for the other person to find when she came to work. JoAnn's husband was a local politician, and once she got the quote, "Politicians make strange bedfellows"; she had a great time with that one. And once for our own amusement we made up a fake manuscript full of dirty-sounding physics terms, phrases like "effect of the giant thruster on the spread F region," which we thought sounded incredibly obscene, though we had no idea what it meant.

My job in the physics department came to an end in a very strange way. There was a graduate student in the department who was really angry and really crazy, and one late-fall day he came into the building with a gun and another gun in a backpack and shot some people. Chris Goertz, our boss, was one of them, and some other people we knew were killed as well. Along with Chris, the murderer shot Bob, who worked with Chris, and a young Chinese Ph.D. student who had gotten the prize he, the murderer, wanted—all in a room on the third floor, where they were sitting in a meeting. There were other people in the meeting, too, whom he didn't shoot. The murders took place on November 1, the day after Halloween, and one of the other men in the meeting said that when Gang Lu came into the room with his gun and started shooting, at first they thought it was a Halloween prank. After shooting the guys in the meeting he went down three flights of stairs and killed Dwight, the chairman of the department, in his office. Dwight was sitting at his desk quietly working with his back to the door and Gang Lu came to the door and shot him. Just like that. I always thought it was strange that Dwight never even saw what hit him—one minute he was in this world and the next minute he was in the next. They say in boojie books that if someone dies suddenly sometimes they don't even know they're dead; they just keep walking along, doing whatever they were doing. And I've always imagined that happening to Dwight, pictured him working, his back to the door, hearing the commotion, glancing around, looking down in horror at his body on the floor.

The Rooms of Heaven

I was up on the fifth floor working when the murders happened. The meeting where most of the shootings took place was two stories directly below, and I heard a little sound, *pop-pop-pop*, and then I heard something like a lot of furniture being moved around. I thought that was the sound of someone rearranging the desks or something, but it turned out it was the sound of people tipping over chairs, shoving tables aside, scrambling for cover. When I first heard the gun I did think that was what it was but then I thought, Naah, it *couldn't* be, and then I decided they must be doing construction work down there and I'd heard a staple gun. I remember I had a little fantasy when I first heard the gun, before I decided it wasn't a gun. In the fantasy there was some murderer down there and I went down and bravely disarmed him because I wasn't afraid of death. At that time I thought I wanted to die, so I could be with Jim Beaman; I couldn't stand the thought of all the time I'd have to live through without seeing him. I used to lie in bed at night and count up how many years I had left; I figured it was probably thirty, maybe twenty if I was lucky.

After I decided it wasn't a gun I forgot about the whole idea of shootings. I went down a long, dim, empty hallway to the bathroom—Van Allen is a big building and fairly sparsely populated—and peed and stared at myself in the mirror and dawdled at the water fountain for a while, filling this little plastic cylinder with a red rubber sponge on top, which is for sealing letters, so you don't have to lick the envelopes. As I was walking back down the hallway to my office a secretary came out of the doorway to the stairwell and said, "Dwight's been shot! He's dead." I said, "Did they catch the person who did it?" And she said, "No, I don't think so. It might be Gang Lu—one of the Chinese graduate students." And then she left. I was confused and didn't know what to do. It was as if I fell into a kind of daze where I couldn't process the information. So I went into my office and sat down at the desk. I picked up the phone and called JoAnn and told her. Then I sat there for a while and worked, sealing envelopes with that thing I had filled at the water fountain. Those letters never got mailed because they had been written and signed by Chris, who was dead by then. Finally I started thinking maybe I should shut the door or something. So I got up and closed the door and sat back down at the desk. Then I stood again and went back to the door and looked out into the hallway and just then somebody came running down the corridor shouting, "They're evacuating the building! Everybody get out!" I thought that meant the murderer was still in the building and hadn't been found, he could be lurking around any corner, hiding in some stairwell. As it turned out, he was already dead, had gone to another office building and shot two more people, then shot himself. But I didn't know that and I was suddenly terrified of being in there, and I was terrified too of getting out, walking down the hallway, taking the elevator to the first floor alone. But for some reason, even more than that, I was worried about whether or not to turn off the business machines. I thought I probably should, since it was Friday and they'd be going all weekend, if not longer. So I did. I closed down the computer program and clicked off the computer and then I ran around the room shutting off the printer, the photocopy machine, the electronic postage meter. My hands were shaking so much it was hard to hit the buttons and that surprised me, because I hadn't known I was so scared. Then I walked down that incredibly long hallway all alone and got on the elevator and rode to the first floor. There were cops standing by the front door ushering everyone out of the building and I left and walked home. On the way I realized that maybe I did want to go on living after all. It was snowing and I couldn't get over the feeling the whole way home that there was a murderer behind me.

26

For years I had a basket of Jim Beaman's dirty laundry under my desk. My desk is as long and wide as a picnic table, with plenty of room underneath. It was a little cramped, having that basket under there all those years, but not too bad. Every so often my foot would bump into it, I always had to keep my legs a little to one side, but for the most part I hardly noticed it.

It was the laundry that was in Jim's room when he died: some T-shirts, a couple of pairs of underwear, a plaid cotton long-sleeved shirt, a sheet, a pair of jeans with a belt still looped through the belt loops. The jeans were the pants he was wearing the day he died; I knew because I found my key to his apartment, which he picked up that day off my kitchen table, in the pocket.

At first I really loved those clothes. I used to take the T-shirts out of the basket and hold them to my face and inhale as deeply as I could. I loved the smell of them, the feel of them; it was as if they had in them some microscopic something left over from Jim's body, molecules, energy, what my friend John Birkbeck calls the life force, the last little bit of Jim remaining on this earth. It wore off after a while, dissipated into the air, or maybe what dissipated was my need for it to be there, or maybe it was both: The life energy went fairly quickly, after a week or two, and my need wore off more slowly, a little at a time. Gradually, after a year or so, I stopped smelling those clothes, touching them, paying attention to them, but I didn't get rid of them. It would have been too painful, too much like an ending, like acknowledging he was gone. I knew he was gone but I didn't want to think about it any more than necessary. I just wanted to let time slip by without noticing. Then, after another year or so I just kind of forgot about them, they were a permanent fixture under my desk. So I left them there some more. Finally, after about three years, I hauled the basket out and looked at what was in it. I was almost afraid to see what had been growing down there during all those years, but the clothes weren't scary, they were just incredibly stale: they smelled, not exactly dirty, but old, dusty, musty, moldy. Especially the belt, which was hard and brittle and darker than its original color. But still I didn't do anything with them. It was just too depressing to think of carting them to the laundromat, getting rid of them somehow. So I shoved them back under the desk and wrote "Deal with clothes in basket" on a list. It took me four more months and joining a twelve-step program to actually do it.

When Jim was alive and struggling with alcohol and cocaine and I was thinking that he was going to stop—that I could make him stop—and the whole thing was driving me crazy, Kathy said to me, "Maybe you should go to some twelve-step meetings for people involved with addicts or alcoholics. Maybe that would help." But I thought, Why should I do that when it's *his* problem? I thought Jim should go to AA or NA and then he'd quit drugs and stop drinking and that would solve everything. I had no idea there was a problem in me as well. And then after Jim killed himself and I was suffering and trying to bring him back from the dead, Kathy or maybe it was somebody else suggested it again, that I try going to some recovery meetings. But I thought, He's dead, what good could it possibly do me now? So I didn't go then, either. Finally, that summer I took stock of the clothes under my desk, I went. In the end what—who—made me go was not Jim Beaman or any other obvious logical reason—any reason related to Beaman—but Bill Ford.

Bill Ford had beautiful blue eyes and the sweet shy manner of a small-town boy from Iowa, which he was. As a kid he'd been a paperboy, a Little Leaguer, an Eagle Scout. He was the youngest of five children. His brothers and sisters all thrived, became doctors and lawyers and successful businesspeople, and for a while Bill thrived too, living in Chicago, making money as a computer analyst. But he'd come back to Iowa City and fallen on hard times, unemployment and other problems. His car was an old red Nissan Sentra, and crammed into the back were boxes containing consumer items from his old life: nice clothes, a VCR, an expensive CD player. All that stuff was there because he had no other place to put it. He slept in the front seat, curled around the stick shift. It shouldn't come as any surprise that alcoholism was at the bottom of his problems. Back in Chicago he'd been sober for five years, then had fallen off the wagon.

I remember the moment I met him. We were at a wedding reception, sitting outdoors at a picnic table. My friend Rudy Martin was there, too, and another guy, and all of us were drinking beer. Sipping it slowly all day long and chatting. Bill kept giving me shy smiles, looking at me across the table, then looking away. I was attracted to him, I'll admit it. Even though I already knew without being told there was something wrong in his life—something a little sick, broken, disordered. Maybe that was even *why* I was attracted to him. I'm ashamed to admit it and I know it doesn't make any sense but I have an awful feeling it's true.

I remember one night when he was at my house and I was cooking dinner for him. It was about a week after I met him at the wedding. That morning when I got up I looked out my front window and saw his car parked on my street, and later in the day I walked by it and saw all the boxes crammed into the back. And that night I saw him riding his bike past my house, going "home," I guess, to his car, and I invited him to come in and have dinner. I remember it was early June and I had fresh peas and I made Bill shell all the peas before I cooked them. It took him about forty-five minutes and at the end there was a little tiny pile of practically microscopic peas—it was early in the year even for peas, and they must not have been ripe enough, old enough to come to anything. I remember Bill saying, possibly sarcastically though I didn't pick up on it at the time, "This is just too much happiness for one person to stand," and I remember having this feeling—a good feeling, kind of a proud feeling, that I had made his night better, that I had introduced something healthy and fresh into his life. At the same time I felt a little guilty, because I knew there was something not quite healthy in this budding new relationship, in the feelings I had about Bill.

It went on like that for a while. He'd stop by my house, sit around for a while, talk. Then take off for the bars. He had all kinds of problems. He had absolutely no money. He got a job that lasted a week, then the paycheck didn't arrive. He had to go to an office and fight about it with someone. Another job fell through. His bicycle got a flat tire. Et cetera. I don't mean to report all this as if he was some kind of person who doesn't deserve sympathy, who should have been avoided by a high-society type like me. It's just that he had a kind of illness and I had a kind of illness. Our two illnesses were related. Both of them, in a certain way, were alcoholism. It's easy to see how alcoholism affects people who drink. They go out and get shit-faced every night, they lose their jobs, their pride, their ambition, they wind up living in their cars. Or they go down some other, equally devastating route as a result of the disease. Because it is a disease, though it isn't quite as easy to see as some other diseases—cancer or polio or diabetes. And it's even less easy to see how alcoholism's counterpart—codependency or whatever you want to call what I had—is a disease. People always talk about it that way in twelve-step meetings—"my disease this, my disease that"—and I have to admit it seems a little spurious to me; I get a little tired of hearing every weird thing somebody thinks or does described as a disease. But when I look back on that moment in my kitchen, see myself cooking at the stove, Bill Ford sitting at the table shelling peas, it seems clear to me that something sick—at the very least unhealthy—*was* going on in me.

One morning I looked out my window and saw Bill's feet sticking out the window of his car. It was about eleven A.M. and the logical conclusion would have been that he was trying to get a little more room in his cramped front seat, sleeping it off after a hard night at the bar. But there was something about the sight of those feet sticking out the window—they had on tennis shoes and white socks, as I remember—that made me think something more dire was going on. The idea came to me gradually. At first, when I saw Bill's feet sticking out the window of his car, I just felt kind of creeped-out. It was like seeing disembodied feet, feet someplace you're not supposed to see feet, feet attached to a dead person. I had that thought and I kept looking out the window thinking it, and pretty soon I started thinking Bill *was* dead—that he had choked to death on his own vomit or died of a stroke or a heart attack or some other alcohol-related illness. Which was really not all that unlikely, all that crazy, after all. Most alcoholics who don't quit drinking do eventually die of it. So maybe on some unconscious level I was merely processing that Bill Ford was dying, out there in his car. But I thought he was already dead. At first it was just a possibility that occurred to me and then pretty soon it was a certainty. I was sure he was dead. But I had to know. But I was afraid to know. I was afraid to go out there and look in the car and possibly see what I couldn't bear to see, what I didn't have to see with Jim Beaman, what I would have rather died myself than see—someone I knew and cared about *dead:* pale, still, greenish, rigid with rigor mortis and who knows what else. Still, I had to know whether he was dead, I couldn't let it rest, and I think that compulsion also grew out of my codependency. I couldn't just think, Oh well, if he's dead, he's dead, nothing I can do about it, nothing my going out there and looking will do to help. I thought my going out there and looking *would* do something to help; I thought my involvement was necessary, that it could somehow *prevent* him from being dead. So I was stuck. I didn't know what to do. Finally it came to me I should ask Rudy Martin, my friend and next-door neighbor—he lived in the apartment next to mine, the place where Martha had lived—to go outside with me and look.

There's at least one important thing you need to know about Rudy: He's blind. He has retinitis pigmentosa, a degenerative retinal disease; he lost his sight gradually when he was a kid. He can see gradations of light and shadow, but that's it. I suppose some people might have thought it was ironic, my asking a blind guy to go outside to look at something. But I hung around with Rudy a lot back then and I took it for granted that he looks at things all the time, he just uses different methods than other people. He looks with his hands, and with the cane he carries when he walks around out in the world, and with his memory and his imagination and his other senses, hearing and touch and smell. And sometimes I would help him look as well. By which I mean I would describe things to him. We would watch TV together and I would tell him what the characters looked like, and I would try to come up with interesting ways of describing the appearances of people both of us knew: I said so and so walked like a cat on tiptoes, and so and so looked loose, as if one of his arms might come off if you grabbed it and pulled. Once we saw a ciacada hatching out of a cocoon attached to the side of our house; the newly hatched cicada was utterly hideous—slimy and alien-looking—and I described it to Rudy in detail so that he could be repulsed by it also. I suppose there was a codependent element in that, too—in my helping Rudy "see." It was really fun, but I can't deny that when I linked my arm through his as we were walking down the street, when I described to him things he wouldn't have known if it hadn't been for me, a certain small, self-serving satisfaction—a kind of pride in being helpful, and nice, and needed—rose up in me like an irrepressible little bubble.

Anyway, that's what I was planning to do if we went out to the car and looked inside and Bill turned out to be dead. I would scream and then I'd tell Rudy, describe Bill to Rudy and he would scream or shout or turn pale or whatever, and the moral support of having him there would make it easier for me.

So I called Rudy on the phone and told him the story and we went outside and across the street and he stood beside me while I peered through the window of Bill's car, past Bill's feet up his calves and his knees and his tan khaki shorts to his chest, rising and falling under a green T-shirt, and into his face. His mouth was open and he was snoring a little, his face was red and slightly pinched, slightly contorted, as if even in sleep he was displeased with having his privacy invaded, with the humiliation of being witnessed in such a state.

I started having trouble sleeping for reasons related to Bill—Bill, and the whole amorphous miasma of my codependent, co-addiction, co-whatever disease—there isn't really a name for it. It was the summer of 1994, three and a half years after Beaman's suicide. I started waking up in the early morning, at four or five or six, lying in bed feeling anxious. I wasn't exactly sure what I was worried about, whether it was Bill's situation, Bill dying of alcoholism out in his car, or my situation vis-à-vis Bill, our relationship. We didn't really have a relationship. But Bill . . . liked me. He was too shy to do much of anything about it but he said he thought about me all the time, I was the one good thing in his life, and once when we were sitting on my front steps he put his arm around me and I didn't stop him. I didn't know how to tell him I didn't return the feeling. And I wasn't even sure how I *did* feel about him. I knew I wasn't in love with him but I felt strangely compelled by his situation, enmeshed in it somehow, as if I was somehow tied, not so much to him as to his problems, with tiny invisible strings.

Rudy Martin once told me that when he was a kid he had this idea that there were invisible threads running between everything, tiny unseen filaments that went between the couch and the chair, the chair and the lamp, the lamp and your foot, and so forth. And when he told me that I thought, I still think, there was some essential truth in it, that on some psychic level there probably are little ribbons of energy connecting everything. And most of all that there are strings connecting all of us human beings. The strings that connect some humans are stronger than others, and there are unhealthy strings, strings made of pain and psychic illness that run between some people. People who suffer from codependency, co-addiction, co-whatever you want to call it, people like me, have trouble with those strings, those invisible filaments woven out of other people's sickness and pain. We have trouble detaching, untying, clearing those filaments away, and the filaments connect us in unhealthy ways; we don't know where we start and the other person stops, and it seems like their problems are our problems. That's the only way I can really describe my connection to Bill, how I was affected by his disease.

Finally, I didn't sleep for a whole night. I lay awake tossing and turning, feeling anxious without knowing why, picturing Bill dead drunk and possibly dying, jammed into the front seat of his little red car. I felt *alarmed*, as if something bad was happening, not just to Bill but to me. Bill was nothing like Beaman; my situation with Bill, was nothing like it had been with Beaman, but somehow, underneath, the fear was the same.

The next day I went to my first recovery meeting. Rudy Martin suggested it as a solution to my misery. Miraculously, as if he'd fulfilled a purpose in my life, Bill drove away a few days later and never came back. He started parking his car on another street, gave up on the idea of having a relationship with me. We didn't see each other for a long time after that, and when we did the terms were entirely different.

A couple of months later, I got rid of Beaman's clothes. It wasn't easy. I had to force myself to reach down into that basket and look again at what was there, take those clothes out and wash them, dry them, fold them, make decisions about which to toss and which to give away. I didn't want to do it, but I did.

27

I'm thinking about those evening rides Jim and I used to take around the Iowa countryside. Once we drove to Muscatine, an hour away from Iowa City, stopped at the Mississippi River and got out, sat on a park bench and smoked a cigarette, stared at a flagpole, a trashcan, the boats bobbing on the muddy water. Then we got back into the truck and drove home again. It was dark by then, it got dark when we were about halfway home. I think of that ride as flat and straight and simple—I see us sitting in the truck facing the windshield, not saying much, the truck speeding forward like an arrow through the dark humid night. Beaman said, that night, that it was soothing for him to take those rides, and that night he needed to be soothed. That's the part I don't like to think about—Beaman's bad moods, dry drunks, the nights he needed to be soothed. I'd rather think about the other times, other rides. When we headed out without a destination, drove slowly on back roads between the cornfields, without any sense of time. Once we came to a crossroads, and there on the left, like something out of a dream of abandonment and loneliness, was a tiny gray deserted church. Another time Jim showed me an old Jewish cemetery, its small stones scattered peacefully along a green-gray slope.

There's something like a memory of that moment, those rides, that comes to me every now and then. But it isn't a memory. It's a strong visceral feeling that is like nothing else; it's not a thought or a memory or a desire or any other conscious process. It's a feeling that comes into my body, almost as if from somewhere outside. It happens unpredictably, without my being able to control it. I can't make it happen but when it does it's unmistakable, though it doesn't last very long. It's something like an odor, a sound—a little snatch of melody—except it isn't anything you could perceive through your senses; it's like the *response* to a smell or a melody. It's like a complex response to a complex chord in a complex symphony, but I don't know what the music is. Or maybe it's more like a smell, a fragrance, because a smell isn't anything real either, it's a secondhand thing, a product, an offshoot of something original, a flower, say, or a piece of fried chicken. But you can get a whiff of it, smell the flower or the chicken without the actual flower or chicken present, and have a complicated feeling in response, a lilac feeling, or a lily-of-the-valley feeling, or a fried-chicken feeling.

And what I'm talking about is an Iowa feeling. It's an Iowa feeling and a Jim Beaman feeling. It's an exotic, multilayered feeling, a morally ambiguous feeling, a feeling that has in it both good and bad, dark and light, beautiful and ugly and every possible variation in between. But none of that really captures it. The closest I can come is to say it feels like, smells like, *magic.* I have a feeling it's the offshoot, the product, the derivative of something unseen, that it arises from the otherworld, maybe. That perhaps it's the odor, the sound, the musical phrasing of death, which I think I smelled, heard, felt without knowing it on Jim Beaman, right from the start.

The color of the other world, I think, must be blue. Or maybe blue is the color of some vital, primal force or element, orgone energy, say, which Wilhelm Reich compared to static electricity and said permeates the universe. There's something about the color blue, anyway. Because after Jim died I had those two little blue dreams—dreams with a bluish tinge, which seemed lit from within by a strange blue light; the light had a kind of buzzing, humming, flickering, electrical quality. They didn't seem like dreams at all, actually, in that they didn't seem to come from inside me; they were more like pictures somebody was showing me, blue postcards someone somehow managed to project before my sleeping eyes, little blue vidoes beamed onto the movie screen of my mind.

Both of them were part of my communications with Y, the dead-guy version of Beaman. One was the dream of the finger tapping, pointing at the book on cocaine. The other was a kind of set picture, modeled on an actual existing photograph of Beaman. In the real photo he's standing against a brick wall, right elbow resting on the wall, hand holding a cigarette; there are cement blocks, a wheelbarrow, bags of mortar, tools lying all around; he's wearing blue jeans, a white open-collared shirt, wire-rimmed glasses, a brown leather belt. He looks as if the camera snapped him in mid-conversation; he looks very handsome and very masculine. In the dream he was standing against the same wall except the wall was a white picket fence; he was wearing the same clothes, wire-rimmed glasses, brown leather belt; he had the same look on his face, the same elbow resting on the fence, the same hand raised although this time maybe not holding a cigarette. But the *feeling* of the dream was different; it had an atmosphere, a clean fresh happy Iowa-farm kind of feeling. Standing next to Beaman, its side to the wall, was a horse, and in the background behind the fence was a farm with a white house and a red barn, a rolling green lawn, a bright-blue sky. The horse was a pure bright glowing white and all the other colors—the red of the barn, the green of the grass, the blue of the sky—were somehow purer, brighter than life, and the entire picture had a quality of wholesomeness, not a moral or an aesthetic quality but just a quality, as if wholesomeness has a kind of being of its own and it got added to the picture like color or composition or texture or style.

Only one thing happened in the dream, and that was a joke. After a pause while I got a good long look at the picture, the horse lifted its tail and pooped: three round horse flops—*plop-plop-plop*—fell on the ground behind it. And that was all. It delighted me utterly, and I woke up and ran into the kitchen like a kid on Christmas morning and we—Y and I—"talked" about it. The dream was a perfect Beaman joke. He loved shit jokes, loved the humble and the scatological. Once at Christmastime, just a couple of weeks before he died, we were in Econofoods and there was a huge replica of a Clydesdale horse standing in the produce aisle, and Jim took three large baking potatoes and put them on the floor under the horse's tail because, he said, it would make everybody happy. And that horse pooping in that dream was a way to make me happy. But maybe there was also another, subtler point to the dream. At least that's what comes to me when I think of it. I think about us and what we could have been. Us if we had gotten married and lived happily ever after, us without the suicide, without the booze and the drugs and the mess. Us in a perfect, ideal world, a potential world, a world like the world that the spiritualists say exists after death.

My father loved farms, and when I was a kid we had farmer wallpaper in the bedroom I shared with my sister when I stayed at my parents' house. The wallpaper had a pale-blue background covered with little scenes showing a stylized farmer in a square straw hat performing various stylized farming tasks, milking a cow with square teats, collecting oval white eggs from a square yellow nest, emptying slop into a square pigs' trough, and so forth. I used to lie in bed in the morning and stare at that wallpaper and dream about the little farmer and his ideal life. My father lived in Massachusetts all his life, he only rode through Iowa on a train once or twice, but I often think he would have loved it here. Out here is where the real farms are, and sometimes the farm life in the Iowa countryside seems to me as innocent, as idealized as the life on that wallpaper. As innocent and idealized as that future Jim and I used to fantasize together: our marriage, our children, our house in the country, our happily ever after. I think even then I knew it was just a fantasy, that none of that was going to happen, though I had no idea what was going to happen instead. Or maybe I did have some idea, on some subconscious level, how our story was going to end. The details of the fantasy were Beaman's doing. He loved to talk about the house, the life, the miniature goats we were going to raise, the secret passageways our kids would think we didn't know about. That house came to seem real to me, and it continued to seem real after he died. It seemed to me that somehow, somewhere out in the country, it actually existed—a shadow house, a potential house, a house made of air and imagination. And I *missed* it. A deep, sharp, strange feeling of homesickness came over me for it at odd, random moments.

When I think about the farm in the little blue dream—the dream with the fence, the horse, the poop—I'm reminded of a real-life house Jim and I saw once. Once, during one of our evening rides, we got a flat tire. It was almost twilight, we were way out on an obscure country road, we didn't have a jack to fix the tire, but just when it looked like the night was going to be a disaster a couple drove up and saved us. They were very young, probably in their early twenties, blond and fresh and innocent. The boy helped us change the tire. Actually, he didn't help us change the tire; he changed the tire for us, while Jim and I stood around and watched and thanked him over and over. Jim loved that couple; when we got home he talked and talked about them, about the boy especially. He said he was just the kind of kid he would like to hire if he, Jim, ever made it big as a contractor; one of his fantasies was that he was going to start a construction company and make a lot of money. And if he did, he said, he would drive back out and offer that boy a job.

After the kid finished fixing our tire, Jim asked him and his wife or girlfriend if they wanted to go somewhere and get a cup of coffee, but they said they lived in a farmhouse down the road and they had to get home. Then they got in their car and drove away, and we got in the truck and drove away. As we were heading down the road toward Iowa City we passed the house they had pointed to when they said they lived nearby. It was a big white farmhouse with a red barn and a wide green lawn. It might have even had a white horse in a corral.

Death is just like going into another room. I've read that in several places, attributed to different people. William Blake supposedly said it, but I've never been able to track down where—I read about him saying it in a secondary source— and an obscure nineteenth-century British church father named H. S. Holland said it, and it seems to me I found it somewhere else with some other famous guy saying it, Ralph Waldo Emerson or Teilhard de Chardin, somebody like that. And I read it in a boojie book, some old book I found in the university library about the British Society for Psychical Research. In it there's an account of a middle-aged widow who's visiting a medium and the medium is communicating messages to her from her dead husband. The widow's all upset, she feels abandoned by her husband's death, she keeps sobbing and saying, "Oh why did you have to leave me." And finally the dead guy gets impatient and says, "But I haven't left! I haven't gone anywhere. Death is just like going into another room."

And I used to try to do that, think of Jim as being in the other room. I always pictured the room he was in on the other side of my bathroom, somewhere beyond the medicine cabi-net. I remember standing there staring at myself in the mirror

right at the beginning, a day or two after his death. I was thinking about a parody of the movie *Ghost* I'd seen on *Saturday
Night Live*. In the movie Patrick Swayze dies but his ghost sur-
vives and they show Demi Moore, his girlfriend, grieving,
oblivious to the fact that he's there, alive but invisible, all the
time. In the parody on *Saturday Night Live* they show the Demi
Moore character sitting around crying, talking on the telephone, doing the kinds of things you only do when you're
alone, certainly not the kinds of things you do in front of your
boyfriend: picking her nose, farting, smelling her armpits. And
Patrick Swayze keeps going, "Oh, honey, don't do that! You
never did that before!" And finally at the end of the skit he goes
off in disgust. I kept thinking about that after Jim died, as a
kind of joke to myself, to try to cheer myself up. As soon as he
died I started imagining he was around as a way to feel better.
But it was hard, conjuring him up; even if he was there I had no
way of knowing it and overall it wasn't very satisfying, though I
couldn't stop doing it.

But I remember that particular day, standing there looking
at myself in the bathroom mirror, thinking about the parody of
the movie, trying to conjure up the ghost of Beaman. After a
while I forgot about the parody and I just stood there staring at
myself in a kind of reverie, full of grief, missing Jim. And I had
an unusual feeling—a feeling so subtle I'm not even sure I was
aware of having it, but it seems to me now I remember having
it. It was as if somehow without knowing it I *registered* something, as if on some level beyond conscious thinking I detected
a vibration, a presence, a disturbance in the air. And after that I
always imagined Jim being in the other room beyond the bathroom mirror.

In real life somebody else's apartment was there—the place
rented by Martha—and if I thought about it long enough I
would always come to that, that all that was there was Martha's
apartment. But in some strange way it didn't matter. It was as if

the real house, the real physical space with Martha's apartment, existed on one plane of reality and the imaginary room where Jim lived existed on another, and the two didn't really conflict, they didn't even intersect, they were simply two different places.

That day when I was in my bathroom, staring at myself in the mirror, sensing Jim's presence, I took off my pink coral cameo engagement ring and put it on the back of the toilet, and I said in my head to Beaman, If you're here, move this ring. Then I took off my clothes and got into the shower. Nothing happened, of course; when I got out the ring was still sitting in the same place on the back of the toilet. And I wasn't surprised or disappointed; I didn't really expect anything to come of it.

But then, in a way, something did come of it. At Christmastime that year, almost a year after Beaman's death, I went to San Diego for a week to visit Patty. Patty had been going to a spiritualist church, a church where they believe in life after death and the possibility of contacting spirits, along with other, regular Christian things. I went to a service on Sunday with Patty, and at the end a man and then a woman, church members who supposedly had psychic gifts, stood up in front and delivered messages from the dead to individual audience members: They'd point to someone in the crowd and say, "Uh, the woman with the red jacket on, there's a spirit here who wants to let you know . . ." et cetera. I didn't especially like the messages. There was one late-middle-aged guy whose daughter had died in a car accident and the daughter's spirit told him to stop being so sad all the time and have more fun, go dancing, take a vacation. Which seemed really cruel to me. I felt like, That poor guy, now he's going to have to feel guilty every time he gets sad. Still, I was disappointed that I didn't receive any messages. I was desperate to have contact with Jim, any contact, whatever I could get, and when Patty said the clairvoyants also gave readings one-on-one I decided to make an appointment.

The woman's name was Margaret; Patty got me her phone number and drove me to her apartment. The reading really upset me, for reasons I can hardly remember. I think it had something to do with trying to take it seriously, with trying to hear Jim Beaman's voice in the voice of a pleasant, female, fortyish churchgoer with California values. Margaret said dead people aren't "allowed" to say anything negative about themselves or the way they lived, they're not allowed to apologize or have regrets, because people have to love themselves in the other world. That idea really bothered me. I hated the thought of Beaman being in a place where everybody's so self-satisfied they can't even say they're sorry, where nobody has any regrets about their life, no matter what they did. I wanted him, I guess, to have a lot of regrets. I thought he should have regrets, that he deserved to have regrets. I was furious at him for leaving me, for never owning up to alcoholism and the damage he'd done because of it. Of course, I didn't have to believe what Margaret said and I didn't, really; I knew the whole episode was stupid. But I couldn't seem to stop being upset. I cried and cried for days afterward, sat on Patty's front steps and stared at the view across the street, smoking and talking on the phone to friends long-distance, endless tears running down my cheeks. Patty said my face looked like a pink blanket with two burn holes in it.

At first it seemed like there was nothing genuine at all in Margaret's reading. She said a couple of things that made a little bit of sense—for example, she said Jim was showing her a picture of Colonel Sanders in her head, saying I had a friend who looked like him, and it was true, I did: I used to be friends with a famous old man who had white hair and a beard and glasses and he did look a little like Colonel Sanders, though I'd never made the comparison myself. But I was too upset and overwhelmed by all the other stuff Margaret said to find that very satisfying. Which was perhaps also why I didn't get it when she said one thing that seems in retrospect as if it might have been a genuine psychic message. She said, "Do you ever take your ring off?" I said, "Not very often." And she said, "Because he says, he can try to move your ring. I doubt if he can do it . . . but he says he'll try." Then she said, "He says the bathroom, in the shower, is a good place to talk to him." I didn't make the connection till a few weeks later, didn't figure out that that might have been what's known in boojie literature as an evidential message. That maybe he was trying to tell me, he did try to move my ring.

Once, back when I was working in the physics department, I heard a report on National Public Radio about a giant radio telescope in New Mexico that was being used to collect signals from outer space. Funding for the program has since been cut, but at the time I heard the story it was still going strong. Its purpose was to scan the universe for signs of life on other planets, as if we earthlings are lonely here on our blue and white ball spinning in space and it would make us feel better to know there's someone else out there. Our office was on the fifth floor and there was a church across the street, and all that summer, when I was working alone, without JoAnn, I used to stare out the window at the steeple and the bright-blue sky and the fat green leaves shivering in the August breeze and the syrupy sunlight pouring over it all and think, How can it be that all this is still there and Jim Beaman is gone? I had that thought over and over, and there was something about it that struck me as strange; it didn't compute, somehow, that all that could still be there but Beaman could be gone. The fact that he was gone made the trees, the steeple, the beautiful blue sky seem not quite real, either, as if his disappearance from the world revealed some flaw, some basic instability or falseness in it. Certainly it spoiled the view for me, not just the view out the window but the view of the whole world. And that day, listening to that report about that radio telescope searching for life in the universe, I stood up and looked out the window and felt for the millionth time the enormity, the absolute incredibility of an entire person's disappearance, and I thought, Why aren't we searching for our own dead people? That would've made a lot more sense to me.

Since Jim's death I've gotten into the habit of keeping one ear cocked to the universe, like that radio telescope in New Mexico. I listen too, but not for anyone so far away and unimaginable as aliens on other planets. I listen for voices from the other room. I listen for anything that might come through. I listen for messages from Jim Beaman. And every now and then I hear something.

Once, as I was drifting off to sleep I heard a tiny quiet voice inside my head say, "I'm very proud of you." I said, "Why?" Nothing happened and I started to fall asleep again, then the voice said, "Because." I said, "Because of what?" but this time the voice didn't answer. Once when I was taking a bath, thinking about a poem I'd written with a reference in it to Jim, wondering how to indicate who he was and what became of him—should I use an epigraph or what?—a very Beamanlike voice said inside my head, "You've got a regular little industry going." Sometimes I get a strong feeling—a Beaman feeling, like the Iowa feeling—accompanied by something I can only describe as a nudge. And occasionally a snippet of music will come to me and the music will say something. Once, for example, when I was thinking about something difficult, painful—Beaman's suicide note—a song suddenly popped into my head along with that little, sort of, nudge. The song was "Get Up Offa That Thing" by James Brown, which tells you to dance and you'll feel better. So I did. I went into the living room, found my James Brown CD, put it on the CD player, and danced around my living room.

Once I felt a slap on the back but when I turned around no one was there. It was the Fourth of July of the year Jim died and I had just gotten out of the psych ward. Some friends invited me to their house for the day, a couple with a set of twins and an older kid. I'd worked with the wife, Robin, at the Office of the State Archaeologist. I liked Robin but I didn't know her very well and I didn't tell her about the psych ward or that I was taking lithium; I was ashamed to have anyone know those things. She offered me a can of Miller and I accepted, then immediately regretted it. I knew I couldn't raise it to my mouth without my hand visibly shaking because of the lithium and I was afraid she or her husband or one of their kids would see me shake and ask me why, or worse yet, that they would see me shake and wouldn't say anything. Maybe, in fact, that did happen. But I doubt it. Because I drank that can of beer in a very cautious way. I held it in my hand for hours, and when it seemed like no one was looking I lifted it to my lips and drank as much as possible as quickly as possible. Then I held on to it again. The beer got warm, I carried it everywhere, set it down on windowsills, on kitchen counters. Finally I finished it.

Later in the day we played softball in their yard, me and Robin and her nice blond husband and the twins, a boy and a girl. We designated certain spots in the yard as first, second, third base, and home—a tree and a bush and a certain patch of dirt and a Frisbee the husband laid on the ground—and Robin got out the ball and the bats and we began to play. The kids went up, got little hits, ran around the bases. Robin struck out. The husband got a hit but Robin caught it. Then it was my turn to bat. The husband pitched me a ball. I swung the bat and got a hit—a pretty good hit, as a matter of fact. The ball flew out over second base, one of the kids had to chase it, I ran to the tree, the bush, the patch of dirt, the Frisbee. Everybody yelled, "Yaay." I stood by a tree, catching my breath. And then it happened. I felt an unmistakable slap on the back, a friendly little whack of congratulations. I looked around but there was nobody there.

Another thing happened four and a half years ago, when my father was dying. My father died a terrible protracted death of cancer, and at the time my brother and I spent about six weeks in western Massachusetts, staying at my sister's, visiting my father every day in the nursing home. My father lived one town over from my sister; my brother lives in Seattle; I live in Iowa, of course. That period when my father was dying was the longest time my sister, my brother, and I ever lived under the same roof. Anyway, I was staying at my sister's, sleeping in her spare room, and one night I said to Beaman, silently, in my head, the way it seems to make sense to talk to the dead: Well, my father's a lot closer to where you are now than where I am, so why don't you try to get a message to me through him. Then I fell asleep and forgot about it. I was always trying to get messages from Beaman back then and usually nothing came of it. I got up early the next morning because I was flying back to Iowa that day; it looked like my father wasn't going to die right away and I had to do a couple of important things at home. My sister drove me to the airport and on the way we stopped at my father's nursing home. He had just woken up and he said, "I had the strangest dream. I was at a convention for bee keepers"—in real life my father actually had kept bees for a while—"I was there with a bunch of other bee keepers and they said, 'Somebody has to be the Bee Man.' And they picked me to do it." And then he told us all about the rest of the dream, how because he was the Bee Man they glued feathers to his hands and arms and he flew way up in the air and all around. He kept saying that phrase, "Somebody has to be the Bee Man. Somebody has to be the Bee Man." But I didn't get it. Maybe I was too upset about my father, too preoccupied with his dying. I went to the airport and flew back to Iowa and a couple of days later I woke up from an afternoon nap on my couch and finally I got it: Oh. Bea-Man.

It's strange, how I react to all those many little signs and messages, how people seem to react to communications from the dead in general. I noticed it when I was reading boojie books: Someone would report, say, a series of communications from a dead husband which came through a medium—not just silly stuff but strong, evidential, convincing messages, with information only known by the dead person. But then after describing it the writer or narrator or receiver of the communication would shrug and say, "But I'm not really sure where those messages came from, maybe it was just me making them up or something." Even some famous mediums said they didn't necessarily believe they were getting stuff from actual dead people. I used to be enormously frustrated by all that pussy-footing around, that refusal to come right out and admit it once and for all: Yes, there is life after death and this along with other evidence obviously proves it. But now I seem to have some of the same reservations. Not that I'm ready to put the old glasses on, see life, death, the universe as one big meaning-less accident, see myself, Jim Beaman, all human beings as future buckets of slop: complex biological machines, when the machine turns off, *poof*, the person is gone. But still. There's something about the whole thing—life after death, communi-cations from dead people—that seems somehow by its very nature incompatible with belief. It's as if there's some kind of problem, some kind of block; even if you want to, even if you have reason to, it's still—on some level, at least—hard to believe.

Maybe it has to do with fear of ridicule, with the difficulty of going against modern scientific ideas; maybe thoughts are like fish or drops of water and tend to get swept downstream on the mainstream current. Or maybe the problem lies in the word "believe." Maybe we don't have to *believe* in life after death, maybe we can simply entertain the possibility. I like that word, "entertain," with its connotations of lightness, airiness, fun, and flexibility, of thoughts that don't have to be pinned down one way or the other like they do with the grim, dour, serious, hard and concrete "believe." Maybe the dead can't *be* pinned down, the way light can't be pinned down according to quantum physics: It's *both* wave and particle. Still, I have a feeling there's something more to it even than that—this difficulty we have believing in life after death. That there's some mystery, some missing piece of the puzzle, something wrong with the way we're looking at the picture. That if we could only look at it a different way, turn the hologram a little to the left or right it would all come into focus, it would all make sense.

I felt it all along. I would try and try to picture Y, try to imagine him there in the room with me, sitting in the other chair at the kitchen table, lying beside me on my bed, really there but somehow invisible, like Patrick Swayze in *Ghost*. Or else I would try to imagine him someplace else, where he was and what he might be doing when he wasn't with me, when he was in the light, as they say in books about NDEs. But I couldn't picture him or any of those things. Every time I tried I got a bored, shallow, dissatisfied feeling, all I could conjure up was sort of a flat, silly, one-dimensional picture, something like a cartoon.

Death is like hypnosis only you can't stop. That was one thing Y said. I've looked for it in the writing but I can't find it; I can't find much of anything in all those scribbled-on pages. The whole experience was an interior event and there's almost nothing left to show for it in the outside world, like something that disappears in a fairy tale when the magic spell is lifted. So probably no one will ever locate that statement on any of those pages, but I remember when I—Y, whoever—wrote it, the pen moving in my hand across the paper: Death is like hypnosis only you can't stop. I didn't make much of it at the time, it was just another thing that was said in a long, long conversation. But I've been thinking about it lately.

The real-life Beaman knew about hypnosis because I hypnotized him once. I'd been telling him about how I'd gone to a hypnotherapist, Charlie Ducey, for a while in Cambridge in 1981. I went to him because I had a phobia of public speaking and a phobia of flying and I had to fly to New York and give a sales presentation; I was an editor at a small publishing house then. I spent all kinds of money on that little talk, went around Boston to every therapist, every workshop I could find to get help with my two phobias, but nothing helped. I went to a public speaking institute where they told you how to make notes and prepare and do deep-breathing exercises, which I'm sure would have been useful to somebody who was inexperienced and a little nervous but wasn't useful to a person who had a phobia. And I took a fear of flying workshop that was held at the airport, but the guy who ran it was sort of a crackpot. He thought food allergies were making you afraid on the airplane and he made you hold little bits of corn or wheat or some other substance in your hand and then his assistant would come along and push on your arm to see if the corn or whatever made you weak—then he'd tell you not to eat that thing before the flight. I was in a panic. Finally, three weeks before the sales conference, someone suggested I go to Charlie Ducey. I did, he hypnotized me a few times, and I was able to fly to New York and get up in front of a bunch of sales representatives and say my little speech.

I loved hypnosis, I loved it so much I didn't want to stop. I went back to Charlie Ducey after the sales conference and said, "I want you to be my therapist so you can hypnotize me more." So that was what we did. I went to him every two weeks for a year, and when the year was over my whole life was different. But that's another story. I loved hypnosis, like I said. I loved sitting on Charlie Ducey's couch—I didn't lie, I sat—going into my trance. There was a certain sensation I had as I was going down down down into it, a kind of prickly, buoyant feeling, a feeling of entering some atmosphere a little thicker, a little more gelatinous—if air can be described as gelatinous—than regular air. The way it worked was this: I'd sit on the couch and Charlie Ducey would say, in his light, soothing, pleasant voice, a voice a lot like Mr. Rogers's: "Picture yourself going down a set of stairs." Or sometimes he'd say, "Picture yourself in an elevator and the elevator is descending." There were numbers on the elevator that descended as you descended down down down to a lower floor: 10, 9, 8, 7, 6, 5, 4, 3, 2, 1. Or sometimes I would ride on a cloud to some other location. When I got there I'd step off the cloud and be in my trance. Whatever way I got there, something would always happen when I arrived. Usually I'd see something and it would have meaning in terms of the problem I'd been discussing with Charlie Ducey on that particular day. Once, for example, I saw myself sitting in a chair in my apartment reading a book. "What's the book," Charlie Ducey said, and I said, surprised to discover it myself, "It's *War and Peace!*" "Hmm, very interesting," Charlie Ducey said, and at the same moment I realized I had mixed feelings, I had war and peace inside about whatever problem he and I were trying to figure out that day—I can't remember what it was anymore. Once in my trance I was sitting at a desk and there was an ugly green blotter on the desktop in front of me. Charlie Ducey said, "Why don't you get rid of it and replace it with one that's a different color?" I said, "I'll try," and then the ugly green blotter turned an indescribably beautiful blue, a pale, airy, celestial blue, the most beautiful blue in the universe. Another time I found a green metal box on the ground. The box was locked and there was a little key in the dirt beside it.

Inside the box were the most fun toys in the universe; they gave off a strong, incredibly exciting feeling, the feeling you get when you play for hours and hours when you're a kid. But they were locked inside the box. Charlie Ducey said, "Why don't you pick up the key and open it," and I said, my voice rising to a little girl's wail, "I can't!" And when Charlie Ducey said, "Why not," I said, "Because, those things can't be mine!" I never did figure out why they couldn't be mine, but just seeing them locked away in a box must've solved some problem on some level, freed up something that had up till then been stuck inside my head. Because a week later I went into Charlie Ducey's office and said, "I've figured out I want to write." And a month later I quit my job, became a freelance editor, and started writing.

I told Jim Beaman about all that one night when we were sitting on my bed, told him how I loved hypnosis, how it was like going someplace real where real things happened but at the same time not going there, or only going there with some part of yourself, some part inside your head. And he said, "Why don't you try to hypnotize me?" So I did. I made him lean back and close his eyes and I said the same soothing things Charlie Ducey used to say to get me into a trance: "You're walking down a set of stairs and when you get to the bottom you'll see something," and so forth. What Beaman saw was himself, stepping out onto his front steps on some Saturday night before we'd met, standing there hesitating, aimless, wondering what to do next. He lay on the bed and said nothing for a while, then he said, "I guess that's it." He came back out of the trance, but then he said, "Let's try it again." So I got him back under using the same methods and this time he saw himself as a teenager, sitting in a recliner in his parents' living room. His father and mother and sister were all in the kitchen, and he had a terrible feeling of being left out, of being an outsider in the family. Then he said in a loud voice, not the dreamy voice you have in a trance, "I've got to stop this," and he sat up and opened his eyes. There were tears in his eyes, which was unusual for him, and he held on to me and said, "Now we can never break up." A few weeks later I asked him whether he wanted to try some more hypnosis and he said, "That was interesting but I never want to do it again."

There's a name they used to call the afterlife in boojie circles: Summerland. The spiritualists called it that. They were a group of mostly British people around the time of World War I, men and women with money and class and education—the kind of people you picture sitting around sipping tea in country houses—who were fascinated by the question of life after death. They formed societies, went to mediums, received many long, cogent messages from dead people. They thought of Summerland as a light, airy, happy place, a place where it's always warm and magic is an everyday thing, where pine needles can turn into real needles and thought is a kind of building material.

I encountered the pine needle in a book called *Life, Death and Consciousness: Experiences Near and After Death*, which I bought and read the first time the year of Jim's death. In it the author gathers anecdotal evidence—personal accounts of near-death experiences, out-of-body experiences, et cetera—to try to paint a picture of life after death. At the end there's a chapter with quotes—descriptions of the afterlife—from dead people, that is, quotes taken from old books written by spiritualists containing messages received through mediums. And here it seems we run into the above-mentioned disbelief problem, the cartoon-character, missing-piece-of-the-puzzle problem. Because it all seems so clunky, unlikely, ridiculous—that a dead person would somehow manage to speak through a living person. And so when I get to this part I break down. I can't just say, this dead guy described the afterlife and here's what he said. Because it's unbelievable that a dead guy would be able to talk at all. Maybe even that dead people exist at all. But let's just say for a minute they can, they do.

So. There's a dead guy in that book, *Life Death and Consciousness*, who's talking about the afterlife, and he says, "It's really quite fantastic here, you can change things with your thoughts. Not the big important things, not the whole scene, because that belongs to everybody. But you can change any little thing that affects only you. For example, if you're sitting under a tree and you look at a pine needle on the ground and then you picture it as a real needle, a steel sewing needle, it turns into a sewing needle."

Death is like hypnosis only you can't stop, Y said, and it seems to me there is a connection between the world where the dead guy sits under a tree and the pine needle turns into a real needle, and the world I went to on Charlie Ducey's couch. It was as if I went to someplace that exists in my own head; I got there by going inside and then down down down like Alice going down the rabbit hole, but when I came to the bottom, came out on the other side, I was not just inside my head, at least the way we think of it—the way people say, "Oh, that's all in your head"—I was really somewhere. It was a real world; I saw real sights, had real experiences there; I look back on what happened during all those little trips to the world of hypnosis as actual memories. But somehow it was an interior world; what happened there was all wrapped up with what was in my mind, with what I felt: I saw myself reading and the book was *War and Peace* because I had war and peace inside my head; the green box, the key in the dirt, the green blotter on the desk were all symbols, out-picturings of something I thought or felt. And the afterlife as the pine needle guy describes it, as countless others I encountered in boojie books, as Y himself said, is a similar place, a real place but a place where what exists is affected by what's inside your head.

And I think maybe that's why it didn't quite make sense, all those times I was lying on my bed, sitting at my kitchen table, standing at my bathroom mirror trying to envision the ghost of Jim, really there but somehow invisible, as if he was covered with magical dust. I think it didn't make sense because I was looking at the picture wrong. I was coming at the whole idea of him from the world of materialism, of large and small, up and down, of beds and ceilings, tables and chairs. I was trying to make the invisible visible. But maybe he wasn't just invisible the way the invisible man is invisible, he's really there, fully formed, there's some magical dust, some vanishing charm that makes it impossible to see him. Maybe he wasn't even in the realm of the visible. Maybe he was in some other realm entirely, in which visible and invisible aren't even an issue; maybe that's why Orpheus can't look at Euridice. And it's not that that's not a real realm, either, a fake, imaginary, pseudo-place, a realm of wizards and fairies and dragons and other spurious stuff. Or that the dead live on but only in our hearts, our memories, not in any real way that counts. Because what counts, what's real, is the definite hard-edged measurable material world, the world we see out there, the world every-body believes in. What I think is that maybe we have it wrong: It's what's in our heads that's real; it's the outside—the hard-edged, measurable, material world—that's an illusion. That Summerland exists but down some rabbit hole of conscious-ness like the one I went down in hypnosis, on Charlie Ducey's couch; that death really *is* like hypnosis only you can't stop.

The Rooms of Heaven

That Summerland is somehow made of consciousness, that maybe *we* are made of consciousness. That maybe everything, in some way we don't understand, is in our heads.

Once when he was alive Jim said, "When you die I'll be waiting for you on the other side. You'll get off the train and look for me but you won't see me right away because I'll be playing a little trick on you, I'll be hiding behind a tree. You'll say, 'Where is he?' And then I'll come out and we'll be so happy."

It seems strange now that he would have said such a thing. I can't remember when he said it, can't imagine any context he would have said it in, but I'm sure he did, because I remember thinking about it after he died. I couldn't wait for that moment—the moment when I got to see him in the afterlife. I wondered what it would be like, whether he'd still carry out his little plan or whether he'd have forgotten about it, become too different, too mature up there in the spirit world to play a little trick like that on me. And I thought maybe too he'd feel too sorry for me to do it. After watching me in my misery down on the earth, suffering year after year because he was dead, maybe he'd feel too guilty to play a little trick on me, would know that after all those years of suffering I wouldn't be able to stand being without him for one more minute. And so I thought maybe—probably—when I arrived on the train he'd be standing by the tracks, right there in full view where I could see him from the window, waiting.

I've come a long way since then. I'm not suffering anymore, I don't have fantasies about death, I hope I have to wait a long long time before I get to see Beaman. I can hardly even remember what it was like to lie on my bed and smoke cigarettes and suffer because he was dead, let alone what it was like to lie there beside him and get to look right at him, the actual him in his real body, which for so long I missed so unbearably. I still miss him, of course, but the missing feels a lot more remote than it used to. He's gotten remote. But I have a feeling that if I could only conjure up a good clear picture of him, see him alive on the other side of my bed, it would all come back and I would miss him just as much again.

I'm remembering how I used to rub his feet with Icy Hot, which smelled like wintergreen and came in a little plastic tub, white with a red lid. The Icy Hot was his idea but the massages were mine. I used to love to rub his feet and also his back, which was truly beautiful, full of dips and curves. When I think of it I think of those old Norelco commercials they used to play at Christmastime, where some cartoon figure would be riding an electric razor up and down a bunch of little ski slopes. I remember once Jim said he wasn't going to last much longer as a tuck-pointer because his body wasn't going to hold out, and that surprised me because his body seemed so strong and healthy and in perfect shape. But he had a more or less permanently strained muscle in one shoulder from tuck-pointing and his feet hurt all the time too. And there was something about that which pleased me, that his body was so perfect—that he was so perfect—and at the same time so . . . I'm searching for the right word. Not exactly vulnerable. Certainly not sick, or fragile, or anything as strong as that. But there were flaws in him, things that were broken, that didn't quite work. His flaw were what made him perfect, to me; they were what made me love him. Pretty big flaws when it comes down to it— addiction, alcoholism, suicidal behavior. But they weren't too big for me to love him. No flaws would have been too big for me back then, maybe not even now, to love Jim Beaman. But the guy whose feet I'm rubbing in this memory isn't Beaman the addict or the drunk, the mean guy with the three-day beard, the guy who skulks around and gets fucked up. He's the tuck-pointer, the workingman. He's been standing on scaffold-ing all day long, hauling bricks, grinding mortar out of joints;

the last thing in the world he wants to do is skulk around and get fucked up. That was the thing about Beaman; there were many versions of him. He was like Michael Keaton in the advertisement for the movie *Multiplicity;* in the movie Michael Keaton gets cloned and the ad shows a whole string of Michael Keatons trailing off beside him. And that was like Beaman. There were a whole bunch of Beamans, and when he was one you forgot about the rest.

But it's his body I was talking about. I'm thinking about it again, how I can picture his body pretty clearly, his back and his feet, the hair on his head, even his face, but still not see him. Those, it seems—his physical features—are not the point. They aren't really what I want to see, to perceive in memory, to conjure up clearly, vividly, like an image on a TV screen. It's something else. Something you can't see in any photograph, something the mere memory of a nose, a mouth, a set of eyes, a pair of lips will not reproduce. I can't say what it is except to use words that are bland, abstract, meaningless: energy, motion, animation. It's what you see when you see a person. It's what you'll never see again in this world when the person is dead, unless you're lucky enough to see them in a lucid dream. It's that energy, that whatever, that I miss, I'm sure of it. I have a feeling that if I could only get a little glimpse of it—him— even for one second, if I could even hear him speak, some place in my heart that is marked Jim Beaman—his place in my heart, just like the cliché—that place, which is frozen, cold, painful, stiff, would melt with a sigh of relief.

Once when I was working in the physics department, not long after Beaman's death, my friend John Birkbeck told me he'd seen some guy around town who looked like Jim. He said he'd seen him three times, at least: Once he was standing with a group of people downtown on Washington Street, and once he was hanging around like he was waiting for somebody in front of Brueggers Bagel Bakery, and once he was walking slowly down Jefferson Street. John said it was eerie how much the guy looked like Beaman, his clothes, his mannerisms, the way he smoked a cigarette. He said it was almost like it *was* Beaman, turning up somehow in ghostly form. My friend John is like that; he loves magical things, spooky things, ghosts, miracles. But he doesn't take them seriously, the way I did back then. I'm sure he didn't literally believe what he was saying; it was all just something he was entertaining. But I did believe it, in a wishful-thinking sort of way. I wanted to believe it, even though I knew it couldn't really be true, that Beaman was somewhere out there walking around, like a cross between a mirage and a miracle. I wanted to believe it so badly, and one afternoon when I was working in the physics department I actually went out and walked up and down Jefferson Street where John had told me he'd seen the guy who looked like Beaman; I walked up and down the sidewalk half dead with longing, hoping to see him. Even if it wasn't him and it just looked like him I still wanted to see him. And of course I didn't. I went back inside my office building, rode the elevator up to the fifth floor, and sat down at my desk feeling empty, dissatisfied, more miserable than I would have if I hadn't had that little tiny bit of hope John Birkbeck gave me.

I never did see anyone who looked like Beaman—nobody, not even once in all those years. But then recently, finally, I did. It was in Kansas City.

Someone I know, Mary Porter, moved there two months ago, and another friend, Jill, called and asked if I felt like visiting Mary Porter for a weekend and I said sure. We arrived on a Saturday afternoon, and Mary said there was a barn dance that night that she wanted to go to. She kept talking about this dance, saying how much fun it was, how all the men and women mingled freely, nobody was shy about asking anybody to dance and so forth. I had some doubts about going; country folksy stuff like that doesn't usually appeal to me, and I'm also afraid of making an idiot of myself trying to do complicated dance steps. But my friend really wanted to go and I didn't want to be a stick-in-the-mud so I said I would.

The dance was held in a huge gymnasium in a long, low institutional building, a school or possibly some kind of modern church. It cost four dollars to participate and we got there early, at seven rather than seven-thirty, for the beginner instruction. I was nervous and I think the guy who gave the beginner instruction might have also had doubts about my ability to do it, because he offered to be my partner for the first dance, as if he thought I needed a little extra help. But I found that when the actual dancing started I *could* do it. There was a band playing on the stage with fiddles and guitars and mandolins and the music was loud and lively. I liked it better than I usually like that kind of music, maybe because I was too busy to spend any time not liking it. So the band was playing on the stage and a guy was up there calling the steps into a microphone and all of us dancers were milling around on the floor dancing, allemande left and allemande right, ladies cross over, stuff like that. I liked the swings best, where one guy would grab you by the waist and swing you around and around three or four times, then hand you on to some other guy. It was a dizzy kind of dancing; you'd swing around and around with a partner, then grab two people's hands and circle around and around in a group of four, then when you were so dizzy you were about to fall over you'd form a line, step up to the person opposite and give a little bow, step back and onto the next swing, allemande left, ladies cross over.

I was having fun. Then, after we'd been dancing for about half an hour, I saw a guy come in who looked exactly like Jim Beaman. Well, maybe not exactly. But close enough. All of his features resembled Beaman's, but some were just a little different, always in a less attractive way. He had a slight overbite and his nose looked like it might have been broken at one point; he was a little narrower in the shoulders; his hair was combed across the forehead in a somewhat nerdy way. But it was the same hair, thick and short and brown, and he was the same height, had the same coloring, and, most of all, he had the same eyes—large, deep-set, blue eyes, dreamy eyes, sad eyes, maybe, a little, with crow's-feet at the corners. Every time I looked at him—and I kept looking and looking at him—I felt a weird little tug in my heart, as if some tiny strings attached to it were literally being pulled on ever so gently. Every time I looked at him I saw Jim Beaman. I saw him, and I didn't see him. It was the strangest feeling.

The Jim Beaman look-alike, whose name, it turned out, was also Jim, had come to the barn dance with a tall thin sandy-haired woman in a lacy black dress. When I first spotted them, standing in the doorway, I thought they were a married couple. Then—from the slightly formal way he held her during the waltzes, from the polite, shy looks on their faces when they talked—I concluded they were on a date, perhaps even a first date. I could tell he liked her a lot—once I saw him glance up at her on the bleachers where she was sitting one out, catch her eye, and smile. I thought it was a proprietary smile, a reassuring smile. It seemed to say, Don't worry, I'm not interested in any of these other women, I'm only interested in you. And that bothered me a little. I seemed to be a little jealous that this Jim Beaman look-alike was there with another woman, that he seemed so firmly attached to her. Not really because I would have wanted to have been his date, his girlfriend, but because it let me know, once again, that he wasn't Jim Beaman. It was like he was a person dressed in Jim Beaman clothing, like the wolf dressed in Grandma's outfit in Little Red Riding Hood. The clothing didn't fit exactly so you knew it wasn't him, you knew it wasn't him anyway because it was a barn dance where Jim Beaman never would have been, and Beaman was dead in any event. But still. I *felt* like it was him. Like it both was and wasn't him.

I asked the Jim look-alike to dance. There wasn't much time between each dance and everyone would be milling around finding a new partner—one of the unspoken rules was that everyone danced with someone different every time—so I went up to Jim (I feel like calling him Jim in quotation marks) and asked him. He glanced over at the bleachers where his date was, or maybe I only imagined that, then he said, "I've already got a partner this time"—he gestured at some other woman, who was not his date—"but I'll dance with you next time." I half expected him to have forgotten when that dance was over but he hadn't. He came over and nodded at me and we lined up across from each other sandwiched between some other partners and waited for the music to start. There was a little time before it did, and I debated, Should I tell him or not? Should I tell him he looks exactly like someone I knew and loved who died? Will it make him nervous that he'll die? Will he think I'm trying to come on to him? But then I did tell him, I just blurted it out. I said, "I'm sorry I can't stop looking at you," and then I explained why. He nodded, looked a little interested, but the whole time it seemed to me that he was focused on that other woman, the woman over on the bleachers. But maybe I was just imagining that. I asked him what his name was and he said it was Jim and I asked him what he did for a living and he said he worked construction. I said the guy I was engaged to worked construction too, he was a tuck-pointer, and the look-alike Jim nodded, a little distantly, about the coincidence, as if it didn't interest him much, and after all, why should it have? He did ask me when he died and I told him, and then I told him how he died too, though the look-alike Jim hadn't asked that. I said, to reassure him in case looking like some dead guy made him nervous, though he didn't seem to need reassurance: "Don't worry, you won't die they way he did, he committed suicide." And he said, "Oh, I don't know." As if it were a possibility. And then the music started.

His hands were calloused, just like Jim's. They were the same size and shape as Jim's but the nails were bitten way down. And he had bad breath, kind of. But I couldn't stop staring into those large dreamy blue eyes. And it was as if I was looking into Jim Beaman's eyes. He took my hand, swung me around, passed me on to another partner. The new partner swung me around, we joined hands, circled left, the ladies crossed over, the caller spoke the calls. I got passed back to my first partner, back to Jim. I looked and looked and looked at him, into that face that was and wasn't Jim's, and I remembered, felt again as I hadn't in years what it was like to be with the real live Jim, not the ghost of Jim, the memory of Jim, but the actual walking talking living Jim. I looked at him and it all came back: the drugs, the spookiness, the love, the sadness.

And the dance continued. The caller called the steps, the fiddle, the guitar, the mandolin played their cheerful manic music, the men swung the women, the ladies crossed over, the partners changed. I kept returning to Jim, to the Jim who wasn't Jim, would come back to swing in his arms, be circled around in a half circle, his arm around my waist. There was a part of the dance where two lines formed, everyone holding hands, and you stepped three steps forward, stamped your foot, and nodded to your partner: I nodded at Jim and he nodded at me. Then you turned to another, corner partner, got swung around by him, and on and on. I kept looking from face to face, then back to the Jim who was but wasn't Jim, thinking how strange it was to find myself there among all those goodhearted people with this innocent, not quite handsome, callous-handed Jim who wasn't Jim, doing something the real Jim never in a million years would have done. I kept thinking about that, looking at that Jim, feeling those little strings tugging at my heart, tears forming in my eyes.

The Rooms of Heaven

And then toward the end of the dance I stopped thinking about it and just abandoned myself to the whole experience: the music, the people, the wild dizzy spinning around and around, there in the middle of a big glossy gym in a church or a school in a city I'll probably never visit again.

Acknowledgments

I would like to thank my agent, Eric Simonoff, for his support of my work and for his good counsel, integrity, and friendship; my editor at Knopf, Robin Desser, for her invaluable guidance and tireless efforts on behalf of the book, and for her warmth, wit, and general loveliness; and Eadie Klemm, Lisa Lustgarten, and Ben Moser at Janklow & Nesbit and Knopf, for their good-humored assistance and friendly voices on the other end of the phone.

Thanks also go to Frank Conroy and Connie Brothers at the Iowa Writers' Workshop for providing me much-needed financial assistance in the form of a 1994 Paul Engle/James Michener Fellowship; to the Ragdale Foundation, for time and space to write during the early stages of the book; and to George and Marge Jansen for keeping my rent low during the many years I lived in poverty as a writer.

For their support, friendship, and contributions to the writing of the book, my profound appreciation goes to Marilyn Abildskov, Joe Blair, Tom Kelley Burns, Dan Coffey, Anne Cremer, Grant Denn, Quinn Dilkes, Patricia Foster, Julie Kastner, Linda Krutsinger, Lynda Leidiger, Jill Levin, Patty MacInnes, Alison Millburn, Tania Pryputniewicz, Jim Robb, Kathy Sheldon, Tom Sleigh, Scott Spencer, Kathy Stahl, Renee Sueppel, and Raymond Tinnian. I owe special debts of gratitude to Jo Ann Beard, whose creative nonfiction served as an example and an inspiration to me; Honor Moore, who

Acknowledgments

helped me develop a key element in the writing process; Chris Merrill, who was my faithful writing companion during much of the writing of the second half of the book; and John Killoran, who read the manuscript and listened to me talk about it so often he practically knows it by heart.

A NOTE ABOUT THE AUTHOR

Mary Allen received an M.F.A. from the Iowa Writers' Workshop, where she was awarded a 1994 Paul Engle/James Michener Fellowship. She has worked in publishing in Boston and lives in Iowa City.

A NOTE ON THE TYPE

This book was set in Janson, a typeface long thought to have been made by the Dutchman Anton Janson, who was a practicing typefounder in Leipzig during the years 1668–1687. However, it has been conclusively demonstrated that these types are actually the work of Nicholas Kis (1650–1702), a Hungarian, who most probably learned his trade from the master Dutch typefounder Dirk Voskens. The type is an excellent example of the influential and sturdy Dutch types that prevailed in England up to the time William Caslon (1692–1766) developed his own incomparable designs from them.

Composed by Stratford Publishing Services,
Brattleboro, Vermont
Printed and bound by R. R. Donnelley & Sons,
Harrisonburg, Virginia
Designed by Soonyoung Kwon